MULTILINGUALISM FOR ALL

DATE DUE

DE 6 08			
DE 1 2 11			
2 13			

DEMCO 38-296

EUROPEAN STUDIES ON
Multilingualism

EDITORS
Guus Extra & Ludo Verhoeven
Tilburg University, The Netherlands

EDITORIAL BOARD (*provisional*)
Ulrich Ammon (Duisburg, Germany)
Lenore Negrin Arnberg (Stockholm, Sweden)
Hugo Baetens Beardsmore (Brussels, Belgium)
Vivian Edwards (Reading, Great Britain)
Koen Jaspaert (Leuven, Belgium)
Bernhard Ketteman (Graz, Austria)
Georges Lüdi (Basel, Switzerland)
Aldo di Luzio (Konstanz, Germany)
Andrina Pavlinić-Wolf (Zagreb, Republic of Croatia)
Håkan Ringbom (Åbo, Finland)
Miquel Siguan (Barcelona, Spain)
David Singleton (Dublin, Ireland)
Tatiana Tabolina (Moscow, Russia)
Traute Taeschner (Roma, Italy)
Daniël Véronique (Aix-en-Provence, France)

Aims and Scope
The series seeks to promote the dissemination of empirical research evidence on the use of more than one language in Europe. The focus is on majority and minority language use at the level of individual and society, and derives from the interdisciplinary approaches of linguistics, psychology, sociology, anthropology, and education. Processes of language acquisition, language shift, language loss and the consequences of multilingualism for such areas as education and language policy are taken into account.

Volume 1   Talking about people. A multiple case study on
adult language acquisition
Peter Broeder

Volume 2   Multilingual Spain
Miquel Siguan

Volume 3   Community languages in the Netherlands
Guus Extra & Ludo Verhoeven (eds.)

Volume 4   Multilingualism for all
Tove Skutnabb-Kangas(Ed.)

EUROPEAN STUDIES ON
Multilingualism 4

MULTILINGUALISM FOR ALL

Tove Skutnabb-Kangas (Editor)

**Roskilde University
Denmark**

SWETS & ZEITLINGER B.V   PUBLISHERS

Library of Congress Cataloging-in-Publication Data

[applied for]

Cip-gegevens Koninklijke Bibliotheek, Den Haag

Multilingualism

Multilingualism for all / Tove Skutnabb-Kangas (ed.)
Lisse : Swets & Zeitlinger. - Tab. - (European studies on multilingualism,
ISSN 0926-6461 ; 4)
Met index, lit. opg.
ISBN 90-265-1423-9
NUGI 941
Trefw.: meertaligheid.

Cover design: Rob Molthoff, LineaForma, Alkmaar the Netherlands
Printed in the Netherlands by Krips repro Meppel
Cover printed in the Netherlands by Casparie IJsselstein

ISBN 90 265 1423 9
NUGI 941

LIST OF CONTENTS

INTRODUCTION[1]

Tove Skutnabb-Kangas

High levels of multilingualism and linguistic human rights

Attaining a high level of multilingual competence has been common for the *élites* in most countries in the world. For them, multilingual proficiency has been part of the symbolic linguistic and cultural capital necessary for maintaining and reproducing their material and political capital (wealth and power). For them, multilingualism is a question of enrichment and benefits.

By contrast, the attempts of *dominated/subordinated linguistic minority groups* to become *high level* multilinguals have in most parts of the world met with considerable difficulty and often direct or indirect resistance and sabotage from the educational system. For them, becoming at least bilingual has been and is in most cases (except if some kind of isolation is possible) necessary for survival, economically, culturally, psychologically, even politically. For them, high levels of multilingualism or at least bilingualism is a question of basic human rights.

In a civilized state, there should be no need to debate the right to maintain and develop one's mother tongue. It is a self-evident, fundamental, basic linguistic human right.

Respecting linguistic human rights (LHRs) implies at an *individual* level that everyone can identify positively with their mother tongue, and have that identification accepted and respected by others, irrespective of whether their mother tongue is a minority language or a majority language[2]. It means the right to learn the mother tongue, orally and in writing and to receive at least basic education through the medium of the mother tongue, and the right to use it in many (official) contexts. It means the right to learn at least one of the official languages in one's country of residence. It should therefore be normal that teachers (including second language teachers) are bilingual. Restrictions on these rights may be considered linguistic wrongs, an infringement of fundamental LHRs.[3]

Respecting LHRs implies at a *collective* level the right of minority groups to exist (i.e. the right to be "different"). It implies the right to enjoy and develop their languages and the right for minorities to establish and maintain schools and other training and educational institutions, with control of curricula and teaching in their own languages. It also involves guarantees of representation in the political affairs of the state, and the granting of autonomy to administer matters internal to the groups, at least in the fields of culture, education, religion, information, and social affairs, with the financial means, through taxation or grants, to fulfil these functions. Many of these principles have been endorsed and codified in a wide range of human rights covenants and charters.[4]

Many ethnolinguistic majorities enjoy most LHRs, and élites enjoy all. It would be perfectly feasible to grant many of these rights to ethnolinguistic minorities, without infringing the rights of majorities. It is urgent to grant them if we are interested in avoiding conflicts where difference in ethnicity coincides with other cleavages in society (as it does in many of the most violent conflicts in today's world). "Questions concerning the rights and responsibilities, the condition and the future of minorities now occupy high points in the agenda of the United Nations, the CSCE, the Council of Europe, the European Community and other intergovernmental and non-governmental organisations", writes Patrick Thornberry, in *Contact*, the Bulletin of the European Bureau for Lesser Used Languages (10(1), 1993).

One of the basic human rights of persons belonging to minorities is – or should be – to achieve high levels of bi- or multilingualism *through education*. Becoming at least bilingual is in most cases a necessary prerequisite for minorities to exercise other fundamental human rights, a point argued in many of the articles in the book *Linguistic Human Rights* (Skutnabb-Kangas & Phillipson (Eds.) 1994) a collection of papers from all over the world.[5]

But there are many reasons for not restricting the right to become bi- or multilingual to minorities, for whom it is a necessity. Ethnolinguistic majority populations should also be given the opportunity to escape monolingual stupidity/naivety/reductionism[6], and to do so at a level which does not stop at studying a foreign language for a few years as a subject in school, something many children are already doing. If one believes – and there are good reasons for doing so[7] – that high levels of multilingualism are an advantage to people, opening up horizons, enabling contact, enhancing development, and as hinted at above, escaping the imprisonment of the narrowing of horizons implied by monolingualism, then everybody should be offered this opportunity. And "everybody" includes majorities, even if many of them are still unaware of the linguistic cages many of them live in and of the fact that they and the rest of the world pay a high price for their monolingualism.

If we are to make virtually monolingual majorities support multilingualism, in the first place by granting minorities linguistic human rights, also in education, and in the second place by them wanting to become high level multilinguals themselves, majorities themselves have to have educational programmes which really *work* in making them multilingual, at the same time as they do not lose content matter. Joshua Fishman has frequently noted that majorities will not start developing (or even allow minorities themselves to organise) educational programmes which lead to multilingualism before they are convinced that they (i.e. the majorities) can benefit too. Offering majorities an opportunity to become multilingual may make majorities great supporters of language maintenance programmes for minorities too.

And in an ideal world, minorities and majorities should of course be given the opportunity to become multilingual together, in programmes which are not geared towards élites (only), but towards ordinary people.

Many people might agree with what has been said so far. But then they start asking: how? What do we do, then, if we want to make everybody multilingual. What are the "recipes"? Are there any?

Comparison and diversity – we know enough for some generalisations

Since schools are part of societies and societies differ, programmes leading to high levels of multilingualism necessarily also vary a great deal – and have to. What fits multilingual élites in Brussels may not be directly applicable in bilingual Estonia or Catalonia. What is new in some parts of Europe or North Americas or Australia may for somebody from India be reinventing the wheel. What is a dream in Moscow, may be reality in San Diego, and vice versa.

My impression is that many of us know too little about the peculiarities of not only other peoples' situations but also about the peculiarities of our own situation. We have to come together and compare. When a group of experienced, highly articulate professional Swedes went to China to study Chinese pre-school education (Liljeström et al, 1982, in English 1985), they claimed that they came back knowing much more about *Swedish* pre-school education, and their *own* ways of thinking. When we see the differences, our meta-educational awareness benefits from comparison.

At the same time we also notice some similarities in contexts, ideologies, organisation and methods that work. I firmly believe that we now know enough about educational language planning for high levels of multilingualism, to start making at least some cautious generalisations which are broader than the ones we have made so far. Even if big universal models in some cases are not my cup of (herbal) tea, there is an urgency to start finding, making, confirming, applying and comparing, on a large scale, some of the generalisations that we fairly confidently CAN make. I will present a short version of some of my own suggestions below.

About this book

This book is based on papers from the symposium Multilingualism for All, organised by AILA's Scientific Commission on Language and Education in Multilingual Settings at AILA's Tenth World Congress of Applied Linguistics (Amsterdam, August 8-14, 1993).[8] The theme for the symposium was the generalisability/applicability of the European Schools model for other contexts. The 9 European Schools, with almost 15,000 children, in 6 countries, with subsections for all official European Union languages, offer education through the medium of all these languages, and their students become high level multilinguals. The position paper by Hugo Baetens Beardsmore (which was sent to the other speakers in advance and was summarized at the symposium by Alex Housen) describes the model as it is now, both ideally and in different countries, discusses the theoretical and practical rationales behind the model and sums up experience so far. It also discusses the benefits and shortcomings of the model, and what the prerequisites for trying out some aspects of it elsewhere might be.

All the other contributors were invited, using the position paper as a starting-point, to describe the educational situation in their own context, and to analyse the applicability of the European School model in their own country/context, both as a general model and in relation to other models. Everybody was asked to consider general principles that educational programmes aiming at high levels of multilingualism should follow. They were asked to consider the following types of question:

– are the rationales which the model is based on sound?
– to what extent can they be generalised to apply in other countries, theoretically, practically, politically, economically, in relation to different types of groups?

- what kind of modifications would be needed in other contexts and why?
- are there aspects of the European School model which they would like to question?
- does the experience from the European Schools make them question theoretical principles or practical experience which they have so far regarded as valid?
- how would they organise an alternative model in their own context?
- what kind of advice would they give to administrators considering a similar model in their country?
- what kind of advice would they give to people who work with the European School model, based on experience in their country?
- are there any rationales for supporting high levels of multilingualism through education which might be candidates for universality, in relation to the necessity of studying L1, L2, L3 etc as subjects, using them as media of education, the order of learning, the progression, teacher bilingualism/multilingualism, homogeneity or heterogeneity of groups in different phases of schooling and linguistic competence, teaching methods, the relative status of the languages involved, attitudes, etc."[9]

Most of the contributors have in their papers combined describing their own educational context with their reflections on the European Schools model, without suggesting explicit alternative models. There is cautious enthusiasm, a wish to learn, reflect, criticize, be inspired. For some, the European Schools model is somewhere in a dream world, for others it is not enough. Most contributors see it as a model the fruits of which are now enjoyed by élites (also but not entirely because of its costs), at the same time as they appreciate the pedago-linguistic rationale behind it and would like similar opportunities to be available for ordinary people. There is some criticism in relation to the traditional pedagogical methods in the schools, but these are not seen as intrinsic to the model. Most contributors see as vital the importance granted to the different mother tongues in the model, the fact that they are used as media of instruction in a non-transitional way. However, some are worried about the non-differentiation between dominant majority mother tongues and dominated minority mother tongues, either in the European Schools or in their own context or both. It is especially the all-pervasive encroachment of English that causes warning signals to be flashed[10] – but there is also at least one apologia for what the writer sees as an inevitability.

What comes out very clearly is the need to be even more diverse, and realistic, and more multidisciplinary in educational language planning. We may wish for a different world and build beautiful models to fit our ideal principles of what we know about how children learn – but we have to start from our specific ideological and material context. This means including as a very central starting-point the historical context of each country. Education is basically a matter of first political and only thereafter pedagogical choices, regardless of how much we would like it to be the other way round.

Baseline recommendations

Still as can be seen in the book, it is possible to make very different kinds of cautious generalisation on the basis of experiments. And it is our duty as researchers to think ahead of today's political situation. In my own contribution to the symposium I drew conclusions about general principles on the basis of several experiments: mother tongue maintenance programmes, immersion programmes, two-way programmes, alternate-days programmes, the European Schools, International Schools, early reading programmes and Kōhanga Reo.[11]

It seemed to me that the principles which have to a large extent been followed in most of those experiments which have reached the best results (i.e. high levels of bi- or multilingualism, a fair chance of success in school achievement, and positive intercultural attitudes), could be formulated as 8 recommendations. I will present them with a few comments, in order to offer the reader one of many possible ways of organising their thoughts when reading the various contributions, one possible baseline which the reader can relate to, agree or disagree with. Here are the principles:

1 *Support (= use as the main medium of education, at least during the first 8 years) the language (of the 2 that the child is supposed to become bilingual in initially) which is least likely to develop up to a high formal level.* This is for all minority children their own mother tongue. For majority children, it should be a minority language. (The European Schools do not follow this principle completely, because they teach also majority children initially through the medium of their mother tongues, e.g. the the Italian-speaking children in the European School in Italy are initially taught through the medium of Italian, instead of a minority language).

2 In most experiments, *the children are initially grouped together with children with the same L1.* Mixed groups are not positive initially, and certainly not in cognitively demanding decontextualised subjects. (Spanish-English Two-way programmes in the U.S.A. are an exception: they have mixed in the same class 50% minority, 50% majority children. All are initially taught through the medium of the minority language, later through both. This may be a relevant factor in accounting for the Spanish-speaking children's sometimes relatively less impressive gains in both languages, compared to English-speaking children in the same programmes. The

mere presence of majority language children in the same classroom may be too overwhelming for minority children, despite the minority language being the medium of education).

3   *All children are to become high level bilinguals*, not only minority children. This seems to be especially important in contexts where majority and minority children are mixed.

4   *All children have to be equalized vis-a-vis the status of their mother tongues and their knowledge of the language of instruction.* Nice phrases about the worth of everybody's mother tongue, the value of interculturalism, etc, serve little purpose, unless they are followed up in how the schools are organised.

There has to be equality in the demands made on the children's and the teachers' competencies in the different languages involved, so that the same demands are made on everybody (both minority and majority children and teachers must be or become bi- or multilingual).

There has to be equality in the role that the languages are accorded on the schedules and in higher education, in testing and evaluation, in marks given for the languages, in the physical environment (signs, forms, letters, the school's languages of administration, the languages of meetings, assemblies, etc), in the status and salaries of the teachers, in their working conditions, career patterns, etc.

It is possible to equalize the children vis-a-vis their knowledge of the language of instruction in several different ways:

A   *All children know the language of instruction* (maintenance programmes, European Schools initially);

B   *No children know the language of instruction* or everybody is in the process of learning it (immersion programmes, European Schools in certain subjects in a later phase);

C   *All children alternate between "knowing" and "not knowing" the language of instruction* (two-way programmes in a late phase; alternate-days programmes (50% minority and 50% majority children, the medium of education alternates daily).

5   *All teachers have to be bi- or multilingual.* Thus they can be good models for the children, and support them (through comparing and contrasting and being metalinguistically aware) in language learning. Every child in a school has to be able to talk to an adult with the same native language.

This demand is often experienced as extremely threatening by majority group teachers, many of whom are not bilingual. Of course all minority group teachers are not high level bilinguals either. But it is often *less* important that the teacher's competence in a majority language is at top level, for instance in relation to pronunciation, because all children have ample opportunities to hear and read native models of a majority language outside the school, whereas many of them do NOT have the same opportunities to hear/read native minority language models. A high level of competence in a minority language is thus more important for a teacher than a high level of competence in a majority language.

6. *Foreign languages should be taught through the medium of the children's mother tongue and/or by teachers who know the children's mother tongue.* No teaching in foreign languages as subjects should be given through the medium of *other* foreign languages (for instance, Turkish children in Germany should not be taught English through the medium of German, but via Turkish).

7. *All children must study both L1 and L2 as compulsory subjects through grades 1-12.* Both languages have to be studied in ways which reflect what they are for the children: mother tongues, or second or foreign languages. Many minority children are forced to study a majority language, their L2, as if it was their L1.

8. *Both languages have to be used as media of education in some phase of the children's education, but the progression in how and how much each is used seems to vary for minority and majority children.*

For MAJORITY CHILDREN the *mother tongue* must function as the medium of education at least in some cognitively demanding, decontextualized subjects, at least in grades 8-12, possibly even earlier.

MAJORITY CHILDREN can be taught *through the medium of L2* at least in some (or even all or almost all) cognitively *less* demanding context-embedded subjects from the very beginning, and L2 can also be the medium of education, at least partially, in cognitively demanding decontextualized subjects, at least in grades 8-12.

For MINORITY CHILDREN the *mother tongue* must function as the medium of education in all subjects initially. At least some subjects must be taught through L1 all the way, up to grade 12, but the choice of subjects may vary. It seems that the following development functions well:

– transfer from the known to the unknown;
– transfer from teaching in a language to teaching through the medium of that language;
– transfer from teaching through the medium of L2 in cognitively less demanding, context-embedded subjects, to teaching through the medium of L2 in cognitively demanding decontextualized subjects.

The progression used for all children in the European Schools seems close to ideal for minority children:

The progression IN RELATION TO THE (minority) MOTHER TONGUE is as follows:

1   *All subjects* are taught *through the medium of the mother tongue* during the first 2 years.
2   *All cognitively demanding decontextualized core subjects* are taught *through the medium of the mother tongue* during the first 7 years.
3   There is *less* teaching *through the medium of the mother tongue* in grades 8-10, and again *more* teaching *through the medium of the mother tongue* in grades 11-12, especially in the most demanding subjects, in order to ensure that the students have understood them thoroughly.
4   *The mother tongue* is taught *as a subject throughout schooling*, from 1-12.

The progression IN RELATION TO THE SECOND LANGUAGE is as follows:

1   *The second language* is taught as a *subject throughout schooling*, from 1-12.
2   *The second language* becomes *a medium of education* already in grade 3, but only in *cognitively less demanding context-embedded subjects*. The teaching can be given in mixed groups, but ideally together with other children for whom the language is also an L2.
3   Teaching in *cognitively demanding decontextualized subjects* only starts *through the medium of L2* when the children have been taught that language *as a subject for 7 years* (grades 1-7) and have been taught *through the medium of that language in cognitively less demanding context-embedded subjects for 5 years* (grades 3-7). Children should not be taught demanding decontextualized subjects through L2 with other children for whom the language of instruction is their L1 before grade 8. In European Schools this is mostly not done even in grades 9-12 in compulsory subjects, only in elective courses.

Table 1. Principles for multilingualism through education

1   Support (= use as the main medium of education, at least during the first 8 years) the language which is least likely to develop up to a high formal level.

Language Shelter	Immersion	Altern. Days	European Schools	Two-Way	Utopian
+	+	+/–	MI+ MA–	+	+

2   Group the children initially together with children with the same L1. No mixed groups initially, and especially not in cognitively demanding decontextualised subjects.

Language Shelter	Immersion	Altern. Days	European Schools	Two-Way	Utopian
+	+	–	+	–	+

3   ALL children are to become high level bilinguals, not only minority children. (Monolingualism is a curable illness. Bilingualism is to be a goal and a positive model for all).

Language Shelter	Immersion	Altern. Days	European Schools	Two-Way	Utopian
+	+	+	+	+	+

4   All children have to be equalized vis-a-vis their knowledge of the language of instruction and the status of their mother tongues:
    A   All children know the language of instruction
    B   No children know the language of instruction
    C   All children alternate between "knowing" and "not knowing" the language of instruction

Language Shelter	Immersion	Altern. Days	European Schools	Two-Way	Utopian
+A	+B	+C	+A,C	–	+

5   All teachers have to be bi- or multilingual.

Language Shelter	Immersion	Altern. Days	European Schools	Two-Way	Utopian
+ (ma?)	+	+	+	+	+

6   Foreign languages should be taught through the medium of the children's mother tongue and/or by teachers who know the children's mother tongue.

Language Shelter	Immersion	Altern. Days	European Schools	Two-Way	Utopian
varies	+?	?	varies	?	+

7   All children must study both L1 and L2 as compulsory subjects through years 1-12.

Language Shelter	Immersion	Altern. Days	European Schools	Two-Way	Utopian
+?	–	+?	+	–	+

8   Both languages have to be used as media of education in some phase of the
    children's education, but the progression is different for minority and majority
    children.

Language Shelter	Immersion	Altern. Days	European Schools	Two-Way	Utopian
+	+	+?	+	+?	+

In table 1 (from Skutnabb-Kangas 1994c, also presented at the Symposium this
book is based on) I have applied the principles to some of the models discussed
in this book (immersion, two-way bilingual and European Schools models) and
some which are not discussed (language shelter (or language maintenance) and
alternate days models). I have also included a "utopian" model which would
get a plus-rating on all the principles. Alternatives, further developments and
discussions about both possible principles and, especially, concrete experience,
are vital.

The languages of a small planet

Observing these principles in my view also respects linguistic human rights in
education. If all education were to follow principles honouring LHRs, high
levels of multilingualism would be likely to follow for both minorities and
majorities. But today the education of both majorities and minorities in most
European and Europeanized[12] countries in my view functions in conflict with
most scientifically sound principles about how education leading to high levels
of multilingualism should be organized. Education participates in attempting
and committing linguistic genocide[13] in relation to minorities. In relation to
linguistic majorities, education today in most cases deprives them of the
possibility of gaining the benefits associated with high levels of
multilingualism. Present reductionist educational language choices (cf.
monolingual reductionism above) do not support the diversity which is
necessary for the planet to have a future. Yukio Tsuda (1994, 58) writes of the
"Ecology of Language Paradigm" as the alternative to the present "Diffusion of
English Paradigm". The linguodiversity needed in addition to biodiversity is
part of the urgent human ecology approach to languages in education and
elsewhere.
When global control to an increasing degree happens via language, instead of

more brutal means (despite some of the signs of the opposite today), the relativity which comes with the multihorizons of multilingual and multicultural awareness must be enhanced on a global scale too, if our planet and our humanity are to have a chance of survival (Skutnabb-Kangas, in press a). It is not only biodiversity which is a necessity for the planet. Maintaining, developing and sharing the knowledge and potential embedded in all our languages and cultures, supporting linguistic and cultural human diversity, is at least equally important for our survival as a species peaceon this planet. Many cultures, and the languages through which their representatives have expressed them, contain more peaceful alternatives for humans to coexist with each other, with nature and with the cosmos[14] than the languages and cultures which dominate today. In a small way, I hope that this book can contribute to enhancing the prerequisites for this necessary diversity. I hope that the collection will inspire teachers and parents, educational administrators and politicians, students and researchers, and enable them to use the knowledge gathered within the covers of this volume to question the power structures and the ideologies and practices which disempower the many and turn them into not only have-nots but never-to-havesexploitation.

Notes:

1   I would like to thank all the contributors to the book for exiting, sometimes challenging (mainly because of technical reasons) and delightful, multifaceted exchange of ideas, in many cases during many years or even decades, with questions on multilingualism and education. Despite the hassle of non-functioning or non-existing mail or phone, faxes and e-mails broken down or not yet installed, conversion-problems, etc, everybody has been supportive and patient, even when required to send the fifth version of the same diskette with courier or from some other institute with a functioning something. Shelley Taylor, OISE, Toronto, stepped in at the impossible last moments, offering to be exploited, native-speaker-language-checking, in the middle of her own last bit of field work with Kurdish children in Denmark. My husband Robert Phillipson, wants it on record that he took over the cooking completely for the last two weeks of editing, when it was my turn. What would editors do without good friends and diversified spouses... thanks.

2   I define "minorities" and "minority languages" in terms of power not numbers. See Andrýsek 1989, Capotorti 1979 and Thornberry 1991 on legal human rights definitions, and Skutnabb-Kangas & Phillipson 1994 on their specific applicability to linguistic minorities.

3 See Phillipson, Rannut & Skutnabb-Kangas 1994 for these rights.

4 See Alfredsson 1991; Phillipson, Rannut & Skutnabb-Kangas 1994; Skutnabb-Kangas & Phillipson 1994; de Varennes (in press), for these rights.

5 This book was one of the results of the symposium organised by the Scientific Commission on Language and Education in Multilingual Settings, at AILA World Congress in Thessaloniki in 1990.

6 For a development of these concepts, see Skutnabb-Kangas (in press b).

7 See e.g. Baker 1993 and Mohanty, forthcoming, for a good combination of summaries of the issues.

8 AILA is the International Association of Applied Linguistics. I was then President of the Commission and convened the Symposium.

9 In addition to the contributors to this volume, Johan Leman (Brussels, Belgium) and Benjamin T'sou (Hong Kong) also gave papers, but they did not write up their presentations. Ali Bentahila (Morocco) was also asked to contribute and was willing, but could not find the money to attend the conference. E. Annamalai could not attend the symposium but wrote his chapter later.

10 See, e.g. Ammon 1991, 1994, Phillipson 1992, Phillipson & Skutnabb-Kangas 1994, Truchot 1990, 1994, Tsuda 1986, 1988, 1992 and references in these.

11 Some of my earlier generalisations have been built into models comparing different educational programmes on the basis of various factors. See e.g. Tables 3, 6, 7 and 8 in my *Bilingualism or not* (1981, in English 1984), 1.3 and 1.4 in *Minority Education: from Shame to Struggle*, and 1 in Skutnabb-Kangas, 1993.

12 Europeanized countries are those countries which were originally colonized from Europe, i.e. Australia, Canada, the United States, New Zealand, for some purposes possibly also South Africa.

13 When the United Nations did preparatory work for what later became the "International convention for the prevention and punishment of the crime of genocide" (E 793, 1948), *linguistic and cultural genocide* were discussed alongside physical genocide, and were seen as serious crimes against humanity (see Capotorti 1979). When the Convention was accepted, Article 3, which covered linguistic and cultural genocide was vetoed by some nation states (the "great powers"), and it is thus not included in the final Convention of 1948. What remains, however, is *a definition of linguistic genocide*, which most states then in the UN were prepared to accept. Linguistic genocide is defined (in Art. 3, 1) as

"Prohibiting the use of the language of the group in daily intercourse or in schools, or the printing and circulation of publications in the language of the group".

The use of a minority language can be prohibited overtly and directly, through laws, imprisonment, torture, killings and threats, as in Turkey today vis-a-vis the Kurds (see e.g. Human Rights in Kurdistan 1989; Helsinki Watch Update 1990; Besikci 1990; "Silence is killing them" 1994, Skutnabb-Kangas & Bucak, 1994). The use of a minority language can also be prohibited covertly, more indirectly, via ideological and structural means, as in the educational systems of most European and North American countries.

My claim is that the use of a minority language is in fact prohibited "in daily intercourse or in schools" every time there are minority children in day care centres and schools, but no bilingual teachers who are authorized to use the languages of the minority children as the media of teaching and child care most of the time. This is the situation for most immigrant and refugee minority children in all Western European countries and in the US, Canada and Australia. Immigrant minority education in these countries is thus guilty of linguistic genocide, as defined by the UN. So is the education that most indigenous first nations have had and that many of them still have (see e.g. Hamel 1994a, b; Jordan 1988).

14 This is the threefold relationship within which we exist, as Debi Pattanayak, so beautifully shows in relation to our mother tongues (1992).

1

THE EUROPEAN SCHOOL EXPERIENCE IN MULTILINGUAL EDUCATION

Hugo Baetens Beardsmore

1. Introduction

This paper was originally written at the request of Dr. David Dolson of the California Department of Education[1] with a view to analysing the extent to which the model of multilingual education provided by European Schools could stimulate reflection on its suitability for adaptation to the California context. I was specifically requested to be as detailed and as concrete as possible, in order to allow administrators, teachers and researchers to get a clear insight into the way the schools operate. At no time was the intention to take over the existing model and transplant it to California as a whole. The aim was rather to see to what extent elements of the long-standing experience gained by the European Schools in coming to terms with multilingual education provision could serve as inspiration, in some adapted form, in meeting the requirements of other multilingual school populations.

It is important to bear the discussion-form nature of this paper in mind, and to react to it in the spirit in which it was written, as a global overview of a complex educational model, designed for a specific target population and with specific goals, but potentially rich in inspiration for ideas and elements which have been well tried in their context.

In the present version I shall follow the format for the California State Department of Education by introducing personal reflections on aspects that could potentially be adapted to other circumstances. Such reflections obviously lack the cross-fertilisation that should result from a discussion paper and may err on the side of over-optimism, lack of awareness of local contingencies and a bias in favour of the model being discussed. They are offered in the light of the very restricted experience, world-wide, of genuine multilingual education provision which is characterised by several ideals, namely, that the entire school population be put under the same constraints with respect to language learning, that all children involved can successfully be led to high-level proficiency in at least two languages, and that attempts be made to respect language and culture of origin while also forging a new, non-ethnocentric identity.

The late twentieth century has witnessed two related phenomena which have serious educational consequences, namely, massive population shifts for people from different ethnolinguistic backgrounds and rapid urbanisation. Urbanisation has led groups of people from the same place of origin to conglomerate in areas of a city where they can find mutual support. It was formerly believed that urban environments represented ideal locations for the gradual disappearance of linguistic heterogeneity, where code and variety differences would get smoothed out into unique urban modes of speech. Today, however, we are aware that this may not be the case and that residence patterns in the form of "urban villages" tend to promote the maintenance of linguistic diversity in cities, particularly amongst immigrants. (1980) provides strong evidence to show how dense social networks, in which interaction predominates among members of the in-group, help to maintain particular speech patterns. This is particularly true with immigrant groups.

The process of European integration is adding a new dimension to linguistic provision in schools as ever more non-immigrant populations are perceiving the need for high levels of proficiency in two or more languages. Both the LINGUA and ERASMUS programmes initiated by the Commission of the European Communities attempt to address the linguistic consequences of greater intra-European mobility, yet these represent no more than a minimal attempt at overcoming entrenched monolingualism. On the other hand, the Council of Europe is responding to a trend gradually emerging in favour of different forms of bilingual education by organising workshops to examine the use of second languages for content matter subjects in mainstream education; the first such workshop is to take place in Germany in September 1993.

At the same time as European integration proceeds there is a growing awareness of the need to support the smaller languages which may potentially come under threat as the pressures for major lingua francas of cross-European interaction augment. The European Communities MERCATOR initiative attempts to address this question.

Hence there is a demand for high-level multilingual proficiency among many sectors of the population, immigrants and their descendants, indigenous minority language groups, and with the breakdown of national frontiers, majority populations who till recently have tended to perceive themselves as not requiring much second language proficiency.

The diversification of linguistic needs, at least in Western Europe, means that the strictly bilingual, i.e. two language, models of education available are not in a position to handle the multilingual requirements of mixed populations with mixed goals. To service such needs one must turn to alternatives to the strictly bilingual model of education currently documented in the literature. To my knowledge there are few sources addressing the question of more than two languages in education programmes, apart from Genesee (1976), Baetens Beardsmore & Lebrun (1991), Byram & Leman (1990), Leman (1993) and the few papers like the present dealing with the European School phenomenon (cf. Bibliography).

European Schools have been specifically designed as multilingual establishments, i.e. where more than two languages function as medium of instruction. These schools have officially existed since 1958 and have acquired a solid reputation for scholastic achievement, linguistic equity, multilingual proficiency among the pupils and the promotion of multicultural awareness. Their organisation will be described below. Before going into details it will be useful to examine some of the more well-known concepts about bilingual education in order to clearly distinguish the philosophy behind the multilingual European Schools.

2. Models of Bilingual Education

Various types of bilingual education have been discussed by theoreticians in the field. Fishman (1976) distinguishes three kinds of bilingual outcome under the headings of maintenance, transitional and enrichment programmes. For Fishman, the major goal of a maintenance programme is to ensure that a threatened language used by minority speakers is rendered viable by an education system which helps to keep it alive. A transitional programme is one where bilingual provision is used to enable speakers to move away from the use of one language into the quasi-exclusive use of another. Most programmes dealing with immigrant education are transitional in nature. An enrichment programme is one where a second language does not replace the first, but is added so as to enable the user to function adequately in the second but at no cost to the first.

The above major goals of a given programme determine the nature of the curriculum, the role languages play and the amount of time devoted to each language. The best known enrichment type is the immersion phenomenon developed for English-speaking Canadians to acquire French, with its different forms succinctly overviewed by Swain & Lapkin (1982). Adaptations of immersion have been successfully developed in Catalonia and the Basque Country (Artigal, 1993) to integrate minority and majority language speakers in smaller language communities, though the model has been misappropriated in some American attempts to apply it to immigrant populations (cf. *Studies on Immersion Education: A Collection for U.S. Educators*, 1984).

An early total immersion programmeimmersion programme, the most popular form in Canada, consists of a radical home-school language switch from the day the child enters the first grade of school. English-speaking children have their initial contacts with the school in French and English is only gradually introduced as they grow older. Most of the children come from the same, majority-language, middle-class background. Both inside and outside the school they feel secure in the worth of their first language, English, which is never denigrated or threatened. In their homes and the environment they are constantly stimulated in the use of their majority-language. Parents who opt for immersion do so consciously on a voluntary basis and are usually well-informed about the implications involved. As middle-class representatives of mainstream society parents are often in a position to provide back-up support for the school's educational efforts and to compensate for the lack of English in the initial stages of schooling. There are few tensions between the values of the home and those transmitted by the school, or between the home and the wider society. Teachers in immersion programmes are all English-French bilinguals who, although they themselves only use French, always react appropriately when a child uses English. With time children are encouraged to interact in French, which gradually becomes the classroom language for all. Very little time is devoted to teaching French as a subject mater, instead the language serves as the medium for acquiring content. Children are initially taught to read and write in French, their abilities in these spheres gradually transferring to English when the language is later added to the curriculum. Linguistic expectations for achievement in French are realistically assessed and in no way match up to native-speaker norms.

The success of the Canadian immersion experience has led some to believe that the model represents an ideal solution for enabling immigrant and minority language group children to insert themselves into standard education, arguing that the experience is the same. Although such children, when placed in a normal mainstream school, are also faced with a home-school language switch, the circumstances are not similar to the immersion experience but represent what Skutnabb-Kangas (1984) and others have called a submersion programme. And in a submersion experience children often fail to acquire the language of the school adequately and fail to make scholastic progress. The same is true in what has been called a "structured immersion programme" in the United States, no more than a euphemism for a submersion programme which contains special English lessons for limited proficiency speakers. Some of the major features which distinguish Canadian immersion from immigrant and minority language groups are the following.

a) Immigrant and minority language children usually do not come from middle-class backgrounds and their first language is not that of the majority society, even if many others in their area of residence may speak the same language as them.

b) Often both inside and outside the school they may be made aware of the lack of worth of their first language, which is denigrated or threatened.

c) Although in their homes and immediate neighbourhoods they can receive stimuli in their first language, this may not be the case in the wider environment, so that what stimuli they do receive may be restricted.

d) Parents of immigrant children placed in standard schools have had no option about the type of programme their children follow, nor are they necessarily well-informed of the implications of the mismatch between the home and school language.

e) Although immigrant and minority group parents may be supportive of the school's educative efforts they are not always in a position to provide the back-up in the home which schools so often implicitly rely upon, through lack of means or knowledge of the school's language.(cf. Skutnabb-Kangas, 1984, 317, quoting a 19 year old Turk; "My mother is illiterate, and though my father reads and writes Turkish fairly well, he has hardly any Swedish at all, and I don't think he even knows the name of my school. Turkish parents can't give their children any help with homework.").

f) Cultural differences may lead to tensions between the values of the home and those of the school and wider society (as Paulston, 1982, 43, or Hawkesworth, 1988, have indicated on the status of girls in certain immigrant communities, for example).

g) Teachers in standard schools are rarely bilingual themselves and therefore cannot react appropriately when a child uses another language.

h) In submersion programmes teachers often spend considerable time on the target language as a subject matter and less on helping the child to acquire content matter through the target language, often a stultifying experience and the opposite of what occurs in immersion.

i) Linguistic expectations for achievement in the target language are often unrealistically compared to age-related native-speaker norms when this is not the case in immersion programmes.

The above are some significant primary differences between the circumstances of immersion and those when immersion turns into submersion for immigrant children placed in ordinary monolingual schools. Heath (1986) provides an account of child rearing differences between minority and mainstream groups and how these affect the linguistic repertoire a child brings to school, which in turn affect language usage in school. Theoretical accounts which explain the totally differing outcomes from immersion and submersion experiences have been provided in *Schooling and Language Minority Students: A Theoretical Framework* (1981). What is abundantly clear, as Hernández-Chávez (1984) has shown, is that it is a total misappropriation to take over the immersion model as a justification for placing immigrant children who know little or no English in standard monolingual English schools.

Other considerations need to be borne in mind when appraising the immersion phenomenon. Although undeniably successful in enabling children to acquire French the pupils are not comparable to native-speakers at the end of the programme. This factor is often overlooked by advocates of the immersion/submersion solution for teaching immigrant children the mainstream second language. Swain (1985) has clearly indicated that after more than seven years in a French immersion programme English children attain near native-like competence in French on written and auditory comprehension tests but reveal striking shortcomings in writing and speaking accurately.

Such productive inadequacies can be explained by several factors, including the lack of opportunity to interact with native-speaker French peers, the reinforcement of erroneous speech patterns by homogeneously English-speaking classmates, the lack of necessity to strive for structural accuracy in order to be understood and probably the small amount of structured teaching of French as a subject within the immersion programme. The results also show the great length of time required to build up a reasonable level of competence via immersion alone.

There is ample theoretical and data-based evidence (Cummins, 1984a; Skutnabb-Kangas, 1984) to indicate that an immersion-type programme is unsuitable for teaching minority-language speakers how to operate successfully in school. The same sources also give evidence to show how immigrant children can acquire high levels of proficiency in the target language if their first language is initially consolidated.

Given such evidence one must turn one's thoughts to discovering a means of providing children from different minority language backgrounds who happen to attend the same school the means of making scholastic progress in a programme that extends the bilingual provision beyond the two-language model. A model for multilingual provision which can serve as a source of inspiration is that developed in the network of European Schools.

These multilingual establishments will be described in detail below, though the description should not serve as a blueprint. As Sharp (1973) and Bentahila (1983), among others, have pointed out, no two sets of bilingual circumstances are identical, and it would be unjustified to take over wholeheartedly a model developed for a particular socio-political context and apply it to a completely different one. Just as the immersion phenomenon is unsuitable if applied to totally different circumstances, so the European School model is not for export. Instead it should be seen as an indication of what can be done in solving linguistically complex educational issues and the fruits of this experience adapted to meet similar, but different needs, elsewhere.

3. Structure

European Schools have been specifically designed as multilingual establishments, i.e. where more than two languages function as media of instruction. These schools have officially existed since 1958 and have acquired a solid reputation for scholastic achievement, linguistic equity, multilingual proficiency among the pupils and the promotion of multicultural awareness.

European Schools form part of a network of 9 schools situated in 6 different countries (Brussels I and II, Mol, Bergen, Culham, Luxembourg, Karlsruhe, Munich, Varese) and attended by approximately 14,500 children. They were specifically designed to provide education for the children of civil servants working for one of the supra-national European institutions. The schools are collectively controlled by the education authorities of the 12 member states of the European Community. Each school consists of different linguistic sub-sections in which everyone follows the same programme irrespective of the language of instruction. The largest European School is in the Belgian capital of Brussels and has about 3000 pupils ranging from kindergarten to the end of secondary education at age 18. At present the Brussels I European School contains 8 sub-sections covering all the official languages of the member states of the European Economic Community except Portuguese, namely, Danish, Dutch, English, French, German, Greek, Italian and Spanish. A Portuguese sub-section exists at the second European School, Brussels II, where there is no Spanish sub-section. A third school is to be set up in Brussels on part of the campus of the Université Libre de Bruxelles, and which will contain all the official languages of the Community.

Priority of access is given to European civil servants' children, ranging from the offspring of cabinet ministers to those of porters and cleaning staff. The schools are under an obligation to admit non-civil servant children if space is available in order to avoid the formation of population ghettos and to balance out the numbers in each linguistic sub-section where possible. One of the schools has a large number of immigrant steel-workers' children, another a large contingent of ex-miners' children. Education is free, except for the non-civil-servant children whose parents pay a nominal contribution (30,000 BF or approximately 750 ECU per annum for primary school, 60,000 BF or approximately 1,500 ECU per annum for secondary school – these feesfees are considerably reduced if more than one child is enrolled).

European Schools have a distinct philosophy as supra-national institutions which aims to reconcile two apparently contradictory goals. On the one hand they attempt to guarantee the development of the child's first language and cultural identity, while on the other they strive to promote a European identity through instruction for all pupils in at least 2 languages, compulsory learning of a 3rd as a subject matter, and options regarding a 4th language. It is important to bear in mind that within Europe this European identity is not self-evident, and that national differences are keenly felt. The schools need to be constantly aware of the need to eliminate prejudice and nationalistic antagonisms in order for them to function harmoniously and to do so they use multilingualism as a tool for both scholastic achievement and harmonious ethnolinguistic relations.

The following principles determine the nature of the programme in the schools.

1. The child's distinct national, cultural and linguistic identity must be maintained, underlining the significance of instruction in the first language.
2. Throughout schooling the child must build up competence in a second language through which he or she will be able to learn content matter and take examinations.
3. The higher the child progresses in the school the more lessons are taught via the medium of a second or third language.
4. All children are to be treated equally so that all are obliged to take on a second and third language, the third language becoming a compulsory component of the curriculum from the first year of secondary education. No sub-section is privileged linguistically.

5. From primary school onwards communal lessons are taught to members of different sub-sections brought together for integration purposes. In the primary section these communal lessons are known as European Hours. The further the children progress in the programme the more lessons are taught to mixed groups from different sub-sections.

6. In final examinations all pupils are expected to take content-matter examinations, both written and oral, at least in their first and second language; the third language might be examined solely as a subject matter or for content matter, depending on the individual's course options.

Examination criteria are theoretically the same whether the pupil is taking an examination through the medium of the first or the second language. They are also comparable to the criteria used in examinations in the different member states of the European Community.

It should be noted that the nature of the programme in a European School does not fit into any clear-cut model as discussed earlier with reference to bilingual education. It is neither an immersion nor a submersion programme. On the other hand it does represent a combination of maintenance, transitional and enrichment programmes. The first language lays the foundations for education, is maintained throughout the programme, but gradually decreases in significance as the pupils get older. Reading and writing are initially taught through the medium of the first language. A second language is introduced as a subject matter from the beginning of the programme and gradually, but not completely, takes over for content matter in secondary education. As the second language gradually increases in significance it represents a type of transitional experience which in theory and in practice will enable the pupil to pursue higher education through the medium of this language if desired. However, the programme has more in common with the enrichment model, since the second language does not take over to the detriment of the first.

Comment

From a purely linguistic viewpoint it is clear that a programme that combines maintenance, transitional and enrichment features is more likely to reconcile the needs and aspirations of all members of a society wishing to improve multilingual proficiency. A linguistic programme that can guarantee content-matter learning in the early stages via the first language supplies the basic function of schooling and should help take away some potential fears of those reticent about bilingual education (cf. Baetens Beardsmore, 1988). The gradual introduction of a second language which takes on ever more importance as one proceeds reconciles the need for content-matter education as a requisite for advanced language competence and the concomitant necessary language security. When this is done without the total elimination of the first language from the school's programme there is an element of continuity which is rewarding linguistically, cognitively and culturally.

There is a striking parallelism between the philosophy that has determined the curriculum in European Schools and the fundamental assumptions behind bilingual education provision for minorities in the United States. In a comprehensive review article, Wong Fillmore with Valadez (1986; 654) summarises the research evidence where the points of convergence with European School practice are clear. Wong Fillmore's points are as follows.

1. Students who are less than fully proficient in the school language will have difficulty deriving academic benefit from their educational experience.

   (This is one factor which determines why European Schools start education in the child's L1 and why there are so many linguistic sub-sections in each school).

2. It takes limited English proficiency students time to acquire the level of proficiency in English that is needed to participate effectively in all-English classes.

   (The European Schools do not introduce the L2 as medium of academically-oriented instruction until the 8th grade, though it does function as a medium of less intellectually-demanding subjects earlier).

3. Instruction in the native language of limited English proficiency students allows them to participate in school, and to acquire the skills and knowledge covered in the curriculum while they are learning English.

   (During the whole of primary education in European Schools basic instruction is given through the L1, including reading and writing, while the L2 is gradually introduced as a subject-matter and as a medium for intergroup activities).

4. Knowledge and skills are more easily acquired by limited English proficiency students in their native language; but computational skills and many literacy skills acquired in the native language can be transferred to the new language once it is mastered.

   (This assumption is borne out by European School practice. Once the L2 gets introduced as a medium for academically oriented subjects in grade 8 pupils rapidly develop the skills to write assignments and prepare for written examinations through the medium of the L2).

5. Pupils need adequate exposure to the language of school in order to acquire it as a second language; this exposure to English is best when it takes place in settings in which the learners' special linguistic needs help to shape the way the language gets used. Subject-matter instruction given in English can provide the exposure that

limited proficiency pupils need, as long as it is appropriately tailored for them. Subject-matter instruction in the school language is an essential component of bilingual education.

(The above principles form an integral part of the European School philosophy. After the foundations of education have been laid in the L1 pupils are gradually exposed to ever more material taught through the medium of the L2.)

6. Formal instruction in English as a second language can help pupils get started learning the language.

(A fundamental difference between European Schools and the Canadian immersion model is the place given to formal instruction in the L2. In European Schools the L2 is taught formally as a subject (which may or may not contain formal grammar, depending on the language or teacher concerned) prior to being used as a medium for content matter. Moreover, once the L2 has become a medium of content matter instruction it continues to be taught separately as a subject throughout the curriculum. It is probably this factor which accounts for the high level of grammatical accuracy attained by European School pupils by the end of the programme when they are expected to be able to write and speak in a way comparable to native speakers. Swain, (1985, 160) refers to findings from an unpublished Ph.D. thesis at the Ontario Institute for Studies in Education that examined grammatical performance and which revealed that learners require opportunities for both formal and functional language practice and, if either one is lacking, they do not seem to benefit as much. In the Ontario study it was noted that if students were in a form-focused classroom, then more informal contact led to superior grammatical performance relative to those students who had less informal contact with the language out of class. However, for students with more informal contact outside of class who had a more communicative-oriented classroom experience, the extra informal contact gave no advantage on the grammar test over their classmates with less formal contact).

The striking comparison between Wong Fillmore's analysis of some of the means of providing minority children in the United States with access to education through English and the actual practice of existing European Schools indicates the relevance of the multilingual model.

On the cultural level the European School model shows an attempt to integrate children from different national backgrounds into a broader, communal, new identity which will not threaten that of origin. Thus the school does not exacerbate ethnolinguistic tensions but harmonises modes of thinking while respecting different linguistic backgrounds. The details of how this is achieved will be examined later.

A further significant point is the notion of linguistic equality striven for in the European Schools. All children, whatever their linguistic background, are put through the same constraints where language acquisition is concerned. This is a far cry from monolingual schools containing minority populations, where only the minorities are expected to go through the strains of adapting to education in a language environment which may be difficult. Moreover, even in cases where special provision is made for minorities, only the latter are expected to make the effort towards bilingualism, meaning transition to the majority language, whereas the mainstream population are not required to make any stringent language-learning efforts. This means there is in-built linguistic discrimination, unintentional though it may be, which cannot fail to be perceived by the children in the school.

Although it is true that some children in European Schools may come from bilingual home backgrounds where both their school L1 and L2 are spoken, and that the linguistic distance between the Germanic or Romance languages may increase or decrease the learning effort for L2, depending on which combination of languages is involved, it is nevertheless the case that all children are subjected to acquiring and working through at least two languages.

4. Language in the Curriculum

Since there are 8 linguistic sub-sections in the largest European School it is important to evaluate the role of language in the totality of the curriculum. Designers of the programme have had to bear in mind the desire to respect each group's first language together with the need to create a harmonious and integrated school population which does not break up into factions based on linguistic criteria. Thought was also given to the possibility that many of the children might wish to continue their studies through the medium of a different language than their first. Two major strategies help to reconcile these goals. On the one hand there is the promotion of bilingualism for all, and on the other there is a good deal of social engineering, about which more will be said later, which both enhances the language learning process and avoids the dangers of fragmentation on linguistic lines.

In the primary school the majority of instruction is given via the medium of the first language. From the very beginning a second language is taught as a subject to all children. The second language is either English, French or German, which represent the L2s used for inter-group communication. The language of the sub-section in which a child is enrolled may not be selected as an L2 so that an

English-speaker has to select French or German as an L2, whereas a Danish speaker, for example, may select from any of the three. Often the language of the host community in which the school is located is selected as the preferred L2 of a particular school so that French is the most favoured L2 in the European School of Brussels while English is the most favoured in the school in Britain.

As in all complex linguistic settings the ideal of equal linguistic treatment for all must be reconciled with practical considerations of making the given entity viable. Thus although 8 of the 9 official languages of the member states are on an equal footing in the sub-sections of the Brussels I European School they are not all exactly equal. A Danish or a Dutch sub-section, for example, may consist of small groups of one class of pupils per grade whereas there may be 3 parallel classes for each grade of English, French or Italian children; this is unavoidable and reflects European population statistics. Statistics for the 1992/1993 school year reveal that in secondary education there were 435 children in the French sub-section but only 148 in the smallest Danish sub-section. Also, the fact that the compulsory L2 must be selected from either French, English or German, makes these languages more equal than the others. The disparity in numbers and functions of different languages within a given school has consequences on language acquisition since the school represents a multilingual micro-community where social forces affect the acquisition process.

Another factor to be borne in mind is that the schools' policy of admitting non-European civil service children means that there are more languages present than can actually be catered for. The European School of Brussels I, for example, has children of 43 nationalities outside the European Economic Community (171 pupils in 1986/1987) on its enrolment and these are distributed among the 8 established sub-sections, with the majority in the English or French sections.

Comment

It is unlikely that a school as complex as the European School is either necessary or feasible in a different context. An adapted version would be a school servicing the needs of three or four language groups in the initial stages, with potential for extension as experience grows. This is precisely the way the European Schools developed since the first establishment in the Grand Duchy of Luxembourg came into existence with four language sub-sections. As further nations joined the European Community and experience with multilingual education grew, additional language sub-sections were added. If a simplified model were envisaged it is likely that the proportion of speakers of each language would be unequal, as is the case in a European School. This should not be a problem as long as sufficient pupils of each language group are available to form a class which could move up as a cohort. Just as the European Schools require lingua francas (i.e. a shared language or languages) for intergroup contacts, an adapted version could use the majority language of the mainstream society outside the school for this purpose. However, there is no reason why linguistic equality could not form an integral part of the programme, whereby all groups would be required to learn an L2, with the mainstream representatives selecting from one of the other languages present in the school and the minorities selecting the mainstream language. This solution has the advantage over standard immersion programmes for mainstream children in that the L2 selected will be a living reality, spoken as a first language by a portion of the other children attending the same school.

5. L1 Instruction in European Schools

In primary school teachers pay particular attention to the quality of the L1 since the multilingual environment in which the children evolve is not conducive to optimal input conditions. The majority of children are not in their country of origin, they are all subjected to L2 experience from the beginning of schooling and there are many languages around them. The particular circumstances usually affect the vocabulary so that teachers have to pay more attention than in a monolingual school to extending the range and precision of lexical usage. Special attention is also paid to spelling in the L1 and is controlled in all lessons once the children have learned to read and write. In all other aspects the nature of instruction in the L1 is similar to what would be found in a monolingual school.

Teachers who use the medium of a given language are always native-speakers of that language, a quality considered essential given the role models they represent and the linguistically mixed population they are confronted with. Most teachers are also bilingual themselves to different degrees, since they mostly work in a country other than their own, and this is considered an asset since it gives them an insight into the nature of bilingualism in the children they teach.

Comment

The insistence on a native-speaker requirement in teachers is important in schools where several languages are used as the medium of instruction. In many bilingual programmes, teachers often teach through a medium which is not their native language, which at times restricts them as role models. It can also cause problems in cases where there is a significant mismatch between a teacher's non-native patterns of usage and the more native-like patterns children bring with them. This can even be the case if the teacher has specialised in the study of the non-native language. Moreover, the fact that there are native speakers of the L1s among the children implies that the teachers' prestige may be adversely affected if language ability is not at least as fluent as that of the pupils. The European Schools insist that the native-speaker requirement amongst teachers plays a significant role in the quality of the linguistic outcome of the programme. In cases where it is necessary to employ non-native teachers who use the medium of a second language these should have full professional proficiency and high levels of linguistic competence since a merely superficial competence in the language to be used as a medium of instruction could lead to potentially catastrophic role models.

6. The Place of the L2 in Primary Education in the European School

From the very beginning of primary school the different L2s, destined to develop into lingua francas for inter-pupil communication, are taught by native-speakers (not the class teacher, note) as subject matter in the same way that foreign languages are traditionally taught. There is one major difference, however, and that is that the L2s in a European School also figure as the L1 for some pupils within the same buildings, something which brings them to life as observable, genuine tools of natural communication amongst children and adults (this is not true for the small European School in Mol, Belgium, where there is no English sub-section). Moreover, these same L2s serve as language of instruction for certain subjects in the 3rd, 4th and 5th grades of primary school so that even in the early stages language learning is not totally divorced from language usage. Second language instruction is designed to be educationally enriching as well as promoting cross-cultural interaction, and its success is partly due to the fact that it goes on throughout the twelve-years of schooling.

In the primary school the L2 is taught by concentrating on the spoken language, written competence being left to the secondary programme. This does not imply that printed matter is completely absent, but that it plays a secondary role and is not the focus of attention, except for Greek children, who because of their different alphabet, are also taught the Latin alphabet symbols. Materials used tend to be specifically designed as foreign language materials for young children but may be supplemented by appropriate materials that would be used with a similar age group in L1 classes, e.g. games, puzzles, etc. Although the goals aimed at in L2 teaching are the same for the three languages involved, slightly different strategies may be used, depending on the L2 in question. English L2 teachers in primary school tend to base themselves on a functional notional approach whereas French L2 teachers may use more written materials than their English counterparts because of the nature of French syntax, where agreement of gender and past participles may or may not be masked in speech but is marked in writing. The focus of attention is on basic grammar and lexis (this process continuing into the secondary programme up to the age of 14, beyond which there is no more structural work on the L2 but the language is used as a medium of instruction for both language and non-language subjects).

Two types of special support are provided for children who arrive in the middle of the school year, perhaps from another country or from a monolingual programme. Pupils with no knowledge of an L2 are sent to *"cours de rattrapage"* or "catching-up classes" during the periods when their classmates are receiving L2 as a subject – they are not separated, however, when the L2 is used for teaching content matter, where such late arrivals may have great difficulty in following in the initial stages. Special remedial language teachers then try to bring the new arrivals up to class levels by tailor-made, intensive teaching which is supplemented by extra lessons outside the normal school timetable, i.e. on Wednesday afternoons which are free for other children. The second type of special provision for late arrivals with inadequate mastery of the L2 in the secondary programme is known as *"cours de soutien"* or "support classes", where further tailor-made instruction is provided, including help with handling content-matter material taught through the L2. These support classes take place when the late arrivals' classmates follow their optional "complementary courses" in the secondary programme (cf. Section 10).

From the 3rd grade onwards physical education is usually taught to mixed groups via the medium of the shared L2, a practice which is continued right through the programme till the end of secondary education. For example, the teacher of physical education might be a native-speaker of French taking a class made up of children from four or five linguistic sub-sections. In theory the teacher will only use French to explain the nature of the game or activity that is to take place. Questioning the children involved reveals that in practice the teacher, in these early stages, will predominantly use his or her native language but may often translate instructions into two or three languages in order to proceed more quickly. This often may go little further than translating a few key words to make sure everyone has understood. Another area where the L2s come into their own is in the set of communal activities known as "European Hours", which represent an important element behind the philosophy of the schools (cf. section 7). By the end of primary school the build up of instruction of and through the medium of the L2 means that approximately 25% of the time-table is taken up via the L2 and as children progress through secondary education this proportion increases significantly.

Comment

Note the major difference between immersion programmes of L2 instruction and the above model. The L2 is taught as a subject before it becomes used as a medium and when this does occur it takes place in cognitively undemanding and highly contextualised circumstances (cf. Cummins, 1981; 1984a) such as physical education or during European Hours, which are described in more detail below (cf. section 7). Once the L2 starts to be used as a medium of instruction it continues to be taught separately as a subject.

7. European Hours

These represent a very important component in the philosophy of the schools. From the 3rd year of primary education 3 lessons per week are devoted to what are called "European Hours". These lessons *may* be conducted in the L2 but are *not intended as language lessons*. In the schools in Luxembourg and Munich the common language tends to be one of the three official L2s, whereas in other schools the medium tends to be that of the out-of-school host community. The primary goal is to group children from the various language sections and, by getting them to work and play together, to make them aware of their common European heritage. They form part of the social engineering (cf. Section 16) designed to break down the fragmentation inherent to the presence of 8 sub-sections. Children are brought together in classes of about twenty to twenty-five, made up of groups of four to five children from different sub-sections for one afternoon per week. Nearly six hundred children are involved in these European Hours in the European School of Brussels I, organised in some thirty groups of roughly twenty children each. Priority is given to co-operative activities based on creative tasks such as sewing, cooking, construction projects, making puppets and often a theme is developed over several weeks, such as preparing for carnival. Teachers are free to carry out any activity they like as long as it mixes children from different sub-sections and encourages them to co-operate with each other. Half way through the school year, in some but not all schools, a different teacher, from a different language background, takes over the European Hours to reinforce the multicultural aspect of education. Some schools, but not all, also use the language of the out-of-school environment if it is French, German or English, in European Hours. All primary school class teachers are involved.

When a theme is introduced in European Hours the following 5 phases are borne in mind;

1. creation of an atmosphere where each child will feel comfortable and be encouraged to get actively involved in a group project;
2. fixing a realisable goal;
3. forming working groups to attain the goal;
4. encouraging communication so as to seek to work together;
5. showing the results to the rest of the school, e.g. through demonstrations, exhibitions, dances, songs.

Observation of a sample lesson during a European Hour revealed the following features. The twenty-two children in the 5th year class were made up of 5 children from the German section, 6 from the French section, 6 from the Italian section and 5 from the Dutch section. Children from the same group tended to cluster and talk to each other in their own languages. The teacher, a French speaker who used no other language, explained the creative activity which consisted of producing a three dimensional work of art using many different materials. Some children in the class had insufficient command of French to clearly understand what was expected (these were recent arrivals at the school). Other children from the same language background would act as informal interpreters or would show their classmates what to do. Once the activity had been explained the teacher would help individual children to perform the activity. Note that although the European Hour is not a language lesson the L2 assumes great relevance by the very fact that it is the only medium common to the whole group. Of the three lessons per week devoted to European Hours, two are classroom activities and one is a games activity conducted outside. No attempts are made to force children to use the L2, though obviously the teacher cannot be expected to know the four languages present in the whole class. By the nature of the circumstances, however, the L2 is perceived as significant as the lingua franca so that children become sensitive to the different roles languages play in their immediate environment and accept the circumstances as natural. Again the activity in the L2 is context-embedded and cognitively undemanding.

A second function of the European Hours is that they represent the first instance of the school trying to promote a new European identity, an avowed policy aim. By familiarising the children with representatives of other European countries the schools hope to overcome prejudice and stereotyped reactions before they have had time to develop. Throughout schooling the programme insists on building up a supra-national, European identity and effects this by gradually mixing children from different countries in as many activities as possible.

How successful the programme is in this respect is difficult to assess. It has been noted that whereas in primary school most friendship circles remain within the language sub-section to which the child belongs, by the end of secondary education the majority of friendship patterns are outside the pupil's sub-section, as revealed by a study among 17 and 18 year olds (Housen & Baetens Beardsmore, 1987).

Comment

The above lessons represent the first attempt by the school to manipulate the population so as to interact across the language barriers, and with time such mixings become ever more significant. In a multilingual school it is vital to avoid segregation which might lead to tensions between groups. It is also vital to produce circumstances where an L2 assumes a natural function but where the linguistic demands are not beyond those that can be expected from limited contact with that language. The mixed group sessions provide non-threatening circumstances for interaction across groups. An adaptation of the concept of European Hours could take on many forms, depending on the context in which the school operates, from metacultural communication sessions to integration of minority and majority cultures within a national or regional frame of reference.

8. Primary School Curriculum

The primary school programme consists of a 5 year cycle in which all sub-sections follow the same timetable and same programme, irrespective of the language of the section. Primary education may be preceded by voluntary attendance in the kindergarten, which may fulfil a useful function for certain children by consolidating language skills in the language of the sub-section which is later to be attended in school. This may be necessary for children who come from bi- or multilingual home backgrounds, or who have travelled about a lot. Table 1 gives the programme for the whole grade for each year, expressed in terms of 30 or 45 minute lesson slots. All subjects are taught through the L1 of the section except those in italics.

Table 1. *Primary school curriculum expressed in number of lessons per week and per grade. Lessons not using the L1 are in italics.*

1st and 2nd grades		3rd, 4th and 5th grades	
L1 as a subject	16 x 30 mins	L1 as a subject	9 x 45 mins
Mathematics	8 x 30 mins	Mathematics	7 x 45 mins
L2 as a subject	*5 x 30 mins*	*L2 as a subject*	*5 x 45 mins*
Music	3 x 30 mins	Environmental studies	4 x 45 mins
Art	4 x 30 mins	Art	1 x 45 mins
Physical education	4 x 30 mins	Music	1 x 45 mins
Environmental studies	2 x 30 mins	*Physical education*	*1 x 45 mins*
Religion or ethics	2 x 30 mins	*European Hours*	*3 x 45 mins*
Recreation	7 x 30 mins	Religion or ethics	2 x 45 mins
Total	33 x 30 mins per week	Total	33 x 45 mins per week

Comment

Of primary concern for reflection is the time devoted to the use of the L2. In the first two grades the L2 as a subject is restricted to five lessons a week whereas in the following three grades the L2 functions both as a subject and a medium of instruction for a little over 25% of the school week. A different proportional build-up might be envisaged in other contexts, but it would be wise not to try and increase the L2 too significantly in the early stages. Some educationists have a tendency to expect quick results from a specific programme with respect to the L2, but need to remember that linguistic development is a lengthy process where ultimate achievement, in at least two languages, is the main concern, not transitional levels in mid-stream. The proportion of time devoted to each language in the early stages depends on a variety of factors, including the status of the languages involved, their roles in the wider environment and the final goals of the multilingual programme, whether to develop high levels of bilingualism and biliteracy, or to develop partial bilingualism/biliteracy.

Canadian immersion research has shown that in the early stages of development the pupils involved have lower results in L1 than do unilingual comparison groups, and restricted results in L2. Leman's (1993) overview of linguistic results in the Foyer Project;(Leman), involving trilingual education for migrants, reveals similar trends. In Canada, Swain (1981) has shown that with time L1 English results are slightly better than those of mainstream, monolingual comparison groups and that L2 French results become near native-like on the tests used. Other research has also shown that with immigrant populations, more, not less instruction in the L1 in the initial stages later helps in the development of the mainstream L2, counter-intuitive though this may appear (Cummins, 1984a).

9. Secondary School Programme

The secondary school programme breaks down into 3 phases, the first of which is called the "Observation Cycle", and which lasts for 3 years from grades 6-8. During the observation cycle the general programme is followed by everyone, though a limited number of options are introduced. In the 8th grade the L3 is introduced as a compulsory subject and the choice of L3 may be made from any of the official languages in the school which have not yet been studied, except for Irish and Belgian nationals. Irish nationals must take compulsory Irish as an L3 and Belgians their second national language (French or Dutch) if this has not been part of their curriculum lower down in the school; these obligations are made so as to align Irish and Belgian children on the national programmes in their country of origin. The L3 is taught as a subject and not used as a medium of instruction, though later on in secondary education it may figure as a medium of instruction if available on the set of elective courses which pupils may decide to follow.

A limited study of the options for L2 and L3 at the European School in Karlsruhe, Germany, for the period between 1985-1990 reveals that the local out-of-school language, in this case German, is not selected by 100% of the pupils in all the sub-sections (Otero-Lamas 1994). The author speculates that the pupils who do not select German are either less willing to adapt to the host environment or else do not intend to stay in Karlsruhe for any length of time. Italians seem to select German more than pupils from other sub-sections. In Karlsruhe it appears that 100% of the pupils select a third language, a considerable number decide to drop it, particularly those in the Italian and English sub-sections. As for the 4th language, which becomes optional in grade 8, the English and Dutch sub-sections appear to take this the least. Since there has been little investigation into L3 and L4 at the European Schools it would be inappropriate to discuss these further.

The L2 takes on a more significant role in the observation cycle. Whereas music and art had been taught in the respective L1s in primary school they are now taught to mixed groups through the medium of the L2. A set of "Complementary Activities" are now offered as elective subjects, from which at least two must be selected in the first year of secondary education (grade 6), and these are also taught through the medium of the L2. Complementary activities consist of such subjects as electronics, computer science, photography, painting, typing, needlework, etc., and are aimed at developing other than purely intellectual capacities. Note that in this phase where the role of the L2 is extended the activities in which it is used are still relatively context-embedded and cognitively undemanding.

In grades 6 and 7 the human sciences (i.e. history and geography) are taught via the different L1s of each sub-section in order to familiarise children with their national origins. In grade 8, however, the human sciences are taught to mixed groups through the medium of the L2 and take on a different perspective. The subject matter is now taught in a European light, bringing out the varied perspectives on European history. For example, a French pupil with English as an L2 will be taught the history of the French Revolution in English by an English-speaking teacher.

There is a fundamental difference with respect to the L2 when one compares the primary and secondary school programmes. In primary school communal lessons taught to mixed language groupsmixed language groups may include native-speaker peers of the given L2, in European Hours, for example. In the secondary programme it is the exception to have native-speaker peers in classes taught through the medium of the L2 since all pupils receive instruction through their non-native language in the same time slot.

In the secondary school programme standard manuals or text-books play a far less significant role than in monolingual schools. Only for the teaching of languages themselves or for subjects taught through the medium of the L1 are standard text books used, and for the different L1s these obviously differ from sub-section to sub-section. For all other subjects teachers rely far less on standardised textbooks than in monolingual schools and are expected to devise much of their own material in order to meet the requirements of their mixed language populations. Whatever materials are used require slight modifications at this level and teachers may provide multilingual glossaries of the specific subject-matter terminology to ensure that the student has the requisite vocabulary in both the L1 and the L2. Atlases used never provide place names in translation, as would happen in monolingual settings (e.g. Londres = London) but instead give place names in the original language.

Since parents express worries about the capacity of their children to acquire more abstract content-matter through the medium of the L2 when the human sciences switch over to the use of this language, briefing sessions are organised where teachers provide reassurance about the nature and outcome of the programme.

At the organisational level the logistics of the secondary school programme are different from those applicable in primary school. Whereas in primary school children had fixed classrooms which represented the "home-base" of their particular sub-section, in secondary school it is not the pupils who have a fixed classroom but the teachers. Thus the 120 teachers in the secondary programme in Brussels I each have their fixed classroom in which they can express their personal identity and subject orientation. Pupils are constantly on the move between classrooms during breaks, since this more easily allows for the assignment to mixed groups which take into account great flexibility inherent in the number of elective courses available. The movement from classroom to classroom also allows for informal interaction between pupils which also enhances opportunities to use their different languages outside the formal setting.

By the end of the observation cycle (grade 8) the amount of instruction not provided through the L1 has increased to approximately 15 periods a week, or almost half of the curriculum.

Table 2 provides the curriculum for the observation cycle in secondary school expressed in lesson slots of 45 minutes per week and per grade.

Table 2. Secondary school programme for the observation cycle (Grades 6-8). Lessons not using the L1 are in italics.

Subject	Grade 6	Grade 7	Grade 8
L1 as a subject	5 x 45"	5 x 45"	4 x 45"
Mathematics	4 x 45"	4 x 45"	4 x 45"
Latin (optional)	-	-	4 x 45"
Integrated science	4 x 45"	4 x 45"	4 x 45"
Religion or ethics	2 x 45"	2 x 45"	2 x 45"
Human sciences (a)	3 x 45"	3 x 45"	*3 x 45"*
L3 as a subject	-	-	*4 x 45"*
L2 as a subject	*5 x 45"*	*4 x 45"*	*4 x 45"*
Graphic & plastic arts	*2 x 45"*	*2 x 45"*	*2 x 45"*
Music	*2 x 45"*	*2 x 45"*	*2 x 45"*
Physical education	*3 x 45"*	*3 x 45"*	*3 x 45"*
Complementary activities	*2 x 45"*	*2 x 45"*	*2 x 45"*
Total	32 x 45"	32 x 45"	31/33 x 45"

a) Taught through the medium of the L2 in grade 8.
b) Those who select Latin may drop either music or graphic and plastic arts.
c) In grade 6 two optional complementary activities must be selected but may be dropped in grades 7 and 8.

Comment

Two important factors need to be noted with reference to the early grades of secondary education. The first is the increase in time devoted to using the L2 as a medium of instruction and the second is the nature of the transition taking place in the curriculum. Whereas in primary school and the first two grades of secondary school matter dealt with in the L2 is mainly context-embedded and cognitively undemanding, by the 8th grade, when the human sciences are taught via the L2, the task has become more cognitively demanding and context-reduced, and therefore more linguistically challenging. However, it is not as though a completely new subject were being taught through the medium of the weaker language since the same area of study had been dealt with in the L1 in grades 6 and 7. Moreover, the provision of multilingual glossariesserves the function of both helping comprehension in the L2 and ensuring that the pupil can acquire the relevant lexis in the L1.

The nature of the content-matter taught in the human sciences is worth reflecting on. Just as the European School gives history and geography in the L1 to consolidate knowledge of the child's origins, a similar strategy could be applied in an adaptation of the model. When the transition to L2 takes place this could serve as the point where mainstream society history and geography are gone into in some depth. (1993) indicates some of the difficulties a geography teacher may encounter when trying to reconcile different perspectives on what is significant in national geography syllabuses and gives suggestions on how to overcome inherent discrepancies in contents, materials and examination requirements.

10. The Middle Cycle of Secondary Education

The middle cycle of the secondary school programme, covering grades 9 and 10, is known as the "semi-specialisation cycle" where pupils have a greater selection of options available, which enables them to specialise their interests. During this period there is a certain amount of variability in the amount of time taken up by subjects not taught through the L1, depending on the combination of elective courses chosen. A glance at table 3 shows that from a maximum total of 31- 35 periods a week, and depending on the choice of elective courses, a pupil can receive 20 periods not taught through the L1, or almost two thirds of the curriculum.

Table 3. Secondary school programme for the semi-specialisation cycle in number of lessons per week and per grade. Lessons not using the L1 are in italics.

Subject	Grades 9 and 10	Elective courses	
L1 as a subject	4 x 45 mins	Latin	4 x 45 mins
Religion or ethics	1 x 45 mins	Greek	4 x 45 mins
Biology	2 x 45 mins	*Economics & Social Sciences*	*4 x 45 mins*
Chemistry	2 x 45 mins	*Plastic arts*	*2 x 45 mins*
Physics	2 x 45 mins	*Music*	*2 x 45 mins*
Mathematics (a)	4 or 6 x 45 mins	*L4 as a subject*	*4 x 45 mins*
L2 as a subject	*3 x 45 mins*		
Physical education	*2 x 45 mins*		
History	*2 x 45 mins*		
Geography	*2 x 45 mins*		
L3 as a subject	*3 x 45 mins*		
Total	27 or 29 x 45 mins		

a) Depending on the pupil's choice
b) Enough elective subjects must be chosen to guarantee a curriculum of minimum 31 and maximum 35 periods per week.

Comment

Of note at this stage is that the transitionary potential of the programme begins to make itself felt in that more time is spent learning through the L2 than through the L1. However, the exact sciences, which have been introduced as compulsory in the pre-orientation stage, are introduced via the L1. It is important to note the maintenance element by which the L1 continues to serve as a medium for some subjects or else an adapted model would clearly become of the transitional type, potentially to the detriment of further development of the original language.

11. The Final Cycle of Secondary Education

The last two years of secondary education, grades 11 and 12, known as the "Specialisation Cycle", have a limited number of compulsory subjects. In 1986-1987 in the European School in Brussels almost every one of the 400 pupils involved had a tailor-made timetable, leading to complex organisational

Table 4. Secondary school programme for the specialisation cycle expressed in subjects per grade per week. Subjects not taught through the L1 are in italics.

Compulsory subjects	Grades 11 & 12
L1 as a subject	4 x 45 mins
Philosophy	2 x 45 mins
Mathematics	3 or 5 x 45 mins
L2 as a subject	*3 x 45 mins*
History	*2 x 45 mins*
Geography	*2 x 45 mins*
Physical education	*2 x 45 mins*
Religion or ethics	*1 x 45 mins*

Elective courses	
Latin	5 x 45 mins
Greek	5 x 45 mins
Physics	4 x 45 mins
Chemistry	4 or 5 x 45 mins
Biology	4 or 5 x 45 mins
L3 as a subject	*3 x 45 mins*
L4 as a subject	*3 x 45 mins*
Advanced course in L1 as a subject	3 x 45 mins
Advanced course in mathematics	3 x 45 mins
Advanced physics and chemistry	2 x 45 mins
Economics	*5 x 45 mins*
Advanced course in L2 as a subject	*3 x 45 mins*
Advanced course in geography	*2 x 45 mins*
Advanced course in history	*2 x 45 mins*
Plastic arts	*2 x 45 mins*
Music	*2 x 45 mins*
Sociology	*2 x 45 mins*
Other subjects	*2 x 45 mins*

n.b. A pupil must have a timetable with a minimum of 31 and a maximum of 35 periods per week.

questions. A new set of elective courses is introduced at this level, known as advanced courses in a particular domain, and consist of a more intellectually abstract approach to the field.

It is impossible to calculate the amount of time devoted to the use of each language at this level, given the great individual variation, though it is clear that the amount of instruction received through the L1 is likely to be about a third of the programme. Religion or ethics, which until now had been taught through the L1, are continued in the L2 as compulsory subjects.

Although there have been no in-depth studies to date on the methodology followed in using the L2 either as a subject or a medium of instruction, observation of a restricted number of sample lessons gives some idea of teaching practice. It has already been noticed that in primary education the L2 is taught as a subject to mixed groups before its introduction as a medium for relatively undemanding cognitive activities. In the L2 language lessons there are no native-speaker peers present (unless children come from mixed marriage bilingual backgrounds, as is sometimes the case), since all sub-sections are being taught different L2s. Teachers concentrate on the spoken language and follow standard practice for teaching a second language to young children. In lessons where the L2 functions as a medium of instruction native-speaker peers are present in primary school, as has been illustrated in European hours discussed earlier.

In the secondary programme no lessons using the L2 contain native-speakers of that language except in certain elective courses in the final grades, such as economics or sociology. Teachers all claim that native-speaker peer contacts develop spontaneously the further up the school the pupil moves, and this has been borne out by interviews. Given the size of the school at Brussels I and the number of teachers and languages involved it is difficult to describe typical teacher-pupil interaction patterns or instructional style when the L2 is being used. Observations of sample lessons have revealed considerable differences, depending on the stage in the programme at which the L2 is used, the nature of the subject-matter being treated, the particular language involved, and the type of training a teacher has received, which reflects that teacher's national background. What does come clearly to the fore, however, is that all teachers are aware of the particular multilingual circumstances of the school in which they work so that all share a few basic principles. For example, when pupils from different sub-sections come together for L2 lessons they automatically tend to group themselves according to language of origin. The majority of teachers try to break up such patterning by encouraging people from different sub-sections to sit together so as to render the use of the L2 necessary and natural. All teachers in L2 classes, whatever their nature, tend to include linguistic features in their teaching, paying particular attention to lexical precision and controlling the accuracy of written production. Teachers observed in L2 medium classes all tended to spontaneously correct minor errors in a naturalistic fashion by merely repeating the correct form before moving on. In the secondary school programme lessons involving the L2 are conducted at a natural pace and the tempo does not appear to be slowed down because of the presence of non-native speakers. Considerable teacher-pupil interaction occurs via rapid and natural question and answer strategies, and indeed to the casual observer it is not self-evident that pupils are receiving instruction through the medium of an L2.

To illustrate the nature of teaching practice four types of L2 lessons will be described briefly.

In grade 8 a combined history and geography lesson was observed being taught via the L2 French by a French teacher. There were 20 pupils in the class, made up of 7 English-speakers, 8 speakers of Greek and 5 speakers of Italian. The lesson was observed during the second week of the new school year, i.e. at the beginning of the phase where the L2 is first used as a medium of instruction for cognitively demanding activities and therefore a new experience for the pupils. The manual being used was a standard text-book produced in France for native-speakers. Content-matter was presented in a highly structured fashion, though with many questions and answers provided fluently and with little hesitation. A Greek and a British pupil were first invited to summarise points dealt with in the previous lesson and prepared for homework. The British boy was requested to correctly identify Neolithic, Palaeolithic and Bronze-Age specimens present in the classroom on a time scale. Population densities were discussed and comparisons made with populations in the different countries represented in the class. Almost all pupils were called upon to provide information at some time. The very few language errors that were made were spontaneously corrected by the teacher repeating the correct forms without dwelling on them. As the lesson progressed the teacher provided a sentence-by-sentence summary of the major points which pupils copied from the blackboard on the right-hand page of their notebooks. On the left-hand page pupils were requested to note down new words, concepts and definitions. For homework pupils were requested to look up the words *"nomade"* and *"sédentaire"* in any French dictionary and to be prepared to discuss these concepts in the following lesson.

The above lesson can be compared with a 10th grade economics class provided in the L2 by a British teacher in the second week of the school year. Again this represented a new experience since economics was a new elective subject for the people involved. There were 13 pupils present, including 2 native-speakers of English, as this is an elective course, 6 Danish-speakers, 2 French-speakers and 3 German-speakers. A standard British manual designed for native-speakers was used, supplemented by photocopies of newspaper extracts. In this introduction to economics very basic concepts were defined by means of rapid questions and answers stimulated by cartoon drawings. All pupils were called upon to help in making the concepts precise, there was no language correction and the pace of the lesson appeared similar to that of a native-speaker class. The quality of English was fluent and not significantly marked.

In lessons observed where the L2 was the subject of instruction, as opposed to the medium, there was a notable difference in approach according to the language. A 10th grade lesson in L2 French as a subject, taught by a French national, concentrated on a literary analysis at a level of abstraction similar to what is likely to occur in the same type of lesson where French is the L1. Of the 21 pupils present, 9 were English-speakers, 4 Dutch-speakers, 3 Italian-speakers, 2 Greek-speakers, 2 Danish-speakers and 1 German-speaker. The pace of the lesson was extremely lively with rapid question and answer strategies directing towards discovering the structure and theme of the text. Pupils intervened with great fluency, though at times pronunciation and gender errors were corrected. The level of abstraction led to problems of lexical availability which were dealt with either by synonym-seeking or by direct reference to grammatical terminology. The liveliness of this lesson might be accounted for by several factors, including the teacher's personality and the fact that in Brussels French is the out-of-school language which provides it with massive reinforcement. What was more striking was that to the observer it did not come across as significantly different from an L1 lesson; pupils obviously coped and enjoyed the activity.

An 11th grade lesson where L2 English was the subject differed significantly from the preceding in that it was far more obviously a language lesson. The class of 24, taught by an Irish national, was made up of 8 Italian speakers, 7 Spanish speakers, 5 French speakers, 2 German speakers, 2 speakers of Greek and one of Danish. An advanced English-as-a-foreign language manual was used as a basis for discussion after certain extracts had been read aloud by the teacher. Discussion developed freely after intensive questions and answers. The teacher concentrated specifically on highly idiomatic vocabulary, there was little correction and no writing involved, though pupil intervention was lively. The difference in nature between the English and French L2 lessons could be accounted for in several ways, primarily the fact that English is not the major out-of-school language in Brussels and therefore might require more language-focused treatment. Although pupils were generally fluent, accents were more marked than in the similar French lesson, as was the occasional grammatical feature. Another explanation for the difference might be that the Irish teacher was qualified in English-as-a-foreign language, where a comparable qualification is rare or non-existent in France. A third explanation might be the differing intellectual traditions in the countries the teachers came from and which were noted in the nature of the lessons, with the French class reflecting a quest for abstraction and generalisation while its English counterpart reflected pragmatic considerations. What was striking, however, was that in spite of these differences, the amount of pupil involvement was equally lively, fluent and spontaneous.

The above descriptions merely serve as illustrations and may in no way represent all L2 lessons in European Schools. Indeed, the actual differences observed may have been purely coincidental since the L2 English programme also contains the study of literature and may just have been absent from preoccupation at the point of observation.

Comment

Several points come to the fore now that the whole programme has been surveyed. In any adapted version it might well be that the majority out-of-school language should function as the lingua franca for the entire population, for many obvious reasons. This should considerably reinforce the acquisition of the major language as an L2 by non-native speakers. Consequently, it is important to reflect on just how much of the timetable can be devoted to instruction of or through the medium of the L1. At all events, it is felt preferable to maintain the L1 right to the end of the programme if the curriculum is destined to have combined maintenance, transitional and enrichment features. Likewise, opportunities could be sought for teaching at least one other subject through the medium of the language with the smallest role in the curriculum (foreign languages not part of the basic programme or classical languages excepted, of course), to provide extra reinforcement.

Since all lessons in a European School tend to some extent to be language lessons, though at times in a low key, it would probably be appropriate to take up a similar stance if an adapted version were taken up elsewhere. The availability of manuals and materials obviously depends on local circumstances, but even when high quality materials are available in European Schools, they have to be supplemented in order to take into account the multilingual and multicultural nature of the populations in each class.

Teaching strategies in European Schools appear to be highly interactive and at the same time well-structured, in that teachers observed were clearly conscious of the need to provide models for note-taking which were precise and accurate.

12. Timetables

The organisation of a school which contains 8 parallel sub-sections is obviously a complex process, particularly in the secondary programme where so many options are available. Two mathematics teachers have special responsibility for all the time-tables and spend much time on computerised scheduling.

Irrespective of the language sub-section they are enrolled in all pupils follow the same curriculum and same timetable, except for new arrivals in the middle of the school year or those who join a European School programme from a standard monolingual school and who need special tuition in order to reach their class L2 level. Such new arrivals follow the same programme as their classmates except during language lessons when they may attend special remedial classes (cf. Section 6); they may also be requested to attend special remedial classes on Wednesday afternoons when the rest of the school has a half-day holiday. The school day starts at 8.10 a.m. and classes end at 16.35 p.m. in the secondary school, a little earlier in primary school.

In the primary school time-tables are fairly straightforward. Since all the children spend most of the time with their class teacher the schedule consists simply of 8 parallel time-tables side by side as if they were in one monolingual establishment. In the time slots devoted to lessons on the L2 as a subject everyone is involved with different languages so that children move to the class where the L2 chosen by their parents is taught. These L2 as a subject lessons do not normally contain native-speakers. Teacher time-tables fit into this distribution, whereby native-speaker primary teachers of the L2s (English, French and German) take on mixed groups instead of their normal classes while the others, e.g. Danish or Greek class teachers, may take on Physical Education to mixed groups. In communal lessons children are split up and directed to a particular class in groups of about 5. All primary school teachers are involved in European Hours which are not considered as language lessons and where any combination of pupil make-up may exist. These lessons are grouped into one afternoon per week so that the time-table is straightforward.

In the secondary school time-tables must be worked out individually. Each child is given a tailor-made schedule which he or she is expected to have readily available as a means of identification. Since there are 2000 secondary pupils constantly moving from class to class on the Brussels I site this personalised time-table is one of the few means of controlling the legitimacy of free periods. As in the primary school, the same time-table applies to a particular grade irrespective of the sub-section, though elective choices may well mean that a given pupil's time-table is very different from that of a classmate. Individual schedules contain the time-slot, name of the subject, teacher's name and classroom number.

To illustrate how pupils are combined and separated according to their sub-section, their L2 option and their elective courses, Table 5 compares two 9th grade pupils and Table 6 two 12th grade pupils.

Comment

Comparing pupils from different sub-sections in the same grade shows how the combination and separation occurs in practice. 12th grade pupils number 91

Table 5. *9th grade time-tables for pupils from the French and English sub-sections. Communal lessons to mixed groups are in italics.*

Pupil No 110 - 9th grade French sub-section.

	Monday	Tuesday	Wednesday	Thursday	Friday
1.	*Phys.Ed.*	Physics	*L4*	Maths	Maths
2.	Physics	Maths	*Music*	*L2*	*Music*
3.	Maths	Maths	*Phys. Ed.*	Biology	*L2*
4.	*History*	*Geography*	*L3*	*L4*	
5.	*L4*	L1	*History*	Chemistry	L1
6.					
7.	Maths	*L4*		*Geography*	Religion
8.	*L3*	Biology		*L3*	
9.	*L2*	L1		L1	Chemistry

Pupil No 38 - 9th grade English sub-section.

	Monday	Tuesday	Wednesday	Thursday	Friday
1.	*Economics*	Physics	Computer	*Phys.Ed.*	L1
2.	Biology	L1	*Arts*	*L2*	*Arts*
3.	L1	*Phys.Ed.*		Physics	*L2*
4.	*History*	*Geography*	*L3*	*Economics*	
5.	Computer	Biology	*History*	Chemistry	Ethics
6.					
7.	Maths	*Economics*		*Geography*	Maths
8.	*L3*	L1		*L3*	*Economics*
9.	*L2*	Maths		Maths	Chemistry

(French sub-section) and number 62 (English sub-section) go to different classes in the first four periods on Monday. In the 5th period both are receiving their respective L1s. In the 6th period both are receiving their respective L3s (where No 91 follows Dutch and No 62 follows French). During the 7th period both are following their respective L2s (where No 91 has English and No 62 has German). In the 8th period both are following history (No 91 in English and No 62 in German).

As far as teacher time-tables are concerned these are designed in European Schools in terms of language, subject matter and level in the programme.

Table 5. 12th grade time-tables for pupils from the French and English sub-sections. Communal lessons are in italics.

Pupil No 91 - 12th grade French sub-section.

	Monday	Tuesday	Wednesday	Thursday	Friday
1.	Maths	L1	Chemistry	L1	L2
2.	*Ethics*	Chemistry	Maths		L3
3.	Chemistry	*History*	Maths	Philosophy	Physics
4.		Physics	*Phys. Ed.*	L1	Philosophy
5.	L1	Maths	L3	Maths	*Geography*
6.	L3	*Geography*		*Phys. Ed.*	
7.	L2	Physics		Physics	Maths
8.	*History*	L2		Maths	
9.				Maths	

Pupil No 62 - 12th grade English sub-section.

	Monday	Tuesday	Wednesday	Thursday	Friday
1.	*Religion*	L1		L1	L2
2.	Maths		Chemistry	*Phys. Ed.*	L3
3.		*Geography*	Chemistry	L1	Biology
4.	Maths	Chemistry	Chemistry	Philosophy	Philosophy
5.	L1	Maths	L3		*Geography*
6.	L3	*History*		Biology	Biology
7.	L2			Chemistry	Biology
8.	*History*	L2		Maths	Biology
9.	*Phys. Ed.*	Biology		Maths	

Primary school teacher time-tables are similar to those in monolingual schools in that each teacher in a given sub-section is responsible for his or her class for a particular grade.

In the secondary school programme attempts are made to enable pupils to have the same teacher for each subject for the whole of one of the three cycles so as to provide continuity. Table 7 illustrates an English language teacher's time-table. This teacher teaches English as a native language and as an L2 to different grades. Time-tables for teachers of non-language subjects are similar to those in monolingual schools so that mathematics teachers, for example, in a French or Italian section, would have very similar or even parallel time-tables, since they do not have to cross over languages or teach to mixed groups. Each teacher is required to teach 23 periods a week.

Table 7. Secondary school programme: English teacher's time-table.

Time	Mon	Tues	Wed	Thurs	Fri
8.10-8.55	6th year L1				7th year L2
9.00-9.45	2nd year L2	2nd year L2	6th year L1	4th year L2	5th year L1
9.50-10.35			1st year L1		4th year L2
10.35-10.50			Recreation		
10.50-11.35	1st year L1	6th year L2		2nd year L2	
11.35-12.20		1st year L1		2nd year L2	
12.45-13.30					
13.30-14.15	7th year L2	6th year L1		6th year L2	2nd year L2
14.15-15.00		7th year L2			6th year L2
15.00-15.45	4th year L2	1st year L1			6th year L1
15.00-16.35					

13. Teachers and Staff

Teachers and directors of European Schools are seconded from their different national education systems for a period of years which differs from country to country. Hence all teachers using a given language are native-speakers of that language, irrespective of the population make-up of the classes, and all must be bilingual. After a particular director's period of office the successor must be of a different nationality.

No special certification is requisite for work in a European School beyond national teacher certification requirements. There is no training available in Europe for working in a multilingual school and most teachers learn how to adapt to the special circumstances of the school while on the job. Some of the British teachers have specialist qualifications in EFL but this is an exception. When new teachersnew teachers are engaged they usually spend two or three weeks in the European School the year preceding their contract so as to become familiar with the system. New teachers are also assigned to the care of an existing teacher who acts as a guide and mentor in the initial stages. Given the complexity of the programme as far as languages and nationalities are concerned new teachers sometimes need time to adapt to the circumstances of a curriculum totally different from any they may be familiar with.

The whole network of European Schools regularly organises in-service re-training sessions or study seminars for different groups of teachers. In 1986/1987, for example, the following courses took place for teachers; a seminar for teachers of Italian as a first or a foreign language, one for teachers of Danish as a first or foreign language, one for music teachers; working group sessions for biology, physics and chemistry teachers.

In order to co-ordinate the activities across grades and across languages non-remunerated co-ordinators are elected among the teachers for a 2 year period, whose task it is to unify the treatment of subject-matter. Alongside the teachers are a group of pedagogic advisers who are responsible for the care and control of each grade, the library and the classrooms, while the natural sciences also have a team of laboratory assistants.

In the primary and secondary school there are teams of remedial teachers whose mother tongues are those of the 8 language sub-sections. The functions of these remedial teachers are to provide extra instruction to new arrivals who may join the school at any time of the year, either in the L1 of the sub-section to which they are assigned, or more usually in the L2. A child who is not up to grade level in the L2 receives special instruction in this language for up to two years, both inside the normal time-table and in the form of extra lessons after class. Lack of proficiency in the L2 during this adaptation period will not hold a child back as the grade moves up since the L2 test results are excluded from the overall grade averages during the adaptation period.

Secretarial support services are made up of personnel who between them speak all the languages of the different sub-sections.

There is a medical service available made up of part-time and full-time personnel. In the largest school in Brussels this consists of a doctor of Italian nationality who speaks Italian and French and a psychologist of Finnish nationality who speaks French and English, both of whom work on a part-time basis. There is a full-time Belgian nurse who speaks French, German and Dutch and a full-time French nurse-secretary who speaks French. The medical team can also call upon the services of 8 people of different nationalities and languages who work as auxiliary staff to help children who suffer from dyslexia, psycho-motor and graphic problems.

Directors, teachers, pedagogic advisers and secretarial staff are all bi- or multilingual so that a pupil can always find someone to help him or her in the dominant language. This is highly important given the fluctuation in pupil turnover as children arrive in the school from a monolingual national system at almost any age.

Comment

The most significant point with respect to teachers is the native-speaker requirement which is adhered to with few exceptions. European Schools are convinced that this is an important element which accounts for their linguistic success.

Another important factor on the organisational level is the multilingual nature of the support staff which enables a child to get assistance in his or her strong language. The fact that all personnel are bilingual is also significant since it gives staff an insight into the facts of life with respect to manipulating more than one language and gives them greater sympathy and understanding about the nature of bilingualism.

The presence of remedial teachers to assist new arrivals to the programme is of great significance since such pupils are not left to struggle alone or to depend on the availability of the class teacher to help overcome the hurdles of insertion into the bilingual environment.

14. Parental Involvement

Although the internal working language of each school tends to be that of the host environment, e.g. French for the school in Brussels, communication from the school to parents occurs either in the three official L2s or in the languages of the sub-sections, i.e. the child's L1. Parent-teacher meetings on the school premises take place either in the language of the sub-section involved, or if a larger, mixed language meeting, in the working language of the school with interpreting available where necessary.

The parents' associations tend to be quite strong since the schools themselves do not undertake the responsibility for transportation or the provision of meals, but delegate this to the parents' association. Hence bussing and catering imply considerable parental involvement and organisation, which automatically bring at least some parents into regular contact with the school.

Parent delegates attend certain school meetings but merely as observers without any discussion power or direct influence. Before children move from primary school into secondary school a parent-teacher meeting is organised to brief parents on the nature of the programme to be followed. In secondary school all parents are invited once a year to make appointments with a maximum of 5 individual teachers with whom they can discuss their child's progress.

Comment

In a school using a language different from that of the home it is vital for parents to understand what is involved in a given programme, so that they may be able to cooperate in the school's objectives with some understanding. Communication with the parents in their own language helps to guarantee co-operation and also takes away some of the fears parents often express about the so-called risks and implications of bilingual instruction. The burden lies with the school to reach the parents involved. With immigrant populations this is even more important. A successful illustration of how immigrant parents have been involved in the Pajaro Valley School District, California, has been given by Ada (1988) in her description of her work with Spanish-speaking parents to develop children's reading and writing skills. Leman (1993) indicates how parental involvement is important in the trilingual Foyer Project destined for immigrants in Brussels. In the United Kingdom and Sweden certain districts have engaged home-school liaison officers drawn from members of the immigrant communities in order to visit parents in their homes and explain a particular school programme and its implications. Part of the success of the

Canadian immersion experience has been attributed to the amount of briefing and parental involvement as a means of collaborating with the programme's long-term goals.

15. Examinations

The European School programme leads to a special diploma, called the European Baccalaureate, which gives access to universities in most countries of the world. Attainment requirements are harmonised across the language sub-sections for many subjects, e.g. mathematics, natural sciences, philosophy, Latin, and the written examinations for these are identical in nature, irrespective of the language in which they are taken. Other subjects, including the languages themselves, are comparable in the nature of the tasks required. The final examination consists of 5 written and 4 oral sub-components, while the compulsory L2 as a subject consists of 1 written and 1 oral examination. In theory the achievement level expected for the L2 is the same as that for pupils who have that language as their L1 in the appropriate sub-section. In practice, however, concessions are made to those taking examinations through the L2 for less complex syntax or slightly less precise or varied vocabulary, though few concessions are made on accuracy.

Examinations do not become an important issue until the semi-specialisation cycle in secondary school, i.e. after grade 8. It is a deliberate policy of the European Schools not to place too much emphasis on examinations or tests until a child has gone through the observation cycle, or the first three years of secondary school. Normally most children move up from grade to grade according to age and not according to test scores, at least until the 8th grade.

Table 8 gives the breakdown of results per school on the European Baccalaureate examination for 1992 (*Schola Europaea*, 1992, No 115, 42) showing that of the 1002 candidates who sat the examinations 95.5% passed.

Comment

It is important to bear in mind that all teachers quite naturally tend to teach towards the particular examination system in which they evolve. Aspects of a curriculum that do not form part of an examination requirement, important though they may be, tend to get less attention as a teaching goal than those that are examined. Since it is ultimate achievement that is the most important factor, both on subject matter and knowledge of languages, intermediate levels of proficiency on the latter, as measured by standardised norms, may not provide

Table 8 Results on the European Baccalaureate per school - 1992.

	No of candidates	Failed	Passed
Luxembourg	159	10	149 = 93.7%
Brussels I	267	17	250 = 93.6%
Brussels II	195	4	191 = 97.9%
Varese	99	7	92 = 92.9%
Mol	57	1	56 = 98.2%
Karlsruhe	61	2	56 = 96.7%
Bergen	45	–	45 = 100 %
Munich	57	1	56 = 98.2%
Culham	62	3	59 = 95.2%
Total	1002	45	957 = 95.5%

the type of result expected for comparable monolinguals in the equivalent grade (cf. Leman, 1993). This was noted in Canadian immersion measures (Swain, 1981) but did not lead to assumptions about the inadequacy of the programme. With more time in the immersion programme, however, it was noted that at later stages grade norm equivalents were attainable.

Of significance in the European School model is the lack of obsession with test scores on language in the earlier stages of instruction, and the reliance on maturation and long-term developments in attaining the certification goals. The primary goal is to respond to educational needs, not linguistic needs, which, although significant and respected, form part of an overall educative philosophy. European Schools do not fall into the stance that García and Otheguy (1985) castigate when they state;

> "...public education in the United States, in its maddening quest for quantitatively defined excellence, has been plagued by standardised tests that are administered in English." (García & Otheguy, 1985, 15).

As Cummins (1981, 1984a), Swain & Lapkin (1982) and Wong Fillmore (1983) have shown, even under the best of circumstances it may take immigrant children from four to seven years to achieve the level of proficiency needed for full participation in school. The European School experience with the L2 bears this out.

16. Social Engineering

Given the presence of 8 linguistic sub-sections in the largest European Schools this leads to a multilingual and multicultural environment. Great care is taken to produce a unified school population by mixing children for as many subjects and activities as possible. These mixtures increase in significance as the children get older and have important consequences on language learning.

One consequence is that within the school everyone interacts regularly in a language that is not their L1 and that inhibitions to experiment in a weaker language are not strong. Interviews with pupils reveal that all are willing to try out a weaker language (including teachers!), that no-one mocks at linguistic inadequacies since everyone in the school has to use a weaker language at some time.

The social engineering has important linguistic repercussions in that it promotes conversational interactions in languages other than the L1 with both native and non-native speakers of the other languages. Wagner-Gough and Hatch (1975) showed that acquisition is a process which relies on conversational interactions, while Wong Fillmore (1986) pointed out the significance of peer-group interaction in promoting language competence. In European Schools the social situation has been so designed that there is great potential for frequent contact between native and non-native speakers of the languages being learnt.

All extra-curricular activities are conducted on the mixed group principle, with conscious attempts on the part of the authorities to prevent single-language or single nationality group activities, thereby reinforcing self-initiated peer negotiation, considered as so important in the language acquisition process. Research results (Baetens Beardsmore & Anselmi, 1991) bear out the significance of this social engineering factor.

17. Research on European Schools

Several investigations have been conducted to measure the linguistic outcomes obtained by the European School system and to explain the processes by which they have been achieved. Baetens Beardsmore & Swain (1985) compared proficiency in French as an L2 as obtained by 13+ year olds in Canadian immersion programmes and those in the European School of Brussels. Standardised test results revealed that highly comparable scores were obtained by the European children after approximately 1300 classroom contact hours with the language and Canadian immersion children after approximately 4500 contact hours. These results in no way showed the superiority of one model over the other, but could be explained by the totally different circumstances in which each programme evolved.

In the European School investigated the L2, French, was the dominant out-of-school language and was regularly used by the pupils in natural interaction. This was not the case in Canada. Given that French was the L1 of some pupils in the European School and also served as the common language for intergroup communication for those who had it as an L2, this led to it being used at least sometimes, and often more, in all out-of-class activities apart from at home and with relatives. Outside classes it tended to be used between friends, at lunch time, in the wider community, and also figured in recreational pursuits like reading magazines and comics and watching television. Thus, unlike their Canadian counterparts who only use French inside the classroom, the European children were in a context which provided immediate stimulus for out-of-class use of French as well as in class.

An interesting observation has been made by an investigator of the European School established in Britain (personal communication), where English tends to be the natural lingua franca since it is present in the out-of-school environment. Parents of Italian siblings studying at the European School there were distressed to note that in spite of their children being enrolled in the Italian sub-section and the fact that Italian was the home language their children tended to interact in English. Also, one German teacher in the German sub-section in Britain began to penalise his pupils for using English during his lessons. This anecdotal evidence points to the overwhelming impact of the out-of-school environment on language usage and should help dispel any fears about the non-acquisition of the mainstream or majority language if a similar multilingual school were set up. On the other hand, where the L2 is not the mainstream language, its out-of-school impact as an aid to acquisition cannot be assumed, and indeed teachers of German as an L2 in the Brussels schools find it more difficult to activate the use of the language in spontaneous interaction.

A second study in the European School of Brussels examined linguistic proficiency among pupils in the final grade of secondary school (Housen & Baetens Beardsmore, 1987). The students had all obtained satisfactory grades both in scholastic achievement and in their different L1s, L2s, L3s and LL4s. Their productive competence in L1 and L2 was sufficiently high for them to take equivalent examinations in either language and it was also discovered that competence in all languages varied in function of a variety of factors. The most important factor was the spontaneous seeking out of opportunities to use a particular language in self-initiated interactions, particularly with peers. This factor interacted with attitudinal and motivational dispositions and was clearly dependent on the nature of the social environment in the school. Given the ample opportunities to use a particular language in social interactions the pupils perceived language acquisition as immediately relevant to their everyday needs and not subordinated to either some long-term goal, as is the case with standard foreign language learning classes, or as an obstacle to be overcome in moving on to other interesting activities, as is the case when language learning is totally divorced from other learning processes. (Dodson (1985) strongly supports this line of argument when he states;

"Just as a child who is already bilingual is motivated to reinforce his second language by his desire to satisfy immediate needs which in themselves are not linguistic needs, so too should a bilingual programme for learners include all those situations, activities and events in which children can satisfy their needs....These needs should be immediate or at worst short-term, not medium or long-term." (Dodson, 1985,9).

A third study (Baetens Beardsmore & Kohls, 1988) looked into this question of immediate pertinence of the language acquisition process as a causal factor in determining the success of the European School system. Current theories on second language acquisition place considerable emphasis on input as a primary source of progression in competence (Gass & Madden, 1985). Krashen (1981) hypothesises that comprehensible input, where the learner focuses on understanding messages and not on form, gradually leads to the acquisition of structure. For Krashen it is sufficient to provide large quantities of comprehensible input, without grammatical or structural lessons, for a learner to progress in a second language. This practice is what mainly occurs in Canadian immersion programmes to date, but it has been noted that the results in grammatical accuracy leave much to be desired if teaching relies exclusively on the absorption of input. In European Schools, however, lessons on the structure of the L2 precede the use of the language in content matter lessons and continue throughout the programme, even after the L2 has taken over for the majority of content matter lessons. This factor probably accounts for the high levels of grammatical precision in the L2 obtained by the majority of European School pupils by the end of schooling.

This is not the place to go into theoretical considerations on the nature of second language acquisition in an environment as complex as that prevalent in European Schools. Housen (1993) presents aspects of this in his extract from the on-going longitudinal study at present being carried out with different L1 populations in two of the schools from the network.

A second major difference between the European School model and immersion models is that the structure of the European School programme forces learners to interact at peer level in the L2. Unlike immersion students who have little opportunity to engage in two-way negotiated meaning exchanges in the classroom (Swain, 1985, 247) European School pupils have ample opportunity, both inside and outside the classroom, to do so. Swain has argued that input alone does not lead to high levels of productive competence and that output is equally important, where the learner is pushed to negotiate meaning by delivering a message that is conveyed as precisely, coherently and appropriately as possible. For a learner to be willing to put in the effort to produce output the attempts must be perceived as immediately pertinent; such is the case in the European School model where use of the target language is immediately rewarding, as it is necessary for establishing friendship circles and conducting co-operative activities in mixed lessons. The design of the European School programme coincides with a prerequisite for success that Dodson (1985) has posited, namely:

> "... a bilingual education programme must include areas which relate to
> the whole range of curricular, extra-curricular and social aspects of the
> children's experience. Nor should it be limited to the mere linguistic
> content of these areas of the children's experience, as the language to be
> learnt does not exist in a vacuum but is fused in the interaction processes
> between individuals and the world in which they live." (Dodson, 1985,
> 12).

For learners to be willing to take linguistic "risks" in attempting to produce accurate output the circumstances must not only be naturalistic but also non-threatening. In Canadian immersion programmes using French in the classroom is non-threatening since all the students come from the same background and are not made to feel inferior because of inadequacies in language. In European Schools the situation is the same, since everybody has to use a weaker language at some time so that feelings of monolingual superiority cannot easily be maintained. In many American schools where limited English proficient students find themselves next to native speakers of English only the former are subjected to the struggle of expressing themselves in a weaker language, which may give rise to feelings of inadequacy and insecurity, thereby impeding the spontaneous arisal of output. Consequently, friendship circles may well form among the in-group of speakers from the same language background, preventing two-way peer interaction. This is why it is felt important to give all children in a multilingual school the opportunity to learn and use a second language, and to make the process pertinent for all. The constant mixing up of children for group activities provides the natural environment for such pertinence to be perceived, as has been borne out by the study by Housen & Baetens Beardsmore (1987).

A fourth study by Baetens Beardsmore & Anselmi (1991) examined the nature and functions of code-switching among adolescents in the secondary programme. Analyses showed to what extent language was used as an identity marker, and how code-switching operated to accommodate cross-linguistic comprehension as well as a clear learning strategy.

18. Conclusions

The fact that approximately 90% of all pupils attending European Schools since their foundation in 1958 have obtained certification leading to higher education clearly indicates that the model is successful both academically and linguistically. This success is not to be attributed simply to the social class make-up of the population or the status of the different languages involved, though they undoubtedly play a role. More important is the care with which the programme has been developed so as to take into account a certain number of fundamental principles which are strictly adhered in order to give the complex situation a chance to succeed. These principlescan be summed up as follows.

1. All pupils are put on an equal footing as far as language requirements are concerned and all are led through the same process of transition from instruction through an L1 into that through both an L1 and an L2.

2. The L1 serves as the basis for instruction as competence in the L2 is gradually built up, while the L1 is never totally abandoned.

3. Transition to the use of the L2 is a gradual process which moves from cognitively undemanding and context embedded activities in the language to more cognitively demanding and context reduced activities as the pupil gets older. An examination of the curriculum shows how this process breaks down into three major phases. The L2 is first introduced as a subject matter while the task of coping with general learning takes place in the L1. In the second phase the L2 is used in naturalistic circumstances that are non-threatening and easy to handle (in European Hours, for example). In the third phase, when more intellectually demanding activities are undertaken in the L2

they are first conducted in areas similar to those that had been previously treated in the L1 (e.g. history and geography) before spreading out into new activities.

4. Throughout the programme both the L1 and the L2 are taught as a subject matter in order to reinforce grammatical accuracy and lexical precision.

5. Testing and examinations are not allowed to determine success or failure until the pupil has had sufficient time to become thoroughly acquainted with a language; ultimate attainment is considered more important than mid-stream progress and there are no unrealistic comparisons with monolingual peers until the very end of schooling.

6. The programme is organised to promote considerable interaction at peer-grouplevel between both native and non-native speakers of a given language so as to reinforce the formal teaching aspects of language acquisition.

7. Using a particular language occurs in naturalistic, non-threatening circumstances which are immediately pertinent to the task in hand, making the operation a rewarding one and a stimulus to further effort.

8. Great care is taken to avoid the formation of linguistic ghettos by mixing children up for as many activities as possible.

9. bilingualare nearly all Teachers in different combinations of languages but always teach through their first language, no matter what the subject or the population make-up of the class they are taking. This situation is possible in Europe with a large pool of qualified teachers to draw from but in some contexts it is probably more feasible to propose that teachers should only teach in the language for which they have full professional proficiency, even though this may not be their first language.

10. Attempts are made to eliminate strong ethnolinguistic perspectives by fostering a European identity and a cross-cultural view of the world while maintaining respect for the pupil's national heritage. In a different context a similar respect for the home language and ethnic heritage could be maintained while promoting a pluralistic cultural identity which reflects the kaleidoscopic make-up of contemporary society.

The positive linguistic and academic results obtained by the multilingual school described in this chapter are not a uniquely European phenomenon based on some supposedly inherent superiority in language acquisition. Similar positive results based on fundamentally similar approaches have been achieved in bilingual education in the United States involving two languages in the curriculum. Krashen & Biber (1988) have posited three requirements as necessary for successful bilingual programmes in the United States, namely,

1. rigorous subject matter teaching such as mathematics, social studies and science in the first language;

2. development of literacy in the first language;
3. English instruction that is comprehensible through daily English as a second language lessons and subject matter teaching geared to the second language acquirer.

Krashen & Biber's examination of seven schools or school districts in which the above principles were rigorously followed showed that in comparison with limited English proficiency students not receiving properly organised bilingual instruction six of the bilingual programmes provided clearly superior results, one produced comparable results and in one case there was insufficient data to draw any conclusions. The results also showed that adequate levels of conversational ability in English were obtained after about two years in a given programme but that adequate levels of formal or academic language took from five to seven years. Once the time factor had been taken into consideration the children involved in the properly structured bilingual education programmes investigated in California were comparable to native speakers of English on all tests used. However, this success was determined by the fact that children in the successful programmes were not exited from bilingual education into mainstream, monolingual education prematurely.

The above results reveal certain parallelisms with the practice of the European Schools and reveal similar positive outcomes. The only major difference between Krashen & Biber's findings and those for European Schools is the number of languages involved on the particular school site. The European School model shows that it is possible to operate a multilingual school made up of unequal numbers of pupils with different language and cultural backgrounds. Success is determined by the care which has gone into enabling the transition from one language to another to take place, as well as the continuous efforts to integrate the school population in order to achieve the desired linguistic, cultural and interethnic goals.

Lest this monograph be interpreted as overly triumphant a word of caution should be noted, as expressed by the Chairman of the Parents Association of Brussels II, Brendan O'Brien (*Schola Europaea*, 1988, No 100, 21-24). While recognising the excellent achievements of the network it is pointed out that the schools have a less than satisfactory record in the case of less academically gifted children. The article in question reveals that in 1984 approximately 55% of the children who started the secondary programme successfully completed the Baccalaureate. Of the remaining 45%, 24% dropped out of the system for educational reasons and 21% left the school for family reasons, change of residence, etc. Although it is not clear what accounts for the 24% dropout rate for educational reasons, the Chairman of the Parents Association notes the major difference between the primary and secondary school programmes and compares with the more familiar monolingual systems as follows:

"In the education systems of our home countries, the programmes of the primary and junior secondary systems provide a general type of education which caters for everybody, irrespective of the ability, talents, qualities, ambitions and plans of the individual. Orientation towards the more academically oriented education only occurs at the end of the junior secondary cycle. Why should it be different in the European Schools where perhaps the need is greater in view of the greater social, psychological and linguistic problems pertaining to living in a foreign country?" (*Schola Europaea*, 1988, No 100, 22).

It is claimed that the system in operation is overtly academic in philosophy, based on the French national system, and not sufficiently child-centred, which leads to less academically oriented pupils being advised to seek alternative education. This obviously accounts for the impressive statistics on European Baccalaureate examinations. Informal discussions with teachers confirm this situation, though several offer anecdotal evidence on the few dropouts they have followed up, claiming that the latter tend to fare particularly well in the monolingual systems they return to. Since there is no hard evidence on such cases no comment can be provided. *Schola Europaea* No 103, p.42 refers to a survey of ex-pupils but it has been impossible to obtain any details on the nature and results of this survey.

The statutes of the Schools do provide for the setting up of a less academically-oriented stream on the proviso that sufficient numbers warrant implementation, and indeed, attempts have been made to satisfy the requirement. It appears, however, that when proposals were put forward in Brussels I, insufficient parents were disposed to switch their children to what they probably perceived as a second-best alternative.

A factor that has not been gone into in this overview is the cost of running European Schools. This is evidently higher than monolingual education. Teacher salaries are considerably more attractive than in national education systems, accounting for many applications for vacancies, which allow the schools to select the candidates they consider most qualified. The materials budget is also much higher than in standard schools. A report presented to the European Parliament (Oostlander Report, 1994) reveals that in 1990 each European School pupil cost 289,031 Belgian francs (± US$ 7,469) per year, compared with 157,742 Belgian francs (± US$ 4,929) for a child in a Belgian school.

The same report was critical of several aspects of European Schools, laying particular emphasis on the fact that they have evolved, over time, from an interesting experimental laboratory into a unique and selective system, due to the high academic standards required for the European Baccalaureate, the lack of success of the less academic option and their extreme isolation from schools in the surrounding environment. The report concludes by making several recommendations. The first is that the network should not be allowed to expand by the creation of new schools. The second is to encourage the European Schools to take in a less restricted range of pupils, so that all who wish can take advantage of their experience with multilingual education. A third major recommendation is that the experience gained by these schools should be put to good use in national schools in the member states so as to provide multicultural education for as many as possible. In other words, the major thrust of the report, which was adopted by the European Parliament in 1994, was that the experience gained by these schools, should be extended to less privileged establishments.

As a model the European School should not serve as a blueprint in a totally different environment. On the other hand, many of the features that have been incorporated over the years are well-tried elements that can serve as guidelines for other societies confronted with similar complex linguistic and educational issues.

Notes:

1   Contract No 106B025-05 California State Department of Education.

2

WORLD CLASS EDUCATION FOR CHILDREN IN CALIFORNIA: A COMPARISON OF THE TWO-WAY BILINGUAL IMMERSION AND EUROPEAN SCHOOL MODELS

David P. Dolson and Kathryn Lindholm

This chapter was written in response to an invitation from Tove Skutnabb-Kangas. She asked us, as well as colleagues from several other countries around the world, to develop an analysis of the applicability of the European School Model to our homeland contexts. For practical reasons we have chosen to limit this analysis to the public school system of California.

During the 1992-93 school year, 1.7 million of the 5.2 million students in the state came from homes where a language other than English is spoken (CDE, 1992). According to figures collected previously, 602,416 pupils were enrolled in foreign language programs (CDE, 1990). These demographic data suggest that while California has a higher than average level of language education activity when compared to other states in the country, the amount of interest in second language, bilingual, and multicultural programs in the state is quite modest by international standards.

One program of special importance is the two-way bilingual immersion model. Originally developed by the San Diego City School District in the mid-1970's, the approach was later elaborated upon and then subsequently promoted by the CDE (California Department of Education) beginning in the mid-1980's. Currently, more than thirty schools in the state are reported to be implementing the model (Christian & Mahrer, 1993; see also note 3).

Among all of the second language, bilingual, multicultural, and foreign language programs organized in California schools, the two-way bilingual immersion approach seems particularly well suited for comparison to the

European School Model. Many second language educators in California consider it an optimal approach for the American setting. Unlike the vast majority of other programs in the United States, the goal of two-way bilingual immersion education is proficient bilingualism and multiculturalism for *all* participants. The stated objectives of the two-way bilingual immersion design appear to be highly congruent with those reported for the European School Model (Baetens Beardsmore, 1993, this volume). Both approaches share the following framework:

1. Participants experience an additive form of bilingualism (or multilingualism). They are able to develop full proficiency in their mother tongue (L1) while gradually acquiring high levels of proficiency in a second language (L2);
2. Participants are offered subject matter and language lessons in both L1 and L2. Languages are kept separate for instruction with the sequence for most participants being large amounts of L1 instruction initially with increasing amounts of L2 instruction overtime;
3. Plentiful attention is given to maintaining a healthy identity with a heritage language group as well as the development of crosscultural knowledge, skills, and abilities needed to perform adequately in multicultural contexts;
4. Emphasis is placed on the authentic integration of students from different language and ethnic backgrounds. Substantial time allotments are dedicated to cooperative or communal hours aimed at fostering crosscultural understandings, experiences, and friendships;
5. Underlying the language and crosscultural aspects of the programs is a solid academic foundation made up of a high quality curriculum which allows students to meet both national and international scholastic standards expected of pupils at specified age/grade levels.
6. In route assessments are linked to the language used as a medium of instruction for the particular subject matter or course in question. Final examinations for the programs are conducted separately in both L1 and L2. Results are judged according to native speaker standards.

This chapter will focus on the programmatic design and student outcomes of the two-way bilingual immersion model as implemented in California. The European School Model is quite admirably and comprehensively addressed by Baetens Beardsmore in this volume and in a companion chapter entitled *The European School Experience in Multilingual Education* (Baetens Beardsmore, 1993). Consequently, in this chapter we will attempt to provide background information on (1) the language and crosscultural educational situation of both language minority and majority students in California, (2) the rationale and the contextual and programmatic features of two-way bilingual immersion programs, and (3), the initial evaluation results of this two-way model. We will conclude the chapter with a comparative analysis of several key elements of two-way bilingual immersion and European School models.

Language Education in California

Minority Groups

Recent demographic trends suggest that racial and ethnic minorities, including language minority groups may soon become the new numerical majority in California. Table 1 illustrates the representation in the state of different ethnic

Table 1. California Language Minority School Enrollment Grades K - 12

LANGUAGE GROUP	NO. OF STUDENTS
Spanish	1.226,846
Vietnamese	73,561
Pilipino (Tagalog)	55,344
Cantonese	45,579
Korean	37,187
Hmong	27,752
Cambodian (Khmer)	26,655
Mandarin	23,329
Armenian	17,904
Lao	16,763
Farsi	15,352
Japanese	11,401
Arabic	9,822
Portuguese	7,285
Russian	6,168
Punjabi	6,049
Hindi	5,877
Mien	4,897
Samoan	3,772
All Other Language Minority	69,877
Sub Total	1.691,420
English	3.403,925
Grand Total	5.095,345

(Source: CDE, 1993)

and language groups. Nevertheless, if we consider past and current educational opportunities as an indicator of future social integration, such groups will invariably maintain their minority status from both a political and an economic perspective.

Almost without exception, language minority education in California has been restricted to compensatory educational models based on a linguistic, academic, and sociocultural deficit model. Language minority students are given English proficiency tests. Based on the results of such assessments, the students are categorized as Limited English Proficient (LEP)[1] or Fluent English Proficient (FEP). Only LEP students are offered placement in specialized language programs (only some of which provide L1 development and subject matter classes) and even then, only for the period of time that the so-called LEP students are considered deficient in English communication skills. Thus, all programs required by law for language minority students are transitional in nature. Once the students are reclassified as FEP, they are no longer protected by the educational laws requiring bilingual and other specialized instructional services (Dolson, 1985). FEP students are rarely offered L1 instruction by school districts. Certainly, they have no legal support in terms of linguistic;human rights to petition the local school for mother tongue classes.

In 1992, 1.1 of the 1.7 million language minority students enrolled in California's schools were categorized as LEP students. Table 2 contains a display of the manner in which these students were distributed among various types of language education programs.

Data in Table 2 was collected as part of the annual language census conducted by the CDE (CDE, 1992). The survey used the following operational definitions for each of the program categories listed in rows 5 through 8:

English Language Development (ELD): A specialized program of English language instruction appropriate for the students' identified level of language proficiency which is consistently implemented and is designed to promote second language acquisition of listening, speaking, reading, and writing. Instruction must be provided by a qualified bilingual teacher or a teacher who is a language development specialist.

ELD and Specially Designed Academic Instruction in English (SDAIE): Each LEP student must receive a program of ELD and, at a minimum, two academic subjects required for grade promotion or graduation taught through specially designed academic instruction in English. SDAIE is an approach utilized to teach academic courses to LEP students in English. The instructional

Table 2. LEP Student Enrollment in Instructional Programs. California Summary

Number Of LEP	(1)	K-6	732,416
	(2)	7-12	332,415
	(3)	Ungraded	13,874
	(4)	TOTAL	1,078,705
Number Of LEP By Program	(5)	English Language Development (ELD)	161,689
	(6)	ELD and Specially Designed Academic Instruction in English	117,650
	(7)	ELD, SDAIE and Primary Language Support	182,343
	(8)	ELD and Academic Subjects Through the Primary Language	359,829
LEP Not In Programs K-12	(9)	Number of Students	257,185
	(10)	Percent of Total	23.9%

(Source: CDE, 1992)

methodology must be designed for non-native speakers of English and must focus on increasing the comprehensibility of the academic courses provided. Instruction must be provided by a qualified bilingual teacher or a teacher who is a language development specialist or any other teacher who has sufficient training to implement the SDAIE methodology.

ELD, SDAIE, and Primary Language Support: Each LEP student must receive a program of ELD, SDAIE, and instructional support through the primary language in at least two academic subject areas. Primary language support may be provided by any teacher or any paraprofessional who has sufficient proficiency in the target language.

ELD and Academic Subjects Through The Primary Language: In Kindergarten through grade 6, primary language instruction is provided, at a minimum, in language arts (including reading and writing) and mathematics, science, or social science. In grades 7-12, primary language instruction is provided, at a minimum, in two academic subjects required for grade promotion or graduation. Lesson content and curriculum must be aligned with that provided to FEP and English-only students in the school district. Primary language instruction must be provided by qualified bilingual teachers (CDE, 1992).

It is interesting to note that 23.9% of the students are listed in row no. 10, "LEP not in programs K-12". This refers to students who (1) are not offered (contrary to law) any specialized instruction, (2) have been withdrawn from a program by their parents, or (3) are enrolled in a program which does not meet the operational definition of any of the programs indicated in rows 5 through 8. Most of the students reported in row no. 10 receive some form of instructional assistance. However, such assistance rarely includes instruction in and through the L1 and almost never implies that the instruction is provided by a bilingual or other qualified teacher.

Public schools in California were required to abide by a mandatory bilingual education act from 1976 to 1987. In 1987, the governor and the state legislature were unable to reach an agreement on renewing the policy for language minority education in the state. Subsequently, programs for language minority students have been governed by a complex combination of state and federal laws, court cases, and CDE guidelines. All of this legal uncertainty seems to have undermined efforts to obtain the human and material resources necessary to support bilingual programs. For instance, between 1987 and 1990, the number of bilingual teachers available for classroom assignments actually decreased slightly while the number of language minority students in the same period increased on average more than ten percent annually (CDE, 1992). The demand for bilingual classroom teachers is estimated to be 22,365 (CDE, 1991). The supply is calculated at 8,033. This results in a statewide shortage of more than 14,332 teachers (sixty-four percent).

Reviews of the literature on the scholastic experience of language minority students in the United States reveal a persistent pattern in which the students:

1. Suffer from very low levels of academic achievement and experience a high rate of drop outs;
2. Often lose proficiency in their L1 but do not necessarily acquire L2 sufficiently for school and vocational purposes;
3. Experience anomie (bicultural ambivalence);
4. Are generally unprepared to deal with racism and prejudice directed at them in the schools and wider society.

Reviews of research on the scholastic underperformance of language minority students in the 1980's were reported by Dolson (1985), Cummins (1989), and Fishman (1989) among many others. More recent evidence that these negative trends continue in California are provided in the work of Ramirez and others (1992), and Berman and others (1992). Studies such as these, coupled with the CDE language census reports on the quantity and quality of specialized language programs, provide an overall picture of the persistence of unfavorable educational conditions for language minority students in California.

Initially, many bilingual educators in the United States mistakenly believed that transitional forms of bilingual education would be sufficient to provide language minority students with equal educational opportunities. What they did not realize at the time is that sociopolitical pressures would reduce the intervention to almost exclusive reliance on the early-exit version of this model with its concomitant promotion of subtractive bilingualism (Hernández-Chávez, 1984). These educators further underestimated the negative effects of minority status on bilingual program teachers and student participants (Cummins, 1989; Spener, 1988).

The results of earlier investigations have been confirmed by the longitudinal study conducted by Ramirez and others (1992) which clearly indicates that the quick-fix versions of bilingual education are severely limited in their ability to address the scholastic needs of language minority students. This implication has stimulated interest among many language minority advocates in more radical program models which attempt to transform the compensatory nature of transitional programs into enrichment models of bilingual schooling (Dolson& Mayer, 1991).

Majority Groups

For decades, secondary schools in California have traditionally offered "foreign language" classes in Spanish, French and German. More recently an extraordinarily small number of classes have been organized to offer other languages such as Italian, Russian, Chinese, Japanese and Portuguese. Table 3 contains information on the number of course sections and corresponding enrollments for second language classes at the secondary school level, grades 9-12. High school foreign language courses are usually taught using grammar-translation and audiolingual teaching methods. A review of textbooks approved by the CDE for Spanish, French, and German courses suggests that these languages are taught almost entirely through the medium of English. Performance is evaluated according to the amount of textbook material mastered. Language proficiency is not often used as a criterion to evaluate either the progress of individual students or the effectiveness of the course. In fact, instructors of foreign language classes are not required to possess even a minimal level of proficiency in the target language as a condition for obtaining a second language teaching authorization.

The crosscultural instruction in foreign language classes is commonly restricted

Table 3. Foreign Language Enrollments in California Schools for Grades 9-12

Language of Instruction	Total Course Enrollment	Number of Classes Offered
German	22,585	1,015
Italian	1,915	70
French	100,938	3,871
Spanish	384,158	12,792
Russian	1,552	72
Korean	34	1
Chinese	1,939	87
Japanese	2,583	102
Portuguese	464	19
Other	7,619	303
TOTALS	**523,787**	**18,332**

(Source: CDE, 1990)

to an extended social studies component which aims at increasing the students' knowledge of the history and cultural traditions of the regions of the world where the target language is spoken. Virtually no attempts are made to develop functional bicultural skills or even to explicitly encourage attitudes that promote identification with specific ethnolinguistic groups. In fact, one rarely sees any form of articulation between foreign language classes and the various heritage language communities resident in California.

Increasingly, the foreign language departments of some secondary schools which enroll large numbers of language minority students offer courses identified as "Spanish for Spanish Speakers" or similar classes for native speakers of other languages. Enrollments in these courses generally consist of language minority students with a smattering of native speakers of English previously enrolled in some form of imersion education or those English speakers who may have attended school in another country.

The national Foreign Language in Elementary School (FLES) program, with its accompanying federal funds, generated a modest amount of interest in Kindergarten through grade 8 schools in the late 1960's. Most of these programs faded by the early 1970's and activity in second language programs at these grade levels has remained paltry. Table 4 contains data which show that in the 1990-91 school year, fewer than 73,000 students were enrolled in such programs

Table 4. Foreign Language Enrollments in California Schools for Grades K-8

Language of Instruction	Total Course Enrollment	Number of Classes Offered
German	2,238	69
Italian	78	5
French	11,798	461
Spanish	53,047	1,830
Russian	299	11
Korean	7	1
Chinese	79	6
Japanese	205	7
Portuguese	124	5
Vietnamese	101	2
Other	4,962	170
TOTALS	**72,938**	**2,567**

(Source: CDE, 1990)

in California. The languages offered generally parallel those of secondary schools.

Instructional approaches do vary in elementary schools. When the language programs are limited to the upper grades (6-8) in schools which are organized departmentally, traditional foreign language teaching methods dominate. These programs have characteristics similar to their counterparts in grades 9-12. The remaining programs are found in schools with self-contained classrooms. Infrequently, full or partial immersion strategies are selected. Most students at these grade levels, however, are enrolled in a second language instructional component provided as part of a bilingual program for language minority students. Note for example, that 53,047 pupils were enrolled in Spanish classes (See Table 4). Most likely, these anglophone students receive from ten minutes to a half hour daily of audiolingual and/or some type of communicative-based instruction. There is usually no formal evaluation of individual student or group achievement in Spanish.

Based on the data contained in Tables 3 and 4, fewer than 603,000 of California's 5.2 million public school students participate in some form of second language instruction. This represents approximately 11.5 percent of the state's total enrollment. With such low enrollment figures in foreign language classes concomitantly hampered by (1) low expectations, (2) antiquated methodologies, and (3) a cadre of monolingual teachers, it is no wonder that student outcomes support the continuance of a population characterized by what Skutnabb-Kangas (1990) refers to as "monolingual;stupidity". As a group, English-speaking students in California tend to graduate from secondary schools with the following characteristics:

1. They are able to speak only one language, English. Even if they know something of another language, it is at a minimal, non-functional proficiency level;
2. They are menacingly ethnocentric, possessing little knowledge or appreciation of other cultural groups;
3. They have pronounced shortcomings in the academic, linguistic and social skills necessary to compete in an international economy;
4. Since little or no attention is given to the development of their crosscultural competencies, they are not well suited to participate in cooperative efforts to address global concerns of commerce, ecology, poverty or peace.
5. They are often unable to recognize racism and prejudice when these behaviors are manifested by their own group. Furthermore, they are not predisposed to stand up collectively or individually against such practices.

Dissatisfaction with the dismal outcomes of traditional foreign language programs and the emergence of reports from Canada on the spectacular results of French Immersion programs led some educators to speculate on the application of immersion education in the United States (California Department of Education, 1984). In fact, an experimental program of full early immersion in Spanish was launched in Culver City, California in 1971 (Campbell, 1984). The results were parallel to those from Canada. Anglophone participants attained high levels of both L1 and L2 proficiency and normal academic achievement even though they were schooled mostly through their L2.

The positive results of immersion programs in Canada and the handful of U.S. experiments, although convincing, did not lead to large-scale implementation of this program model in California or other parts of the U.S. (Rhodes and Schreibstein, 1983). Apparently, both lack of interest in and the scarcity of funds for elementary school foreign language education combined to limit the establishment of immersion programs to a few scattered attempts. Only later would interest re-emerge as some educators considered the possibility of integrating foreign language education for majority students with bilingual programs designed for language minority students.

Description of the Two-way Bilingual Immersion Model

Two-way bilingual immersion education combines features of full bilingual education for language minority students and early total immersion education for English-speaking students. For language minority (non English-speaking students), academic instruction is presented in and through their first language, Spanish, and they receive English language arts and, depending on the particular program and grade level, portions of their academic instruction in English.[2] For English-speaking students, academic instruction is provided in and through their second language, Spanish, and they receive English language arts, and depending on the program design, some portion of their academic instruction in English.

The definition of two-way programmes;definition of encompasses *four criterial features*: (1) The program essentially involves some form of dual language instruction, where Spanish is used for a significant portion of the students' instructional day;[3] (2) the program involves periods of instruction during which only one language is used; (3) both native English speakers and native Spanish speakers are participants; and (4) the students are integrated for most content instruction.

The *major goals* of the program are that (1) Students will develop high levels of proficiency in their *first* language and in a *second* language, (2) Academic performance will be at or above grade level as measured in both languages, and (3) Students will have high levels of psychosocial competence and positive cross-cultural attitudes.

Rationale and Theoretical Underpinnings

Two-way bilingual immersion has been constructed on three major theoretical and conceptual building blocks so that it can meet the language and academic needs of both native and non-native speakers of English: (1) Social context of language education; (2) Effective schools, and (3) Language development (see Lindholm, 1990, 1991, 1992).

The *social context of language education* refers to the attitudes and policies that are held regarding the language education program and its participants. There are several features from this body of literature that have influenced the development of the two-way bilingual immersion model. (1) The model is additiveadditive bilingualism for both English-speaking and Spanish-speaking students. This additive aspect is important in two regards. First, all students are provided the opportunity to acquire a second language at no cost to their home language and culture (Lambert, 1987). Second, Spanish-speaking students are given the chance to further develop high levels of Spanish proficiency rather than to advance through the usual process of Spanish language loss (Lambert, 1987; Veltman, 1988). (2) Encouragement of positive and equitable interactions between teachers and students and between Spanish-speaking and English-speaking student peers fosters equity in the classroom (California Department of Education, 1982; Cummins, 1986; Kagan, 1986). (3) Balancing the proportion of Spanish-speaking and English-speaking students in each classroom facilitates an environment of educational and linguistic equity and promotes interactions among native and non-native English speakers.

Two-way bilingual immersion, like immersion education, is grounded in *language acquisition* research in several respects.

1) Languageinput to the students is adjusted to their conceptual and linguistic level, using many features of sheltered instruction, including "motherese", to facilitate language comprehension and acquisition on the part of the students (Krashen, 1981; Long, 1980).

2) Balanced with the need to make language comprehensible for second language learners is the necessity to make language input challenging for students operating in their first language (Swain, 1987, 1991).

3) Concentrated exposure to language is important to promote language development. Several studies have shown that it takes somewhere between four and seven years to develop full proficiency in a second language (Collier, 1987; Cummins, 1981; Krashen & Biber, 1988; National Commission on Excellence in Education, 1983; Swain, 1984). Part of the importance for developing full proficiency relates to the Threshold Hypothesis discussed by Cummins (1979, 1987) and Toukomaa and Skutnabb-Kangas (1977). They speculate that there may be threshold levels of linguistic proficiency a child must attain to avoid cognitive disadvantages and to allow the potentially beneficial aspects of becoming bilingual to influence cognitive growth. This hypothesis assumes that a child must attain a certain minimum or threshold level of proficiency in both languages to enable bilingualism to exert a significant long-term effect and to positively influence cognitive growth. Cummins and Toukomaa and Skutnabb-Kangas in fact, argue that there are two threshold levels of linguistic proficiency a child must achieve. Attainment of the lower threshold level of bilingual proficiency would be sufficient to guard against cognitive disadvantages. However, for long-term cognitive advantages allowing the potentially beneficial aspects of becoming bilingual to influence cognitive growth, achieving the second threshold, or a higher level of bilingual proficiency, is required.

4) The two languages are kept distinct and never mixed during instruction. Several reasons for keeping the languages separate include:

   a) it improves the quantity and quality of teacher delivery, particularly the teacher's preparation (e.g., vocabulary, materials) for lesson delivery in Spanish;

b) students need sustained exposure to the minority language in a variety of contexts to obtain native speaker levels;

c) Spanish needs sociocultural and political protection to assure that English does not encroach in the domains of language use because of its dominant status;

d) avoidance of language mixing and switching allows for more reliance on comprehensible input, negotiation of meaning, and comprehension checks in both languages.

Over the past several years, a large body of literature has amassed on *effective schools*. There are several critical characteristics of effective schools that have implications for the success in implementing the two-way bilingual immersion model.

1) The bilingual program is integrated within the total school program, strong support for the program is given from the school district administrators and local Board of Education, and the principal is very supportive of and knowledgeable about the program (Troike, 1986).

2) Parental involvement and collaboration with the school.

3) Students receive their instruction from certified teachers who have native or native-like ability in either or both of the language(s) in which they are instructing.

Program Features

A number of program features will be discussed in this section, including 1) Language distribution and use, 2) Curriculum and instructional approaches, 3) Instructional strategies in Spanish and English, 4) Characteristics of teachers, students, and classrooms, and 5) Cross-cultural and self-concept components.

1. Language Distribution and Use

Table 5 depicts the two most common instructional designs. In California, most programs follow the 90:10 model whereas outside of California, the majority of programs use the 50:50 model. We will focus our discussion on the 90:10 model because, as Table 5 illustrates, the 50:50 design is similar to the 90:10 model in grades 4-6.

As Table 5 shows, the distribution of languages for instruction varies across the grade levels in the 90:10, but not 50:50, design. In the 90:10 model, at Kindergarten and first grade, 90% of the instructional day is devoted to content instruction in Spanish and 10% to English. Thus, all content instruction occurs in Spanish and English time is used to develop oral language proficiency. Reading instruction begins in Spanish for both Spanish-speaking and English-speaking students. At the second and third grade levels, students receive 80% of their day

Table 5. Two-Way Bilingual Immersion Program Models: Percentage of Spanish and English Instruction by Grade Level

Grade Level and Language Distribution	90:10 Model	50:50 Model
Kindergarten & First		
Spanish Instruction	90	50
English Instruction	10	50
Second & Third		
Spanish Instruction	80	50
English Instruction	20	50
Fourth & Fifth[a]		
Spanish Instruction	50	50
English Instruction	50	50

[a] Includes sixth grade if there is a sixth grade at the elementary school.

in Spanish and 20% in English. As in the previous grade levels, all content is taught in Spanish, with the exception of music, art, or physical education which may be taught during English time at some school sites. In second grade, English time is still largely spent in developing oral language proficiency. Students begin formal English reading in third grade. By fourth and fifth grades (and sixth grade, if it is included at the elementary school site), the students' instructional time is balanced between English and Spanish. The content areas taught in each language depend on the available curriculum materials and supporting resource materials and on particular needs at each school site. However, an attempt is made to assure that students are given opportunities to develop academic language in each of the major curricular areas.

As indicated previously, teachers never mix the languages during instruction. In most school sites at the early grade levels, teachers may team together so that they are models of only one language. At the upper grade levels, language separation may occur by time of day (1/2 day in Spanish, 1/2 day in English), by unit (one unit in English, one unit in Spanish), or by week (one week in Spanish, one week in English). The most common strategy for both the 90:10 and the 50:50 designs is to separate the languages by time of day, so that students study in one language in the morning and another language in the afternoon.

2. Curriculum and Instructional Approaches
The instructional curriculum is based on state and local school district

guidelines. Thus, the curriculum that the bilingual immersion students receive is equivalent to that for students at the same grades not enrolled in the two-way bilingual immersion program. Schedules are carefully structured for teaching all required academic subjects using methods appropriate not only for specific grade levels, but suitable also for enabling both English-speaking and Spanish-speaking students to acquire language skills in both English and Spanish. Instructional approaches include whole language, discovery math, integrated thematic subject matter, writing process, and cooperative learning.

3. Instructional Strategies in Spanish and English

Instructional strategies vary by language and grade level. In the early grades in the 90:10 model, Spanish is used to teach content and it is usually not taught as a subject area. There is little variation across school sites in the use of Spanish for almost exclusive teaching of content. In addition, students are typically grouped heterogeneously, rather than by ability, when they are grouped at all. School sites, and even teachers within a grade level at a particular site, vary in the teaching of Spanish grammar at the upper elementary levels. Some teachers believe that Spanish grammar will be learned as Spanish is used and thus they do not think that it is necessary to teach the students Spanish grammar. Other teachers consider Spanish grammar important to teaching content and incorporate grammar instruction, such as subject-verb agreement, gender agreement, different verb tenses, sentence structure, and so on, into their content lessons.

During English time there is considerable variation in how English instruction is carried out and whether it is used as the language for content instruction in the early grade levels. In some school sites at the early grade levels, students are separated for English time, with the Spanish speakers receiving English as a Second Language (ESL) strategies and the English speakers working on further English language development. In other school sites at the early grade levels, the students are kept together for English time, and all students are given oral input through content such as music, stories, drama. Unfortunately, not enough attention has been paid to English time in many school sites where English time has been used for assemblies, P.E., or other activities that do not provide a good basis for the development of academic English.

4. Student Population

As indicated earlier, classroom composition is a balance of native English speakers and native Spanish speakers. In many school sites, segregated communities surrounding the school make it virtually impossible to include equal numbers of Spanish-speaking and English-speaking students. Typically in the first or second year of model implementation, schools may have more difficulty recruiting a balanced population. After one or two years, though, most schools are able to balance their populations without difficulty. The populations represented in the two-way bilingual immersion model are heterogeneous by school site. Many times the Spanish- and English-speaking populations are not comparable in important ways that we will briefly describe below.

Spanish Speakers. As a group, Spanish speaking children can be characterized as largely immigrant and who have parents who belong to the working class and have typically 5-6 years of formal education. It is important to note that there is variation within this group, though. On the one hand, some Spanish-speaking students are U.S. born or have parents who are highly educated and middle class. On the other hand, some Spanish-speaking students live in run-down inner cities or in rural areas in broken down trailer homes without electricity or indoor plumbing. Some of these students' parents are very involved in their children's education and understand how to promote achievement in their children and other parents are not involved for various reasons or have no formal education to enable them to help their children with their schoolwork.
In programs in which the language combinations include Korean, Chinese, or Portuguese, there is also diversity with respect to immigration status and socioeconomic status. However, language minority students in these language groups are more likely to be middle class and to come from homes with educated parents.

English Speakers. The English speaking population is also diverse in social class and parental education as well as in ethnic composition. In some schools, most of the English speakers are middle class and Anglo. In other schools, the majority of English speakers are African American students living in the poor and run-down sections of the city. In still other schools, the English speaking population is diverse, including middle and working class Anglos, African Americans, Hispanics, and Asian Americans.

Social Class and Language Group Confound. In many schools, a social class and language group confound exists whereby the English speakers come from middle class and educated families and the Spanish speakers come from working class and undereducated (by U.S. standards) families. These differences must be acknowledged to assure students equal educational opportunity in the classroom by both their teacher and their fellow students. These differences must also be recognized in the interpretations of the evaluation results.

5. Staff

Teachers in two-way bilingual immersion programs tend to have appropriate teaching certificates or credentials, have good content knowledge and classroom management skills, have native or native-like proficiency in one or both languages in which they are instructing, and are trained with respect to the two-way bilingual immersion model and appropriate instructional strategies (e.g., educational equity, cooperative learning, second language development). In reality, however, the quality of teachers does vary by school site and even grade level within the same school, in large measure because of the tremendous shortage of bilingual teachers in the United States.

At some school sites, teachers do not work together as a team but rather plan and teach in isolation. In other school sites, teachers at the same grade level plan together and team for instruction. The amount of coordination and planning within and across grade levels varies by school site, but a higher level of coordination across grades is almost always associated with more successful programs.

Many classrooms have an instructional assistant for some amount of time, though the amount of time, and whether there is any assistance, varies by school site and even grade level. In some classrooms, there is an instructional assistant all day and in other classrooms, there may be a four- or six-hour a day assistant that is shared among two or three classrooms. In addition, some classrooms have parent volunteers for a few hours a week.

6. Cross-Cultural and Self Concept Components

Psychosocial and cross-cultural competence are carefully integrated into the two-way bilingual immersion model in various ways. These features are built into the model through the social context components of additive bilingualism and positive and equitable interactions between teachers and students and between Spanish-speaking and English-speaking students as indicated above. In the ideal - and successful - models, teachers are trained to treat all students equally, whether they are Spanish or English speaking, rich or poor, ugly or cute, shy or extroverted, African American or Korean or Anglo or Hispanic, boy or girl, disabled or not. Each student is expected to perform, to participate in different roles in the classroom or group, to serve in leadership roles, and so on. Further, students are expected to treat each other with respect and with equity.

Of course, this component is the most difficult to implement because teachers are socialized in the United States (like most countries) to believe that cute kids and middle class kids know more, that boys are better at math and girls are better at reading, that Asians work hard and Hispanics and African Americans are not as motivated. The stereotypes and expectations that guide our behaviors are the most difficult to retrain.

Early Evaluation Results

Evaluation efforts have sought to determine the levels of first and second language proficiency; the levels of reading, language, and mathematics achievement in Spanish and English; and the level of psychosocial competence and cross-cultural attitudes.

To provide information about the students' progress in two-way bilingual immersion programs, data will be presented and briefly discussed from one school site in San Jose, California. This school site was selected because it has implemented a 90:10 model for the past seven years and we have good longitudinal data for the students. Another reason for selecting this school is that the program at the school site is exemplary in its degree of implementation and best represents the potential of the bilingual immersion model. The district recommended the implementation of a two-way bilingual immersion program at the Kindergarten and first-grade levels in September, 1986 because the bilingual immersion model was considered the most promising model to promote high levels of bilingualism, biliteracy and academic achievement as well as positive cross-cultural attitudes necessary for true school integration. During the past few years, the school has received funding by the U.S. Department of Education, through Title VII, to develop its program. River Glen has just completed its seventh year, with children participating in Kindergarten through fifth grade. Most graduates of the program go into a bilingual immersion program at the middle school. However, in this program students only receive 1.5 of their 5 periods in Spanish; one Spanish Arts course and one content course taught in alternating units of English and Spanish.

At River Glen, about 63% of the students are considered low-income, based upon participation in the Free School Lunch program. Almost three fourths of the school's population is Hispanic (72%), with 25% White Non-Hispanic, 1% African American, and 2% Asian American.

A total of 323 students were included in the evaluation research sample; 61 Kindergartners, 62 first graders, 49 second graders, 36 third graders, 32 fourth graders, 20 fifth graders, 21 sixth graders, and 20 seventh graders. Two additional groups of students were also selected from the same district to enable appropriate comparisons. A sample of 125 Spanish speaking first-through fifth-grade students was selected from a high quality transitional programmes;late exit. These students were of similar backgrounds as those at River Glen. In addition, 322 English speaking first- through fourth-grade students from a regular school in a middle class neighborhood were selected as a comparison sample for the English speakers.

A number of testing instruments were administered to the students. The Comprehensive Tests of Basic Skills, Form U (CTBS-U) is designed to measure achievement in English in the basic skills normally found in U.S. state and district curricula. La Prueba Riverside de Realización en Español (La Prueba) consists of a series of progressive tests designed to measure the academic achievement of Kindergarten through Grade 9 native Spanish speakers. The Student Oral Language Observation Matrix (SOLOM) is a rating scale that assesses oral language proficiency in children in five domains: (1) Comprehension, (2) Fluency, (3) Vocabulary, (4) Pronunciation, and (5) Grammar. The Cross-Cultural Attitudes Scale assesses students' attitudes toward individuals from other cultures and language backgrounds and toward other languages.

Tables 6 and 7 provide data relating to the percentage of students who were rated as fluent proficient on the SOLOM by language background and grade level. Looking at the results from the perspective of the students' English language proficiency (see Table 6), it is clear that the English-speaking students were considered fully proficient in their native language, as expected. The results are even more dramatic for the Spanish speakers. In spite of the limited quantity of English in the instructional day, the Spanish speakers showed growth in English language proficiency across the grades, with almost all of the native Spanish speaking third through fifth graders scoring as fluent English proficient. Turning to Spanish oral language proficiency (see Table 7), almost all Spanish-speaking students were fluent in Spanish and the English speakers made great gains in Spanish oral language proficiency across the grade levels (See Table 7). By fourth grade, most of the English speakers were rated as Fluent Spanish proficient. Thus, the objective that students would be proficient in two languages was met by most native English and native Spanish speakers.

To better understand these language proficiency results, it is important to recognize that when teachers use the SOLOM to rate students' language proficiency, they are instructed to rate the students' language relative to other, *monolingual* students at the same grade level. Thus, students must demonstrate continued development in each language just to maintain the same rating they

Table 6. English SOLOM: Average Score and Percent and Number of Students Scoring Fluent/Non Fluent by Grade Level and Language Background

| | English SOLOM | | | | Average Score |
| | Non Fluent | | Fluent | | |
	Number	Percent	Number	Percent	
Kindergartners					
LEP	20	87.0%	3	13.0%	16.3
EP	0	.0%	38	100.0%	25.0
First Graders					
LEP	17	60.7%	11	39.3%	16.6
EP	0	.0%	33	100.0%	24.7
Second Graders					
LEP	5	22.7%	17	77.3%	21.8
EP	0	.0%	26	100.0%	25.0
Third Graders					
LEP	0	.0%	16	100.0%	22.1
EP	0	.0%	18	100.0%	25.0
Fourth Graders					
LEP	1	5.6%	17	94.4%	22.3
EP	0	.0%	13	100.0%	24.9
Fifth Graders					
LEP	1	9.1%	10	90.9%	22.2
EP	0	.0%	9	100.0%	24.9

Note. The top score on the SOLOM is 25; a score of 19 or above indicates proficiency in the language.

received the previous year. If a student's language development does not keep pace with normal *monolingual* development, then the rating is lower even though the student may speak the language just as well as or slightly better than s/he did the previous year. Thus, to note decrements across the grade levels does not mean that the students are losing the language, but rather that students are not making the same level of growth expected of a *monolingual* child at that grade level. Clearly, this rating places high expectations on the students to develop language *as a monolingual would*, and does not take into consideration that the child is learning two languages. These are important points to keep in mind in understanding the SOLOM results.

The majority of the students performed exceptionally well on the achievement test in Spanish (see Table 8). At most grade levels, average percentiles were in the 80s and 90s. Percentiles dipped at the sixth grade level, the grade at which

Table 7. Spanish SOLOM: *Average Score and Percent and Number of Students Scoring Fluent/Non Fluent by Grade Level and Language Background*

	Spanish SOLOM				Average Score
	Non Fluent		Fluent		
	Number	Percent	Number	Percent	
Kindergartners					
LEP	0	.0%	23	100.0%	24.9
EP	23	60.5%	15	39.5%	17.7
First Graders					
LEP	0	.0%	28	100.0%	24.7
EP	17	51.5%	16	48.5%	18.3
Second Graders					
LEP	3	13.6%	19	86.4%	23.1
EP	11	42.3%	15	57.7%	18.7
Third Graders					
LEP	1	6.3%	15	93.8%	23.9
EP	9	50.0%	9	50.0%	18.4
Fourth Graders					
LEP	0	.0%	18	100.0%	24.1
EP	5	38.5%	8	61.5%	18.9
Fifth Graders					
LEP	0	.0%	11	100.0%	24.7
EP	2	22.2%	7	77.8%	21.7

Note. The top score on the SOLOM is 25; a score of 19 or above indicates proficiency in the language.

students changed from the elementary to the middle school program. Despite the drop in the middle students' exposure to instruction taught through Spanish, they did surprisingly well. Among the students in general, over three fourths of the English and Spanish students scored above the 50th percentile, and about two-thirds of the students scored above the 75th percentile, in reading, language, and mathematics achievement. Statistically, we would only expect 25% of the students to score this high. Thus, in Spanish reading, language, and mathematics achievement, the students were making much better than average progress. In addition, in content areas such as science and social studies, achievement was also exceptionally high, with average percentiles in the high 60's to 80's. These achievement results attest to the fact that the students were learning content in Spanish. Their high scores in reading, language, mathematics, social studies, and science demonstrate that they were

Table 8. Spanish Achievement Scores in Percentiles for Native Spanish- and English-Speaking Students at each Grade Level

Grade Level: Language Background	Reading	Language	Mathematics	Social Studies	Science
First:					
Spanish speakers	83				
English speakers	81				
Second:					
Spanish speakers	94				
English speakers	93				
Third:					
Spanish speakers	85	83	90	81	90
English speakers	91	92	97	96	97
Fourth:					
Spanish speakers	97	97	92	97	94
English speakers	89	92	87	87	93
Fifth:					
Spanish speakers	96	98	97	95	96
English speakers	95	98	98	97	98
Sixth:					
Spanish speakers	62	65	78	77	80
Seventh:					
Spanish speakers	76	91	88	84	89

Note.There were too few English speakers in the sixth and seventh grade cohorts to provide reliable data.

developing strong reading comprehension, vocabulary and study skills, mathematics computation and problem solving skills, as well as science and social studies concepts.

English achievement varied considerably, as expected (see Table 9). It is important to remember that students did not begin English reading instruction until third grade, and thus scores prior to third grade represent transfer from Spanish reading instruction and perhaps parental or other extracurricular input (e.g., television programs, older siblings or peers) in English reading.

It is critical in the interpretation of these results to understand that it is much more difficult for all of these students to catch up to their peers, statistically, because almost all students show gains from one year to the next, and a student

Table 9. English Achievement Scores in Percentiles for Native Spanish- and English-Speaking Students at each Grade Level

Grade Level: Language Background	Reading	Mathemathics
First:		
Spanish speakers	16	47
English speakers	25	63
Second:		
Spanish speakers	17	52
English speakers	37	61
Third:		
Spanish speakers	17	52
English speakers	48	79
Fourth:		
Spanish speakers	29	52
English speakers	60	83
Fifth:		
Spanish speakers	33	79
English speakers	70	94
Sixth:		
Spanish speakers	30	63
Seventh:		
Spanish speakers	48	56

Note.There were too few English speakers in the sixth and seventh grade cohorts to provide reliable data.

must make these gains to maintain the same percentile. In order to increase even five percentile points means that students must score much higher than other students who are also growing in knowledge. In addition, they must demonstrate greater growth in English when they are receiving considerably less instruction in English. Thus, to make gains in English achievement requires making greater growth than monolingual English speakers who are in English only educational programs.

In English reading achievement by third grade, English speaking students scored average to above average. By fifth grade, 85% of the English speakers were scoring above the 50th percentile, and over 50% of the students above the 75th percentile. The English speaking students' performance was also slightly higher than English speaking counterparts in the regular English only instructional program. Among the Spanish speakers, performance in English reading increased steadily across the grade levels. However, their reading achievement in English did not approach average until seventh grade. Mathematics achievement in English for both groups also increased over the grade levels up to the fifth grade, with over two thirds of the English and Spanish third through fifth graders scoring above the 50th percentile. Although their scores were average to slightly above average, the sixth and seventh graders scored lower in mathematics than did the fifth graders, and lower than they had when they were in fifth grade.

Comparisons of the Spanish speaking two-way bilingual immersion students with Spanish speaking students in a high quality transitional bilingual education program in the district indicated that the bilingual immersion students scored higher in every area: Spanish reading, language, and mathematics, and English reading and mathematics. Similarly, when the English speaking fourth and fifth grade two-way bilingual immersion students were compared to English speaking mainstream fourth and fifth grade students in a middle class school, the bilingual immersion students scored higher in English reading and English mathematics than their monolingual English peers. This level of achievement is remarkable because of the much greater emphasis in the regular English programs on English. For the English speaking bilingual immersion students to perform at higher levels in English than monolingual English students who are being educated only in English clearly demonstrates that the English speaking students are making excellent progress in English. The Spanish speaking students also made excellent progress in Spanish content areas and English mathematics, and they were making good progress in English reading as well.

In analyses of the students' cross-cultural attitudes, we find that the students have very positive attitudes toward speakers of other languages, toward the second language, and toward students who are different from them (Lindholm, 1994). Also, there are no significant differences between the English speakers and Spanish speakers in their cross-cultural attitudes. Thus, these results demonstrate that both groups of students are developing positive cross-cultural attitudes.

The results are consistent with those of other evaluation studies. However, the performance of students at River Glen is typically higher than the achievement of students at other school sites implementing the same model. With more schools now implementing the two-way bilingual immersion model, we have just begun to systematically examine the outcomes of students at different school sites and look at the outcomes in relation to the extent of actual model implementation.

We have also conducted analyses to determine whether the data provide evidence that higher levels of bilingual proficiency are associated with higher levels of achievement in both English and Spanish (Lindholm & Aclan, 1991). Preliminary results demonstrate some significant findings and clear trends to suggest that High proficient bilinguals (those who receive the top score in both their languages) outscore Medium proficient bilinguals (those who score at the top in their native language and are rated proficient, but not at the top of the scale, in the second language) who score higher than Low bilinguals (those who are very fluent in their first language, but not yet fluent in the second language) in Spanish and English reading, and Spanish and English mathematics. These results provide further evidence that highly proficient bilinguals may be developing a threshold hypothesis over students who have low and even intermediate levels of bilingual proficiency.

In conclusion, the results are very positive for both native Spanish and English speakers in that they demonstrate gains in both Spanish and English proficiency; high levels of Spanish reading, language, mathematics, social studies, and science achievement; and satisfactory to well above average reading, language and mathematics achievement in English; and positive cross-cultural attitudes.

Comparative Analysis of the Program Models

This chapter represents a first attempt at comparing the two-way bilingual immersion design as implemented in California to the European School Model as described by Baetens Beardsmore (1993, this volume). Instead of an exhaustive account of as many variables as possible, both antecedent as well as transactional, this analysis will focus on a small number of factors which the authors consider fundamental to the integrity of each model. Our analysis should be considered exploratory in nature but could very well serve two purposes. First, the issues raised in this chapter may be of value to researchers as they attempt to identify priorities for future studies. Second, for practitioners intending to replicate, in whole or in part, either of the two models in their local educational contexts, our analysis can serve as a cautionary statement regarding specific features of the programs.

Second Language Teaching

A major difference between the two-way bilingual immersion and European Schools models is the language teaching;methods the second language to the students. In the European Schools model, a traditional foreign language grammar-based approach is used for the first several years. The focus is on grammar and vocabulary up to about age 14. Beginning at about third grade, the second language is also used as a medium of instruction. In contrast, in the two-way bilingual immersion model, from Kindergarten, students are taught content through the second language. There is considerably less attention paid to grammar. While the model calls for language objectives and the incorporation of grammar in the content, unfortunately, the importance of the incorporation of grammar and language objectives has only recently been recognized as students reach the fifth and sixth grades without sufficient grammatical understanding. Thus, the two-way bilingual immersion model is beginning to incorporate more grammar, but still differently than the European Schools model. That is, in the bilingual immersion program, grammar is incorporated into the content teaching, not taught separately.

A second difference in methodology concerns the types of competence that are highlighted. In the European Schools model, the focus is on the spoken language and written competence is left to the secondary program (except for Greek children who are taught the Latin alphabet system). Written materials may be used, but they play a very secondary role. In two-way bilingual immersion, reading and writing in the non-English language are incorporated into the program from the beginning. Students write in journals and complete other written assignments from Kindergarten or first grade. Literature is used to expose students to the second language. Exposure to English literature and writing in English varies according to whether the model is 90:10 or 50:50. In the 90:10 model, students are exposed to English print by first grade and are expected to read and write by third grade when formal English reading and writing instruction begins. In the 50:50 model, students are taught to read and write in both languages in the early grades.

Thus, the methodologies in teaching the L2 contrast in the European Schools and two-way bilingual immersion models. In the European Schools model, the approach is more focused on grammar and spoken language; thus, students receive more grammar instruction and fewer reading and writing experiences. In the two-way bilingual immersion model, reading and writing are introduced immediately, but there has been little attention paid to grammar. Over the course of their elementary years, the approaches become more equivalent with both models using the L2 as the language of instruction for subject matter.

One last contrast in second language teaching concerns the administrative and societal expectations for student achievement and proficiency. In the European Schools model, students receive a much more rigorous curriculum and a longer school day than in California (and most of the United States) where there are minimum standards and the school day may be as short as four hours. Thus, clearly European Schools model students have more opportunity to develop language proficiency in the second, L3 and L4 languages as well. Overall, their levels of language proficiency will be much stronger than the students in the California public schools.

Language Group

There are significant differences between both majority and immigrant minority populations in the European and U.S. contexts. The history and geography of these regions seem to have fostered more of an international crosscultural perspective in Europe and a greater tendency towards intranational mono-cultural attitudes in America. Even so, the motivation of families from the groups which enroll their children in either the two-way bilingual immersion or European Schools appear to be more similar than different. Both sets of groups see an increasingly interdependent world where multilingualism and cross-culturalism are not only desired but considered absolutely essential for psychosocial, cultural, economical and political wellbeing. These families believe that the ability of children to function in a heritage language and culture along with those of one or two other groups are important personal and societal attributes.

What fundamentally distinguishes enrollments in two-way bilingual immersion education from those in European Schools is the inclusion of large numbers of caste-like minority students in the U.S. programs. Ogbu and Matute-Bianchi (1986) describe such students as coming from ethnolinguistic groups which have become incorporated into a society more or less involuntarily and permanently through slavery, conquest or colonization and then relegated to menial status. This description matches almost perfectly Latino groups such as Puerto Rican and especially Mexican origin pupils who constitute approximately half of all two-way bilingual immersion participants.

Like immigrant minorities, caste-like Latinos/Latinas are the recipients of instrumental and expressive exploitation and discrimination practices. The group is viewed as a source of cheap labor which is operationalized through creation of a job ceiling. The job ceiling is then enforced by limiting access to educational opportunities or by providing substandard educational experiences. The victims are then blamed for these circumstances through negative stereotyping (uncivilized, lazy, inferior, etc.). The major difference for caste-like minorities according to Ogbu and Matute-Bianchi (1984) is that they tend to develop an "institutionalized discrimination perspective" and an "oppositional cultural system" to cope with their subordinated status.

The adoption of an institutionalized discrimination perspective reflects the fact that some caste-like minorities are eventually persuaded by the majority, to some degree, that their inferior status is justified by inherent biological, social or cultural traits. Because of this, many are convinced that it is impossible for them to advance socially or economically as individuals or as a group in a majority-controlled society. This leads many caste-like minorities to embrace an oppositional cultural system consisting of various survival strategies such as (1) passing, (2) clientship, (3) collective struggle, and (4) deviant behavior, including gang membership and criminal activity.

In California, a numerical majority of all participants in two-way bilingual immersion programs come from Mexican origin families. Providing students from this caste-like minority group with a proper education is a challenge far greater in size or scope than anything experienced within the European Schools Model. In fact, according to the description of such schools by Baetens Beardsmore (1993), none of the language groups in that setting would be categorized as caste-like minorities.

Two-way bilingual immersion programs appear to address, at least in part, the needs of caste-like minority groups. Cummins (1994) among others has observed that these programs benefit both minority and majority students. However, two-way bilingual immersion programs seem to generate interactional effects that result in accelerated learning on the part of minority students, allowing this group of pupils to close the scholastic gap that traditionally separates them from their majority student counterparts. In fact, two-way programs are somewhat more powerful than other multicultural interventions since the incorporation of the heritage language, and culture creates a context in which other important sociocultural interventions can be nested. For example, strategies such as cooperative learning (Holt, 1993), Family Critical Literacy (Ada, 1989), Descubrimento (DeAvila, Cohen, and Intili, 1981), and Anti-bias Curriculum (Derman-Sparks, 1989) are more frequently being adopted as components within many two-way bilingual immersion programs.

Political Status of Program
Viewed from the perspective that two-way bilingual immersion programs have the potential to empower students by providing them with awareness and skills needed for proper participation in efforts to promote social justice, the programs are often seen as threatening to those who would maintain the status quo. Cummins (1989) reports on the various strategies used to undermine educational programs considered to be likely vehicles for sociopolitical change.

Table 10. Neutralizing the Threat of a Good Example: Two-way Bilingual Immersion Education

---

A. GOAL

Ensure that the economic and political interests of the dominant group are not threatened by deviant initiatives that might empower minority groups or enlighten majority group members of the existence of social injustice.

↓

B. METHOD

Exert economic and political pressure to ensure that implementation of the deviant initiative is destabilized and outcomes are negative. If positive outcomes emerge despite this pressure, then either ignore, deny or distort them.

↓

C. OUTCOMES

The failure of the deviant initiative under these conditions will demonstrate that attempts at subordinated group empowerment are ill-conceived and ill-advised. Dominant group control can be re-established under the guise of equality and justice.

Source: Adapted from Cummins, 1989 (p. 125)

Referring to the what he calls the "threat of a good example", Cummins identifies the goals, methods, and outcomes utilized in efforts to delegitimize such programs. We have adapted Table 10 to correspond uniquely to the two-way bilingual immersion program context.

In refuting claims of effectiveness associated with two-way bilingual immersion education, opponents commonly use the three strategies listed by Cummins (1989; see also Cummins 1994): (a) limiting the framework of discourse, (b) denying/distorting empirical realities, and (c) ignoring logical contradictions. Often opponents of the program attempt to align their arguments with what they claim is an overriding concern for the well being of language minority students. That is, under the guise of promoting equal educational opportunity, attempts are made to eliminate two-way bilingual immersion programs, since this educational approach is deemed to be harmful to the very students it was specifically designed to help.

Since the inception of the two-way bilingual immersion concept, opposition to this and other two-way bilingual programs has paralleled the same unsubstantiated arguments used against transitional bilingual education. A well-documented history of the sociopolitical debate surrounding bilingual education has been compiled by Crawford (1989). Crawford carefully depicts and analyzes the various attempts to portray bilingual schooling as educationally harmful and fundamentally un-American. Just last year, a commission charged with monitoring state governmental agencies referred to the California Department of Education's promotion of native language instruction in bilingual programs as inappropriate, unwarranted, not feasible, and counterproductive (Little Hoover Commission, 1993). A recent report regarding the reauthorization of the federal bilingual education act summarizes the position of English-only advocates into two damaging assumptions: (1) that language minority students who are economically and educationally "disadvantaged" are incapable of learning to high standards and (2) that instruction in the native language distracts these students from learning English (Stanford Working Group, 1993). Ramirez and others (1992) correctly identify transitional bilingual education programs, the most common design in the United States, as early-exit models. The fact that two-way bilingual immersion is structured to promote full development of two languages means that the notion of exiting students from the program is contrary to the enrichment nature of the intervention. Seen as a radical form of bilingual education, the model has become a target for English-only and other anti-bilingual education groups.

For example, the READ (Research in English Acquisition and Development, Inc.) Institute of Washington D.C., formed by individuals known to favor English-only policies, has disseminated a study entitled *Bilingual Immersion: A Longitudinal Evaluation of the El Paso Program* (Gersten, Woodward, and Schneider, 1992). The study has co-opted the term "bilingual immersion". This is actually a report of an experiment in Texas in which Mexican-American children were enrolled in an intensified English-based reading program. Earlier, the primary author, Gersten, referred to such programs as "immersion education" although they in no way resembled the immersion programs of Canada. This type of program has been categorized as "structured English immersion" or "sheltered English" by more responsible researchers (Ramirez, 1992). Apparently, the author and his colleagues from the READ Institute wanted to disassociate themselves from the structured immersion and sheltered English labels. The use of the term bilingual immersion in this instance is an inappropriate attempt to pass off the English-based program in Texas as something other than compensatory education and only confuses educators as to the enrichment nature and positive outcomes associated with authentic two-way bilingual immersion education where the goal of the program is to develop high levels of proficiency in two languages.

In California, with one exception, two-way bilingual immersion programs are operated as strands of classrooms found within so-called regular English-medium schools. This has meant that the programs have had to defend themselves against ever-present insidious encroachments of monolingual mediocrity as they attempt to maintain fidelity to the theoretical model. One of the more serious threats has been the assignment of majority staff members who do not possess sufficient proficiency in the minority language to fulfill their professional functions in the program. When teachers are unable to teach the core curriculum in the minority language, it is impossible to maintain the scope and sequence of the program. Lack of minority language proficiency and awareness of minority language educational practices among principals and other administrators has created additional obstacles. This has tended to reduce the effectiveness of "best decision" judgements needed to adapt the two-way bilingual immersion model to local conditions. Monolingual administrators have not been generally effective in promoting the program at the local school and in the wider community.

Based on the reports of the European School Model (Baetens Beardsmore, 1993, this volume), we assume that little or no minority stigma is attached to either the participating students or to the programs themselves. In fact, it appears that there is little controversy surrounding the schools, which are seen, for the most part, as enrichment opportunities (but see Baetens Beardsmore's discussion of the Oostlander report, p. 67).

Grouping Practices

Unlike the European Schools Model, two-way bilingual immersion programs group minority and majority students together during most language and subject content classes taught through the minority languages. This means for example, that Spanish-speaking and English-speaking students are initially grouped together for language arts, math, science, and social studies and instructed through the medium of Spanish.

For English speakers, this educational experience resembles the full early immersion design as practiced in Canada (Genesee, 1987). The variation, of course, is found in the fact that native speakers are mixed with the second language learners. In California, the mix of the two groups is viewed as positive for the English-speakers. In immersion programs, participants often fail to gain full native-like proficiency in the second language (Swain, 1984). By providing English-speaking participants with daily opportunities for interaction with native speakers, it is hoped that these students will become more native-like and avoid the stigmatization of speaking an "immersion" dialect of the second language.

For Spanish speakers, the inclusion of native speakers of English in Spanish medium instruction, although somewhat unique among instructional strategies, is thought to be beneficial to the minority students. By and large, before and after these students enter public school, they have and continue to experience L1 loss and underdevelopment. These students are not prepared to encounter the same type of L1 instruction which would be provided in their home countries. Instead, the promoters of two-way bilingual immersion believe that a specialized engagement with Spanish should be provided, similar to that suggested in "sheltered" second language programs. The thinking is that sheltered Spanish instruction best approximates the needs of Spanish-speaking students experiencing L1 loss (including those minority students who possess very little functional proficiency in their L1) and English-speakers in the process of L2 acquisition. Secondly, in response to their minority status, Spanish-speakers have been observed to benefit to a greater degree than their English-speaking counterparts from cooperative learning groups taught in their heritage language (Kagan, 1986).

In addition to the linguistic, academic, and social rationale, mixing English and Spanish speakers during language and subject matter classes has a political basis. First, most minority groups which have participated in the struggle for equal educational opportunities, have traditionally done so on the basis of ethnic and racial integration. Separation of "white" majority students from language minority students (often children of color) is not widely-accepted, at this time, by many minority group leaders. The fear is that students will be isolated and segregated into substandard educational environments. Secondly, in the past, political pressure by the majority group has restricted most efforts at mother tongue schooling in the United States to transitional, early-exit models which underutilize the minority language and lead to subtractive forms of bilingualism. As a strategy to reduce pressure to transition Spanish-speakers into English-only classes, two-way bilingual immersion education is structured on the premise that the scholastic well being of English-speaking students is dependent on the continued enrollment of Spanish-speakers in the program. The overall performance of majority group participants is inextricably linked to the long term involvement of the minority pupils. Thus, two-way bilingual immersion is likely to be viewed by both the majority and minority school communities as "our" program rather than "their" program.

Summary and Conclusions

Clearly, both the European Schools and the two-way bilingual immersion models are progressive experiments in language and crosscultural education. The programs share many theoretical underpinnings and are aligned, for the most part, on a common research foundation. Still, both models seem to be in relative early stages of development and in need of further refinement.

For example, the European Schools Model seems exceptionally well suited to educate students from the various countries in the European Community. On one hand, students will develop home country linguistic and cultural skills while on the other, gain multilingual/crosscultural skills and the academic foundation needed for the multinational regional setting. Still, experience with the model is limited. Baetens Beardsmore (1993, this volume) alludes to problems which occur with the "less academically oriented" students, an issue which will take on added significance if more and more working class families begin to enroll their children in the model. Also, the model surely will have to consider the implications of enrolling European minorities (e.g.: Sámi from the Nordic countries or Basque- and Catalan-speakers from Spain and France).

By contrast, educators involved in promoting and implementing the two-way bilingual immersion model in the U.S. are consumed by the demands associated with caste-like minority students. Serving this group of students has resulted in minority status for the program itself, leading to a whole host of social, financial, and political dilemmas - including the possibility that the experiment will be aborted prematurely. Even if the programs are able to withstand the sociopolitical challenges, there are many design and implementation issues which need to be addressed by further research. Not least among these would be the identification of effective grouping strategies, strategies which would allow both minority and majority students to experience adequate language, academic, and psychosocial growth. Furthermore, the two-way bilingual immersion model has been implemented mainly at the elementary level. There are a number of implications to be studied in terms of the proper adaptation of the design to the secondary school setting.

Chilton-Pierce (1992), among several other leading contemporary psychologists and philosophers, suggests that human development consists of two components, intellect and intelligence. He defines intellect as the ability to use the mind, an aptitude which has supported the significant strides made in creating our technologically "advanced" society. This is contrasted with intelligence which he defines as abilities to use the heart. Here, Chilton-Pierce claims that humans are still at a relatively primitive state of development. As beings, we have not learned how to care for and respect our natural environment. We have made little progress in finding ways to coexist peacefully with our fellow humans. War and other forms of violence, such as subordination of groups (minority status), poverty, and pollution have become the norm. What is exciting about the European Schools and two-way bilingual immersion models is that they hold out the potential for us to find ways to develop both the intellect and intelligence of our future generations.

Notes:

1   Editor's note: The term LEP is still used in most official documents, despite its pejorative connotations: minority children are labelled negatively, in terms of what they do *not* know, and with English native speakers as a norm. California Department of Education, Bilingual Education Office, has worked quite some time trying to find positive alternative terms and David Dolson has been instrumental in this. See also, e.g. Wink, 1993.

2   In California, all but eight of the two-way bilingual immersion programs currently being implemented enroll approximately balanced numbers of students who are native speakers of English and Spanish. In the remaining sections of this chapter, we will refer to the language minority students as Spanish speakers and the language majority students as English speakers.

3   In California, as indicated previously, the Spanish/English language combination accounts for 49 of the 57 bilingual immersion school programs (Christian & Mahrer, 1992, 1993; Christian & Montone 1994). However, there are also Japanese/English (1 program), Chinese/English (3 programs), Korean/English (3 programs), and Portuguese/English (1 program) language combinations. Across the United States, the Spanish/English language combination is also the most prevalent (160 of the 176 programs), but there are French/English (1 program), Chinese (Cantonese)/English (4 programs), Haitian Creole/English (1 program), Japanese/English (2 programs), Korean/English (3 programs), Navajo/English (2 programs), Portuguese/English (1 program) and Russian/English (2 program) language combinations as well (Christian & Mahrer, 1992; Christian 1994, Table 6).

3

MULTILINGUALISM FOR AUSTRALIANS?

John Gibbons

The task of this chapter is to examine the European Schools model of bilingual education described by Baetens Beardsmore in this volume, in order to examine its applicability to Australia, and also to determine what characteristics distinguish these Europeans School programmes from bilingual programmes found in Australia. There is no doubt that the model has had an extraordinary measure of success in Europe, and is encouraging for proponents of bilingual education for all children. The particular value of the European Schools model to Australia is that it shows a set of conditions that can make maintenance bilingual education work (maintenance bilingual education is where two language are used to teach content subjects, one language being the dominant language of the majority group – in Australia this would be English; the other language of instruction is the home language of minority children, and this language is used in school with the objective of maintaining and developing this mother tongue, so that the minority language child can become fully bilingual). Pleasure in this success is however tinged with caution: while the approach is obviously highly developed and exciting, it also demands a high level of resources – by Australian educational standards it is expensive.

The assumption made here is that differences between the European Union (EU) and the Australian contexts will explain the differences between Australian and European Schools bilingual programmes, and will motivate those instances where the European Schools model cannot be directly applied in Australia. Contextual differences and their outcomes will be discussed under three headings – language status context, policy context, and context of long term educational objectives. Some other issues raised by Baetens Beardsmore are also addressed subsequently.

Hereafter the capitalised expression "European School" will be used to refer specifically to the EU run schools described by Baetens Beardsmore, not to Europeans schools in general. My direct personal knowledge of bilingual programmes in Australia is also mostly limited for geographical reasons to schools in New South Wales, so comparisons will be made primarily with these. Baetens Beardsmore's chapter (this volume) makes use of an important distinction between maintenance, transitional, and enrichment bilingual education. There is however another important distinction that I wish to make. This is between *bilingual education as a route to education*, and *bilingual education as a route to bilingualism*. For children who come to school with little or no knowledge of the majority language used in mainstream education (in Sydney for example, according to Abdoolcader (1989) this is the case for around a third of children entering Catholic schools), the main point of bilingual education is to ensure that such children can be educated at all in the early years of school. If their mother tongue is not used as a medium of instruction, then their education may be set back for a year or more until they master enough of the language of the education system to understand the education offered to them. Jim Cummins (1984a) also maintains that it can take up to seven years for second language children to reach the point where they can perform their potential in a way similar to peers for whom the language of education is a mother tongue. This then is the bilingual education as a route to education issue which has been fought through the US courts in such cases as Lau v Nichols. Since the justification for such bilingual programmes is education rather than language, they are often transitional, with bilingual ability sacrificed in a transition to 100% L2 instructional medium – see also for example the programme discussed in Gibbons, White & Gibbons (1994).

However in Canada, the French immersion programmes have had as their objective the learning of French – here bilingual education is a route to bilingualism. The initial sacrifice is educational. At first the children do worse educationally, although later they do as well as or better than their English medium educated peers – see Genesee (1987), and Swain & Lapkin (1982). The same has been found in Australian immersion programmes – see Lorch, McNamara, & Eisokovits (1992: 7-8).

The form of bilingual education that has the best track record without doubt is the enrichment type, usually involving immersion. Its effectiveness has been demonstrated in many settings, including Canada, Ireland and Australia (Clyne, 1986). However maintenance bilingual education as a route to education has had mixed results, as is shown in the survey by Cziko (1992). The success of this type of bilingual education appears to be very much dependent on the conditions under which operates.

In the past, most enrichment bilingual education such as the Canadian immersion programmes, has had bilingualism as its main objective. By contrast, education has usually been the main objective of transitional and maintenance bilingual education, such as that found in some Sydney Catholic Primary Schools and intended for linguistic minorities.

The European Schools model of bilingual education presented by Baetens Beardsmore is maintenance bilingual education, but its purpose seems to be predominantly bilingual education as a route to bilingualism, or perhaps a balance between the educational and linguistic objectives. It is then a new form of bilingual education.

These two contrasts may explain some of the differences between the European Schools and the Canadian Immersion Programmes. In the latter there is a willingness to sacrifice content to language, hence the initial retardation in general education produced by using only the second language as medium is accepted as a short term cost of learning the second language fast and well. In the European Schools education is rated as highly as language, and the programme is partly intended to "shelter" home minority languages, so rather than endanger content and home language by using a poorly understood second language as medium of instruction, initially the second language is taught by more traditional second language teaching approaches. In effect both the European Schools and immersion forms of bilingual education seek a long term balance between educational and language outcomes, but the initial short term requirements are different. Furthermore, in the European Schools, there are two types of student in the school. As we have noted, there are those from a language minority background, whose mother tongue needs "shelter" at school: for them a total immersion in a second language is not appropriate and there is a maintenance agenda. For the other group, those from a language majority, enrichment is desirable. Once more a balanced approach is needed to accommodate the needs of both groups.

I shall now turn to a comparison of contexts, to see how the model compares to the Australian context, and what light the contextual differences throw on the model and its applicability in Australia.

The Language Status Context

A partly united Europe affords a very different socio-political context from that of Australia. The European Schools epitomise the united aspect of a sometimes divided European Union. Europe has many languages; all the languages of the constituent nations have official status (even if "working languages" have more effective status than non-working languages). In Australia there is one official language – English. This one language can be used throughout Australia for all situations other than the home – in particular it is the expected language for public and official uses. This language is overwhelmingly powerful in the context of Australia, and dominates all others. Furthermore this internal language is a viable international language – for example, in our region it may well be the language that a Korean executive uses with an Indonesian executive. The Australian context resembles the situation in individual European nations like Britain or France before they became part of the European Community. In the European Schools it is the supra-national context of the EU which provides the stimulus and purpose of the European Schools. That supra-national context, and therefore that purpose and stimulus, is absent in Australia. This difference pervades all the lower level differences between bilingual education in the Australian context and in the European Schools. A reality that mitigates against bilingualism among Australians is the overwhelming social, economic, political and cultural weight of English.

An example of the effects produced by this weight of English can be drawn from the behaviour of children in bilingual programmes in Sydney who share a language other than English (LOTE). It is common for children whose proficiency in a common LOTE is much higher than their proficiency in English, to talk to each other in English even during the LOTE medium periods of the bilingual programme. The common playground language of a European School is unlikely to exert that degree of influence (see below).

The Policy Context

Australia is probably unique in the degree to which the National Language Policy has officially accepted and embraced the languages of recent immigrant minorities, putting multilingualism alongside multiculturalism as a national ethos. The considerable extent to which minority languages are officially supported by government funding of designated television and radio stations is also worthy of remark. Furthermore, the National Language Policy document (Lo Bianco 1987) openly espouses bilingual education, and discusses examples of it at some length. Unfortunately, while providing in principle support, it makes no specific recommendations for funding of bilingual education. It was not however the final word on Australia's language policy. It was followed by the National Language and Literacy Policy titled "Australia's

Languages". The original Green Paper which proposed the policy had a significant difference in detail, its title was "The Language of Australia", which implied that there is only one language in Australia – namely English. While the title changed, the ideology of the policy did not (reflecting the views of the Minister at the time – John Dawkins). The policy carries with it very significant funding targeted at adult literacy in English, and limited funding for the maintenance of aboriginal languages, the teaching of second language and some other language issues. But it deliberately and specifically excludes funding for the maintenance of non-aboriginal minority languages, and funding for bilingual education in non-aboriginal minority languages, despite protests from many prominent Australian academics. Helen Moore (1991) writes "the Minister is opposed to language maintenance in mainstream schooling". The overwhelming majority of funding in the policy goes to the teaching of English, and most of the remainder goes to the teaching of second languages, rather than maintenance. Despite pluralistic and multicultural rhetoric in principle, in practice implementation with regard to minority languages in mainstream education is at best assimilationist. The funding for maintenance of minority languages in mainstream education continue to be negligible, and for bilingual education in minority languages is almost non-existent. This is why less than one percent of non-Aboriginal minority language children receive a true bilingual education, despite the potential benefits that such an education carries.

As a consequence, the type of program described in Gibbons et al. (1994) is mainly a product of commitment at the school and system levels. The major use of bilingual education that is now emerging in Australia is enrichment bilingual education for English speakers in fee paying private schools. This takes us back to the previous comment that the European Schools model is "expensive"; the reality is that bilingual education for minority children in Australia will probably never receive sufficient funding to make the European Schools type of bilingual education possible for most minority children. As an illustration of what this policy climate produces, I should perhaps mention once more the case of the Campsie bilingual programme in Sydney (Gibbons et al., 1994). The description of the programme recounts the continuing problem of lack of funding, and the fact that this prevents the extension of the program through the school – it is therefore transitional. (One School Principal in a depressed moment described his transitional bilingual programme as a form of humane linguicide, preferable only to the callous linguicide taking place in most schools in Australia.) The poverty of St Mels, Campsie, in comparison to the European Schools can be seen in the difference in school fees. Baetens Beardsmore describes the fee of 750 ECU as "nominal". At Campsie the school fee in the same year was less than 300 ECU per year, but even then many parents were on some form of fee relief.

Long Term Educational Context

In the European Schools, the assumption is made that children will return to their home country. By contrast, in Australia as in most countries with large migrant intakes, whatever their initial intentions, few migrants return to live in their country of origin. In Australia this often extends even to political refugees, who do not return to their home country after the regime has changed. Therefore a main concern of Australian education is to prepare children for life in Australia. This contextual difference makes some of the European Schools approach inappropriate to Australia.

Looking first at the curriculum, in the European Schools it is a mixture of the home country curriculum and a "European" curriculum. The target is the fairly culturally neutral European Baccalaureate. Consequently it is feasible to use teachers from the relevant European country. Their teaching qualifications, experience, style and orientation derive from that country. The teaching methods and much of the teaching material can also be drawn from the relevant European nations.

If we compare Australia the situation is very different. Since teachers are preparing children for life in Australia, the curriculum is Australian. In general, educational material from the children's heritage country has proved inappropriate to mainstream Australian education particularly because of the background assumptions it makes and the teaching approach it assumes. Material in Australian bilingual programmes (although not necessarily in second language instruction) tends to be translations or LOTE adaptations of English medium educational material designed for Australia. This does in fact cause considerable problems in the first few years while immersion programmes are developed, since the generation of new sets of materials places considerable demands on scarce resources.

With regard to overseas teacher qualifications, many of these are not recognised in Australia, and teachers with such qualifications are expected to retrain. According to the Principals of schools with bilingual programmes that I have spoken to, knowledge of and sympathy with Australian curricula and Australian educational practices is as important as LOTE proficiency. As a consequence many bilingual teachers are second generation migrants – Greek

Australians, Lebanese Australians, and so on. First generation migrant teachers tend to become aides, entrusted with the language but not the curriculum.

An example of the differences this may produce, can be found in Sydney International School. This is a fee paying school whose programmes were originally inspired by the Canadian immersion programmes. It provides bilingual education from Kindergarten to university entrance for mainly English speaking students in a choice of six languages – French, German, Modern Greek, Italian, Japanese and Spanish (although Spanish is fading through lack of demand). The main problems faced by the school arise in the secondary school. There are nowadays increasingly prescriptive government guidelines concerning the secondary curriculum, as in Britain, and state examinations can be taken only in English, on the Australian curriculum. The consequence has been that despite the best intentions the school has found itself forced to provide all classes in English, other than five hours per week. Five hours per week is of value of course, but it cannot lead to the proficiency levels of the Canadian French immersion schools, where according to Swain (personal correspondence) 70% of students leave high school willing to undertake university study through the medium of French.

From this example one can see the enormous contextual advantage provided by a multi-national EU and the baccalaureate system, and the difficulty of applying the European Schools system to Australia. In European nations where there is a single dominant language, the national education systems resemble that of Australia more than the European Schools bilingual system. Nevertheless, as Europe slowly becomes more united, and supra-national and pan-European considerations take on more salience than national ones, there is a potential for the European national systems to evolve towards the bilingual system currently in use in the European Schools – indeed there is a policy of the steady "europeanising" of education throughout the EU. Sadly, the potential is much less in Australia, as integration with our Asian and Pacific neighbours is much slower and more difficult, and there is at present no political or economic structure equivalent to the EU.

The equivalent to the 'European Hours' in Australia is perhaps more far reaching than these. There has been substantial reform in the curricula used in Australia intended to reflect changing understandings of Australia and its society. Predominant among these are: (a) that Australia was not an 'empty land' when European settlers arrived just over 200 years ago, but has instead an indigenous culture extending at least 40 000 years into the past, which has been supressed, sometimes brutally – to quote a common slogan "White Australia has a black history"; and (b) that modern Australia is home to people from a very large range of ethnic backgrounds, and their history and culture continue in Australia and are to be recognised across the curriculum. To the extent that these perceptions penetrate all areas of the primary curriculum, rather than being restricted to particular hours, Australian education is possibly more developed in this area.

Children of Lower Academic Ability

A major concern of myself and many other proponents of bilingual education (see for example Lapkin, Swain and Shapson, 1990) is the effect that it has on children of lower academic ability. The issue is whether, in additive bilingual education, the learning of content subjects is negatively affected in the long term by the difficulty that such children may have in attempting to learn science, history, social studies etc, through the medium of a language they speak less well. Does bilingual education add even more to their learning difficulties, so the disadvantaged are further disadvantaged? Do they do worse than lower ability students educated only in their mother tongue?

Baetens Beardsmore mentions lower academic success rates among such children. Similar problems have been found in Singapore (and described in the government's Goh Report) as well as a number of other contexts. Cummins (1984a) makes a strong case that "submersion" in a majority language has a negative effect on language minority students. The exception to this appears to be the Canadian bilingual programmes, where both majority English children and minority children are immersed in French. According to Swain (personal communication) this is because educators, when using a second language in which none of their learners are proficient, are forced to take a range of measures (see Swain, 1991) to make the curriculum accessible and intelligible, including extreme explicitness. These accommodations are particularly beneficial to the lower ability student, and they compensate for the extra burden of the poorly known language of instruction. It may therefore be the case that the European Schools' use of conventional language teaching rather than immersion in the early stages in fact disadvantages such students.

Turning now to language learning, Gardner (1979) and others have shown that intelligence plays a much more significant role in learning a language through conventional classroom instruction than it does in learning through immersion. Immersion bilingual programmes appear to be far more successful in promoting bilingualism among low ability children than conventional language instruction (see Genesee, 1987: 80-83), so long as the mother tongue is adequately supported. Once more there is a possibility that lower ability children are disadvantaged by this particular aspect of the European Schools model.

The Role of the Playground Language

A complicating factor in these issues is the exposure of the children to the second language outside the classroom. They may in some sociolinguistic contexts have the opportunity for immersion in a second language outside the home and classroom. In this case school immersion is less necessary for language learning, and conventional second language teaching may serve a remedial function, filling in gaps left by the natural learning process. Equally, they may arrive at school with sufficient second language proficiency for education through the medium of the language not to pose severe problems. However, this would not be the case with children who speak a dominant host language as a mother tongue – for example English speakers in London. One would expect their results to be less impressive, resembling those from late partial immersion in Canada.

Motivation

Baetens Beardsmore early on refers to the perceived "need" for bilingualism in the EU. This is essentially a pragmatic or instrumental reason for becoming bilingual. Recent Australian government policy similarly makes no secret of its view that economically useful languages, particularly Japanese, should be the main focus of second language learning in Australia. The question is, how well does this instrumental orientation conform to the motivations of European and Australian students and parents, particularly where home language maintenance is involved.

Recently (see Gibbons, 1994) I have examined parents' reasons for selecting particular second languages, in a private primary school in Sydney, which has subsequently opted for an Indonesian bilingual programme. It was quite clear among this group that the 60% of parents who wished their children to learn European languages mostly wished these languages to be learned for cultural, integrative or maintenance reasons. The 40% of parents interested in Asian languages had mostly pragmatic, utilitarian and instrumental reasons. These findings are matched by those from an unpublished study of motives for language learning among modern language students at the University of Sydney performed by Sakurada and myself. It would be interesting to examine in a similar way language choices in the European Schools.

Conclusion

There is much to learn from the European Schools model of bilingual education. It demonstrates unequivocally that the maintenance of minority languages through bilingual education can be highly effective, with only positive consequences for long term academic progress (which, as we have noted, is not always the case elsewhere). The system of providing second language instruction as a precursor to second language immersion is an alternative to direct immersion which may prove attractive to those establishing immersion programmes for English speaking students in Australia. We did however note that this may not always benefit the language development of low ability students.

The manner in which the differences in context create many of the differences between the European Schools model and Australian bilingual education are also instructive. They act as a warning, by now familiar, that language education policies which are effective in a particular context cannot always be easily transferred to another context, although there will be aspects and insights that are generalisable. There is evidence that bilingual education can benefit almost all children in almost all contexts. The challenge in any particular context is to find, as the European Schools have done, the particular form of bilingual education that works.

4

LANGUAGE(S) IN INTERNATIONAL EDUCATION: A REVIEW OF LANGUAGE ISSUES IN INTERNATIONAL SCHOOLS

Maurice Carder

"An American parent was surprised when his six-year-old, who was slowly working her way through her ABCs, appeared one evening with her name written in the Greek alphabet. Wondering just what was included in the first grade curriculum, he asked his daughter where the letters came from. 'From Demitri', she said. 'He sits next to me in class and these are the way letters look in his country." A six-year-old learning the relationship between Greek symbols and the English alphabet is typical of the unplanned learning that often occurs.

Young people like these have been called third-culture students by sociologist Ruth Useem since they are neither wholly of the culture of their own country nor of that of the country they are living in. Her work shows that they are a remarkable mixture of innocence and sophistication – they know how to order a meal in five languages but not who was the winner of last year's World Series or FA Cup.

Among the culturally shellshocked are a very few young people who do suffer from not being rooted firmly in a language or culture of their own. The most extreme case I have met was a former student who, years after graduation, complained about not being totally comfortable in any of his languages (he had attended an English-language school, but talked Cantonese with his parents, and Danish with his friends). The fact that he was driving a BMW at the time makes me think that not even this turned out to be an insurmountable handicap!

A serious problem for young people who return to their own country after a prolonged absence is a certain social awkwardness. After a teenager has been out of his or her native culture for a while, he or she loses touch with the language of social discourse – the current jokes, the sports teams, and the top musical groups. An international student who mentions the Swahili word for "hamburger" or the last time he or she was in Paris may meet with disbelief or hostility. They learn that it is better to keep a low profile for a while, listening to what everyone else is talking about before beginning to unfold.

Sometimes the problems of re-entry are almost amusing – like the boy who was accepted to medical school back home in Mexico City and worked his way to the top of his class – until the authorities discovered that he had been promoted from the seventh grade to the ninth grade at his school in New Delhi and insisted that he go back to complete the eighth grade. (He managed to avoid that fate!)" (Keson 1991, 57-59).

Introduction: setting the scene

International Schools serve the needs of those in the world who are frequently on the move, such as diplomats, those involved in international business, UN personnel, overseas forces employees. But they are also there to create an "ideal" education for a world with rapidly shrinking boundaries and a changing social structure.

The *European Council of International Schools* (ECIS), founded in Geneva in May 1965, the oldest, largest association of international schools, serves the interests of some 60,000 young people, the largest component of which are US and British citizens, but including also students of many other nationalities, with widely varied cultural and linguistic backgrounds. Some ECIS schools

> "have over 2,000 students on roll and one has only 24. Some are urban – in the heart of cities like Paris, London and Rome ... and some are rural – in a Swiss mountain village, beside a Finnish Lake, in the Bavarian countryside. Some had 85% British or American enrolment and others have fewer than 10% from any one country. Typically 50-60 different nationalities are represented, with no single one in the majority." (ECIS 1992.).

The *International Baccalaureate Organization* (IBO), based in Geneva with other offices in Buenos Aires, New York, Singapore, and Cardiff (the examination office) and with representatives in India, Mexico, the Caribbean, and the Middle East (Sultanate of Oman), is a non-governmental organization holding consultative status with UNESCO and the Council of Europe. It is responsible for the *International Baccalaureate Organization diploma*, a credential recognized worldwide for university entrance. Only students in affiliated *International Baccalaureate* (IB) *schools* can take the IB examinations, and all students take the same IB examinations irrespective of where they are taken. There were in 1990

> "some 400 such schools in 58 countries in every continent. The variety is enormous: national and international; state and private; large and small; rich and poor. However, all schools are accepted on common worldwide criteria and by common procedures. Growth has been rapid over the last few years, and the controlled expansion of the project is some 10 per cent annually." (Blackburn 1991, 16).

"The *International Schools Directory*", published and updated by the ECIS every year, described in 1993 some 300 schools in about 70 countries. It also gives a brief description of the language programme and foreign languages offered. A typical entry will read: "The language of instruction is English and there is an ESL programme providing intensive tuition with students transferring to regular classes as soon as they are able. All fluent English speakers are required to learn German and then French".

This chapter will give a general overview of what constitutes international education, followed by a review in general terms of the curriculum in international schools (including new programmes under development for the middle years of schooling and for the primary level) and, specifically, of the languages part of the curriculum offered by the International Baccalaureate (IB) for the final two years of schooling, leading to the IB Diploma (and mention of the IB's new Language A2 examination will be made). The programme offered at the Vienna International School will be described. I have used quotes extensively, as International Schools represent a widely diverse type of institution, each school being quite different from each other. Although I have visited many International Schools, I have worked in only one, the Vienna International School. Because of this, I feel it is only fair to quote directly from those who have a much broader experience of the many different types of school around the world. Discussion will revolve around the concepts of "international humanism" and "élitism" as much as the merits and challenges of bilingualism.

The format of the chapter by Hugo Baetens Beardsmore will to some extent be shadowed though not strictly adhered to and some of the questions posed by Tove Skutnabb-Kangas for discussion in the initial call for papers at the symposium the book is based on should be answered.

Principal organizations involved in International Education: ECIS, IBO

Before detailing what international education means and discussing the role of languages in International Schools, we have to look at the organizational structure behind some of them. It is not possible to state exactly that only certain organizations are responsible for the administrative and curricular structure of international schools. Many of them grew out of national systems, serving the needs of particular nationals abroad, for example military personnel from Britain and the USA who were serving in various parts of the world after the Second World War. The *United World Colleges* were born as a result of their founder, Kurt Hahn, giving a talk at the NATO Defence College in Paris in 1957.

"At the NATO Defence College was born the concept of the Atlantic College. If middle-aged officers, who until recently had been fighting one another, could so convincingly bury their differences once engaged on a common task, then why not, he asked, attempt a non-military staff college for teenagers from the countries of the Atlantic Alliance? 'We would aim to make the boys attending (this college) feel loyal to the common cause of the free world. Are our ideals in safe-keeping? Are our young as much in earnest about their faith as their contemporaries who live under Communist rule? These colleges could become the source of a movement which would help restore morale throughout the NATO nations'". (Sutcliffe, 1991, 27).

There are, however, two bodies that come immediately to mind in any discussion of international education, namely the ECIS, *European Council of International Schools*, and the IBO, *International Baccalaureate Organization* (see above).

ECIS is a non-profit corporation administered by a sixteen member professional staff based in England. It provides all areas of administrative and organizational back-up, for example school accreditation, teacher and executive recruitment, in-service training, fellowships in international education, and specialist publications. ECIS schools cater for some 60,000 students. Some schools offer a standard US college-preparatory programme or a standard

GCE/GCSE/IGCSE programme, or a combination of these. Some prepare also for the German Abitur, the French Baccalauréat, the Swiss Maturité, the Spanish Bachillerato and other national examinations. Each year, the number of schools preparing for the diploma of the International Baccalaureate Organization (IBO), grows. ECIS schools are

"in most instances independent in ownership and management (but this does not apply in all cases and the membership includes state-run schools with international English-medium streams), and occasionally may come under the sponsorship of a particular multi-national company/organization or one or more of the embassies.

They are community schools, mostly non-competitive in requirements for entry, designed to serve a varied constituency and a broad range of abilities – though some are selective and a few cater to specialized needs.

Their patrons are employees of multi-national corporations or national or international governmental agencies – though some are expatriates of no pattern at all, and some are local nationals who simply prefer the ECIS school to any available alternative.

Many of their students are 'third-culture', neither a product of the culture of the country in which they are studying nor of the country of their legal nationality, because for most of their lives they have lived in a variety of alien settings." (ECIS 1992, xvii).

IBO developed from The International Schools Association. It is

"registered as an educational charitable foundation under Swiss law, and as such is governed by an International Council of Foundation supported by a Standing Conference of Governments and Heads of IB schools.

The Council meets annually, usually in Geneva, and is the supreme governing body of the organization. The current president is Dr. Piet Gathier, formerly Director General of Secondary Education in the Netherlands. The Council elects one-third of its membership from participating schools; one-third from participating governments, and one-third are ad personam members distinguished in the fields of international affairs, education, and business. Recently elected ad personam members include: HRH Princess Sarvath El-Hassan of Jordan; Signora Susanna Agnelli, Under-Secretary of State for Foreign Affairs in Italy; and leading international businessmen such as Dr. Curt Nicolin (Sweden) and Dr. V. Krishnamurthy (India). The Standing Conference of

Governments arrangement ensures essential governmental participation in the project, for example in the field of recognition and equivalence, but also in the academic independence of the organization.

Participating schools play an essential role. The IB arose out of the needs of international schools and was largely created by them. Representatives of schools are actively involved in the governance of IBO and in the continuing process of IB curriculum review and development on the Curriculum Board and Subject Committees. As a result, the schools influence the programmes they teach. It is this partnership between schools, administration, and examiners which makes IBO different from many national examination systems.

A Board of Chief Examiners, largely independent of the main administration structure, is ultimately responsible for the setting of question papers, assessment, and the award of grades. Chief Examiners are usually university professors who are distinguished in their own field and of many nationalities. A team of 1,100 assistant examiners worldwide assists the Board of Chief Examiners, and the examination administration is handled by the Examination Office in Cardiff." (Blackburn, 1991, 15-16).

"Most mainland European countries now accept the diploma as a valid university entry qualification. The diploma fulfils the general matriculation requirements of all British universities and in present-day Britain, it is no disadvantage for a British student and a considerable advantage for a non-British student to hold an IB diploma. In North America, IB students use their diploma or groups of certificate subjects to gain credit, and many leading universities give up to one year's earned academic credit on this basis.

IB students have now entered more than 800 universities throughout the world. However, simply possessing the diploma is no magic key to university entry. High grades will still be required by top universities. Strict faculty and department requirements will often have to be met. But, it does work – and better than anyone could have imagined ten years ago." (Blackburn, 1991, 24).

What is International Education?

To give an adequate description of this vast field would require a volume on its own; indeed, in 1991 such a work was published (Jonietz & Harris, 1991). Much of what follows in the general part will be based on articles in this volume. All unreferenced quotations in this chapter derive from contributors to this volume. Perusal of its writings reveals not only the many different facets of the schools involved but also the varied approaches to the area of the many contributors. Some quotes may help to explain. It is necessary to quote so extensively in order to demonstrate the difficulty in giving a clear, concise definition of international education:

"It is so difficult to define. I would put it, I think, that the purpose of international education is to teach our kids how to welcome diversity not just tolerate it: diversity in language, diversity in culture, and diversity in race seem to me one of the few desirable aspects of the human condition, and yet, most educational systems ignore the possibility or in some cases work flatly against it. I would have thought that those seem to me to be the two aspects, speaking quickly off the cuff, that appeal to me. I want to say you really do see this in IB schools. Diversity is not something to be tucked away in somebody else's back garden but is welcome. Whether I go to an IB school in East Africa or the north of Italy or wherever, I do see students who are getting this kind of experience." (Blackburn 1991, 222).

"If I had a pound for every essay that has been made at defining international education, I would surely be a good deal richer than I am now. If I had read them all, however, I am not sure that I would be much farther along towards a comprehensive definition: what constitutes or should constitute an international education remains a complex and controversial matter. Much more research and experimentation are undoubtedly required, but needed even more are greater imagination and bolder outreach ... First let me recall what I wrote in a recent article in the International Schools Journal (Autumn 1988): "We must ... stop thinking of 'internationalism' as a merely cosmetic appliqué to attract more numbers to what remains essentially the same old school. Internationalism is more than a mix of student nationalities and languages and cultures and religions, no matter how well stirred ... It is more than a market strategy, to be manipulated for the gaze of the public. We must stop playing with the bits and pieces coincidental to our heterogeneous collection (of students and teachers) and face up to the fact that in and of itself (that collection) may constitute an international school, but not at all necessarily an international education. The two concepts are not inextricably intertwined ... (and because we have one it does not ineluctably follow that we must have the other.)" ... We must discover ... a way to use the riches of our heterogeneity to create an educational programme genuinely different from that available in any domestic setting, an eclectic synthesis drawn from the best that is known about teaching and learning from wherever in the world it may be found. We must become a truly discrete branch of the profession, committed to the identification of those elements which are basic to the concept and practice of global citizenship, and skilled in the art and science of transmitting them to those for whose education we are responsible. What I should like to do then, is to explore further 'those elements which are basic to the concept and practice of global citizenship'." (Mattern, 1991, 209).

"An international school system will be non-prescriptive in that its membership will be strictly voluntary, based on shared needs, purposes, and philosophy. It will be a system in the literal sense: A set or assemblage of things connected, associated or interdependent, so as to form a complex unity; a whole composed of parts in orderly arrangement according to some schemes or plan; an organized scheme or plan of action, especially one of a complex or comprehensive kind; an orderly or regular method of procedure." (Blaney, 1991, 199).

"Pick up any current magazine or newspaper and you will find many people (philosophers, financiers, consultants, politicians, businessmen, educators, environmentalists, and performers) who tell us that our planet is very small, and that we have much in common with others around the world. They suggest that we must open our national boundaries in education and other areas not to destroy them but so that we can grow and profit from the knowledge and experience of others. It is possible that international schools and international education may have something to share with all of us which may help to improve the quality of our individual or national lives." (Jonietz, 1991,).

"The aims of international education in the 1990's are reflected in the goals of the various organizations involved. They seem to see their mission as: offering to the international community a high calibre academic program which focuses on education for global understanding and ends in an internationally recognized diploma." (Jonietz, 1991, 4).

"The aims of the IB are still the same: to promote international understanding and to promote student mobility." (Blackburn, 19991, 15).
"... the biggest growth area is seen in the number of independent, community-based, English language of instruction schools offering education to 'third culture' students (neither a product of the country of residence nor of their original nationality). Since 1964, these schools designed for a population of mobile students and parents have also developed a population of mobile teachers and administrators.
The question is – what is it like to be part of an international school? 'Typical' is a difficult word because these schools are in a variety of continents as well as locations (urban and rural), they have different funding bases, their populations represent different national groups, they may be affiliated with different examination boards or national organizations, they may be supported by different national or community groups, and they may be independent or receive some or all state funding. However, they are alike in their international goals and their multicultural, multilingual, and multinational populations." (Jonietz, 1991, 53-54).

A group of Primary school teachers/administrators who formed the *International Schools Curriculum Project, Age 3 – 12* (ISCP) (now 70 member schools world-wide), are developing a shared curriculum between international schools. They define international education in terms of this shared curriculum, as "a well-designed framework of written curriculum documents, instructional methodologies and assessment techniques used in many international schools" (from "The International Educator", Spring 1993). A social studies curriculum is being piloted, the science curriculum is complete and the one for mathematics will be created in 1993-1995. The project is committed to

"achieving a deeper internationalism among the overseas schools community by developing a curriculum that instils an empathetic, cross-cultural awareness" (ibid.).

The inter-active language and literature curriculum framework, being developed at present, is envisioned

"as a major vehicle for moving teachers and students beyond the superficiality of most cross-cultural curriculums so they can experience a more profound empathy with other cultures. Recognizing the important links between language, culture and thinking, the ISCP has designed the inter-active language program to meet the needs of ESL students. In the process, they are paving the way for a more culturally sensitive learning environment.

Given that in most overseas schools, instruction is in English and the underpinning philosophy is generally Anglo-American even when English speakers are in the minority, the four-component interactive language program incorporating language arts, ESL, host country or other modern languages, and support for the student's mother-tongue, makes good educational sense and shows a genuine respect for the cultures that make up the school's community." (ibid.).

They recognise that more than a shared curriculum is needed, though, for "getting beyond the most superficial levels of cross-cultural empathy" (ibid.), and ask themselves how this could be done:

"However, a rigorous shared curriculum doesn't necessarily move us towards a deeper internationalism, that more profound empathy with other cultures and concern with international issues which characterizes a true global citizen... If education points a possible way forward and if we are in the education business, then where should we start in an effort to get below the surface and work towards a deeper internationalism?" (ibid.).

In order to counteract "the deep-rooted nature of cross-cultural suspicion and resentment" that "events in the former Yugoslavia provide one of many chilling reminders of", and the ignorance of "Germany's neo-nazi youths ... about even the most basic historical and political features of the original Nazi party." (ibid.), an inquiry-based approach is recommended and detailed. Focusing the curriculum on fundamental concepts like interdependence, scarcity and conflict is recommended and "local, regional and global perspectives are ... being integrated into academic subjects that lend themselves to an inter-active approach." But this is not enough; critical thinking should be at the core of international education:

"A more profound impact will only be achieved if we examine the way students learn and teachers learn. We must in fact look at how people in schools think. If we don't take on this challenge then the result will be teachers who are unable to really understand cultures that are different from their own. These educators will fall back on their own traditional responses and most likely will accept the 'black and white' summaries of complex international issues which often pass for 'political analysis' in the western news media ... On the other hand, if we educators encourage our students to think clearly and critically then perhaps we are taking a few small steps towards developing students who can respond to challenging international issues with more than knee jerk, nationalistic responses." (ibid.).

According to this group of International School staff, languages play an important role (and this will be detailed in a later section) in becoming truly international:

"An appropriate inter-active language programme for international school students is one of the most important components of this program. If these activities include a genuine respect for the cultures that make up the school's community and a thoughtful response to complex cross-cultural issues with all their attendant complexities of politics and ethics, then our schools will be one step closer to embodying a true internationalism. In Roland Barth's words, if we can forge ahead, we will be on our way to becoming a true 'international community of learners.'" (ibid.).

The International Baccalaureate: curriculum, diploma and the role of languages

Curriculum

To understand the treatment of languages in the curriculum of international schools, especially those such as the Vienna International School (VIS) which has played a large part in the development of international curricula, it is necessary to understand the context of the overall curriculum plan and underlying philosophy, which generally takes an idealist stance when compared with other systems.

The International Baccalaureate Diploma is the goal of students who graduate from the Vienna International School (VIS), (as in many international schools), but this examination, with its accompanying syllabus, is intended only for the last two years of schooling. A major challenge for international schools around the world has been how to enable mobile students to slot in to different educational systems every time their parents are moved. Schools may have British, American, or some other school system, and students come from any number of national education systems. Over the years, therefore, there have been efforts to develop a more stable curriculum that would eventually be shared by international schools worldwide, bearing in mind always that such schools are largely independent and can not be coerced into accepting such a curriculum.

One example of this trend has already been given above: the development of the International Schools Curriculum Project, Age 3-12, at the primary level, and the language and literature programme of this will be presented below. At the middle level, the efforts led to the formation of the ISAC (International Schools Association Curriculum), later renamed IBMYP (The International Baccalaureate Middle Years Programme), which initiated developments on the curriculum for the middle years of schooling, i.e. the 11-16 age range. The programme is working closely with the IBO. In 1988, the curriculum was advanced enough to be introduced in a group of pilot institutions, both state and independent, in Europe, North America, and Latin America. Many other schools, national and international, have let it be known that they intend to adopt the programme in the near future (Jonietz, 1991, 8).

The schematic representation of the plan (Figure 1) gives a clearer idea of the conception:

> "The child schematically represented at the centre recalls that his or her own personality is and should constantly remain the focus of the whole teaching/learning process.
> The distribution of the components of the curriculum around and inside a polygon illustrates the concept of global education.
> The two-way arrows underline the concept of interaction between the components of the curriculum." (Renaud, 1991, 10-11).

A comment on the language area is presented by Davis and Ellwood (1991, 62) in the following extract:

> "All schools can aim for such a programme; where the international schools have an immediate advantage over many (though not all) national schools is in the vital resource presented by the diversity of individual backgrounds, languages, cultural biographies, and cognitive styles of their students. There in the schools is the basis for an awareness of the problems of the real world and the need for communication in

one's own language and the languages of others. Modes of learning and thinking styles are complicated by the multicultural nature of international education. Any innovative curriculum model will have to consider the following aspects of language: the problem of students with no real mother tongue to help create identity, the methods of reinforcement of the mother tongue, the frequency of instruction, and the variety of foreign languages on offer; not to mention the complex issue of bilingual instruction of content areas. Learning how to learn rather than what to learn will also be a major concern."

This curriculum again shows the humanistic ideals fundamental to much international education.

The International Baccalaureate Diploma

The *International Baccalaureate* (IB) *Diploma* is the goal of students in many international schools. The diploma described below (based on Blackburn 1991, 16-19), is a group diploma examination in which each student must choose six subjects – normally three at Higher and three at Subsidiary level – with definite distribution requirements.

The curriculum consists of six subject groups:

Group 1 Language A (first language) including the study of selections from World Literature.

Group 2 Language B (second language) or a second language A.

Group 3 Study of Man in Society: History, Geography, Economics, Philosophy, Psychology, Social Anthropology, Organisation and Management Studies.

Group 4 Experimental Sciences: Biology, Chemistry, Applied Chemistry, Physics, Physical Science, Environmental Systems.

Group 5 Mathematics: Mathematics, Mathematical Studies, Mathematics with Further Mathematics.

Group 6 One of the following options:

(a) Art/Design, Music, Latin, Classical Greek, Computing Studies

(b) A school-based syllabus approved by IBO.

Alternatively, a candidate may offer instead of a Group 6 subject: a third modern language, a second subject from the Study of Man in Society, a second subject from Experimental Sciences.

At both Higher and Subsidiary level, each examined subject is *graded* on a scale of one (minimum) to seven (maximum). The award of the Diploma requires a minimum total of 24 points.

This pattern ensures that every IB student will continue to study a combination of the social sciences and languages, together with the natural sciences and mathematics. This is a proscribed pattern, unlike the British A and AS level arrangements or the American College Board examinations, but candidates may also offer single subjects for which they receive a certificate. In addition, the balance of higher and subsidiary level subjects meets the needs of the specialist university systems and the needs of a broad general education.

There are several other distinctive features in the IB pattern. Every diploma student must write an extended essay – a piece of personal research work of some 4,000 words; follow a course in the Theory of Knowledge; and spend the equivalent of one half-day a week on some form of creative activity or social service (CASS; see Figure 1). These are essential requirements for the diploma.

The role of languages

The present situation
IBO has three working languages – English, French, and Spanish – and all subjects are examined in these languages. The number of candidates registering for the exams in English has grown very rapidly since the late 1980's, whereas the number of candidates registering in Spanish shows marginal growth, and in French there is no growth at all (Blackburn 1991, 18). Spanish has never made a claim to be a world language (though it is in a strong position as a regional language in the Americas) and French, though it has made such a claim, is clearly not in a leading position. Given the low numbers of candidates registering in Spanish and French, perhaps English could be isolated as the sole IB working language, thus releasing more funds and energy for the general mother-tongue and foreign language programme, which is very extensive.

Languages play a central and fundamental role in any international examination system, and all students must take both Language A and Language B:

Language A – This is the language students choose as their best language and is usually their mother tongue or the language of the school. This is taken with a course in World Literature which accounts for 30 per cent of Language A marks. Many students are being educated outside their own country. It is essential that these students do not lose touch with their own language,

Figure 1. Schematic Study Plan / Représentation du plan d'études

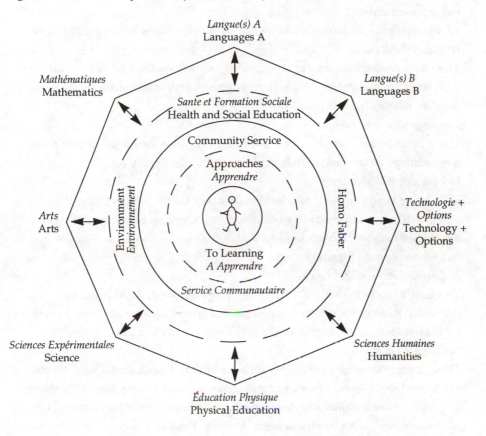

literature, and culture. This is the essential basis on which to add an international dimension. It is also necessary if they wish to return to higher education in their own country.

Language B – This is the language the students choose as their second examination language – usually for them, a foreign language. This is also obligatory.

A wide range of languages are offered and examined on a "regular" basis, and other languages may be offered on special request from schools.

The Vienna International School (VIS) gives students a rough guide to language courses, relating them to the IB, as follows:

LANGUAGES: A note on all International Baccalaureate Language Courses.
Courses offered in T3 and T4 cater for all abilities and ambitions in the languages,

and are available in English, German, French (Language B only) and Arabic, subject to enrolment.

At all levels great emphasis is laid on oral work and lessons are conducted in the language concerned.

The final examination includes an extended oral test (in the case of Language B with an external examiner) and written papers. A proportion of the marks come from the school's internal assessment.

Language A Courses

These courses are intended for native speakers of a language or for those approaching that standard of fluency. There is a strong literary bias.

IB Language A Higher Level

This course brings students to a level appropriate for the study of this language and literature at a university in a country of this language. Four important works are studied in depth, the works of six authors of various periods are studied and five works of world literature.

IB Language A Subsidiary Level

This course brings the student to a level appropriate for study of any subject at a university in a country of this language. The works of six authors of various periods and genres are studied and five works of world literature.

Language B Courses

These are for non-native speakers who have already been learning with success for around three years. (In exceptional cases it could be the student's native language). It needs ability and dedication to tackle these courses on shorter study of the language. The literary content is lower than in Language A, and the emphasis is on increasing fluency in speaking, reading and writing.

IB Language B Higher Level

This course brings the student to a level appropriate for study of this language at a university in a country where it is not the language spoken.

IB Language B Subsidiary Level

This course gives the student good general fluency in using the language.

Changes in spe at secondary and primary levels

There is an identifiable group of students in IB programmes in international schools whose linguistic needs are not thoroughly challenged by the Language A/Language B distinction. These are largely those who, in addition to a mother-tongue (in which they are proficient to an academic level), have a near-native level of competence in another language. It is frequently those who do not have English (usually the language of instruction) as their mother-tongue, but who have been at an international school long enough to have acquired a level of academic competence in the language.

The IBO therefore set up a project to investigate the issue and a feasibility study was published in 1989 proposing a new nomenclature of the *IB language exams*:

Language A1 (which would retain all the features of the previous Language A);

Language A2 (a programme and assessment designed for near-native speakers with a high level of competence in the target language, who are currently poorly-served by the Language A1/Language B suite of IB Languages);

Language B (which remains as previously).

The IBO has now set up a working party to develop the programme, and it is currently establishing definitions of the target group, aims of A2 and an outline syllabus and programme. The typical candidate will be bilingual (in the sense that their second-language competence will be at a level approaching that of native-speakers), and there may be extensive motivation for candidates to do Language A2 by awarding a Bilingual Diploma to those candidates offering at least Language A1 + Language A1 or Language A1 + Language A2.

Some of the aims of the new programme could include such areas as developing the students' ability to use the Language A2 as an effective tool for further study, encouraging students' recognition of the relationship between or among their languages, and promoting the use of language(s) for personal growth, development and relationship with the international community. The syllabus could include some of the literature blocks from the Language A1 syllabus and some topic blocks, including such matters as language, bilingualism, nationalism, biculturalism, etc.

A pilot programme will be starting soon, and the first examinations will take place in May 1996.

Once on stream, this examination will give the IB diploma a sophisticated language programme which will provide students with more choice, will challenge them further, and provide a comprehensive picture of their language capabilities.

At the *primary* level, the work of the International Schools Curriculum Project (described above in the section "What is International Education") includes comprehensive new plans for *all* language subjects. They see the problem as follows (from "The International Educator", Spring 1993):

> "Most of us who teach in international schools would probably admit that when we say 'international' we really mean 'Anglo-American.' The medium of instruction is English and the underpinning philosophy is generally Anglo-Saxon.

However, there is another, conflicting fact of life in our schools. For many, students who speak English as their first language are in the minority. Despite this fact, the tendency has been to design language programs, whether 'whole language' or the more traditional types, around philosophies, practices and resources based on language arts programs designed in Britain or North America for English mother-tongue students.

Another problem is the separation of language arts and ESL programs, each with its own learning outcomes and teachers, though these teachers may be working with the same students.

The instruction occurs as if there were two different students to whom two different languages are being taught.

If we are to develop an appropriate international education for our students then perhaps we should take a fresh look at their real needs. Given the profound links between language and culture and between language and thinking, then re-examining their linguistic needs seems to be a good place to begin."

The ISCP has, on the basis of their analysis of the problems, as outlined above, set itself the challenge of developing (between 1993 and 1995) a total language and literature programme which incorporates four inter-active strains:

"1. *Language Arts*: A core program of skills, concepts, content and attitudes within the various language modes, integrated as far as possible with other learning areas in the curriculum.

2. *ESL*: A program of language support for those students for whom English is not the first or preferred language, closely linked to the language arts program and showing the strategies to be employed by ESL teachers to support ESL students within that core program. Again, the ESL program should be linked, in terms of topics and vocabulary to the integrated core of the school's program.

3. *Host Country or other Modern Language*: Most international schools offer instruction either in the language of the host country or in another modern language. Again, efforts should be made to establish this program as one related strand in a total language curriculum with clear links to the other strands in terms of content and expectations.

4. *Support for the student's Mother-Tongue*: Recognition of the student's mother-tongue goes a long way toward recognizing the student's culture, a worthy aim in its own right. There is also an impressive body of

research to demonstrate the importance of a strong mother-tongue for the acquisition of another language so there is a more pragmatic reason for supporting the mother-tongue as our students work to acquire English. Support can include providing assistance by helping communities find a suitable teacher, providing classrooms after school, assisting with administration, developing a collection of library resources in a range of languages or simply providing advice to parents about keeping up the mother-tongue at home.
A four-strand inter-active language and literature program would begin to address the needs of our students in a more comprehensive manner. If it were supported by a policy of language-across-the-curriculum with every teacher seen as a language teacher, it would be even more powerful" (Bartlet 1993).

The plan reveals the concerned efforts to penetrate the "international" label, an admittance that international education is underpinned by a generally Anglo-Saxon philosophy, and an outline of the language programme, which involves accepting that English has become the international language and language of international communication, while making every effort to integrate with the host country through instruction in the environmental language, and support the students' mother-tongues wherever possible. There is also the more ambitious aim of seeing "every teacher as a language teacher".
After presenting some of this complex background, I shall be focusing on language issues in Vienna International School (VIS) (where I have been working for twelve years).

From general to specific: Vienna International School

General description
I shall present some general aspects of the VIS curriculum, including the role of languages in it. The mother tongue programme and the ESL programme will be discussed in some more detail. There will necessarily be some overlap and repetition. The role of teachers and other staff and parental involvement shall also be touched upon.
The ECIS Directory (ECIS 1992, 19) describes the school as follows:

"The Vienna International School was formally established in September 1978, having developed from the 'English School' of Vienna.

Its student body represents 78 countries. 65% of the students have parents working in UN, UNIDO, IAEA, UNWRA, IIASA, OPEC or who belong to the Diplomatic Community. Other parents represent the international business community and 13% the local Austrian community.

In September 1984, the school moved into its permanent new campus located near the UN office complex. The school facilities include large modern classrooms, a media centre, 6 science laboratories, 3 computer labs, 5 indoor gymnasia, a theatre, dining facilities, track and outside playing fields, outdoor theatre and a small ecology area.

In curriculum matters the school works in close consultation with the UNIS in New York and the International School of Geneva.

The language of instruction is English and there is an English-as-a-Second-Language programme providing intensive tuition with pupils gradually transferring to regular classes. All fluent English speakers are required to add German, and, once they have reasonable facility in this, to add French or their mother tongue.

In the Secondary School the curriculum in the first five years up to age 16 is based on consecutive courses. A general course for all in the first three years leads on to a common core of English, German, Maths and Physical Education with a choice of five option groups which include Science, a Humanities subject and a creative subject. Students either enter for the London Overseas GCE O level exams or are internally assessed. The final two classes total 180 and the school has developed diplomas at three levels: International (the International Baccalaureate), Academic (at least five subjects from the IB range) and General (a broad general education suitable for two-year colleges and similar intermediate courses). Equivalence to Austrian Matura is available.

The school is accredited by the Austrian Ministry of Education and is accredited with ECIS. In addition it is an overseas centre for the University of London O and A level examinations."

The language of instruction of the school is English only, i.e. there is no bilingual instruction. Throughout the school there is a strong ESL programme (English as a Second Language) which is compulsory for those whose language level in English demands it – it is timetabled largely against English and French. The host country language, German, is taught as a subject from Primary 2 upwards. Both English and German are compulsory.

Either French or Arabic can be chosen as Foreign Languages from Middle One upwards, and Spanish is offered as an optional additional Foreign Language.[1]

Mother-tongue support is strongly encouraged – the school provides facilities and administrative back-up, though parents have to cover costs (much of which can be reclaimed by some UN employees). It is largely an after-school activity, though from the Middle School upwards other mother-tongues can be taken in the French/Arabic/ESL slot.

For the International Baccalaureate students must take two languages (one Language A and one Language B), and may add a third (A or B).

The Primary Curriculum

The description of the *Primary Curriculum* is taken from the School *"Students' and Parents' Handbook"* (VIS 1993a), and that of the *Secondary Curriculum* from *VISTAS*, Middle House (VIS 1993b).

> "The working language for all pupils is English, both for those whose mother tongue is English and for others who will be taught English as a second language in order to bring them to a level of fluency which will enable them to take part in all other lessons of the curriculum.
>
> ESL and German (see below) are not entirely mutually exclusive, but it is not the school's policy for any child to attend German until the child's English is very strong. The school has the responsibility for the decision, but will of course consult parents over it. This policy is particularly important to bear in mind where a child's mother tongue is German.

2. Subjects in the Curriculum

As the language of instruction is English, all lessons with the exception of German are given in English and the textbooks are entirely in English. In much of the work of the Primary School there is significant integration, rather than division, of subjects. The work is class-teacher rather than subject-teacher based. The subjects include: English; Mathematics; Social Studies (including History and Geography); Science; Creative Activities (including Art/Craft); Music (including Music/Movement); Physical Education; German and/or English as a Second Language (ESL); Computer Studies.

A synopsis of the Primary School curriculum is contained within the VISTAS booklets which are available to all parents.

3. English as a Second Language

Children remain in their normal classrooms as much as possible. The ESL teachers take non-English speaking children out of their classrooms, for one or more periods a day. Such work starts in Primary 1, and at this stage it is all oral work. Reading and writing are gradually introduced from Primary 2 and developed in the higher classes.

4. German

Starting at Primary 2 level all children not involved in the ESL programme will be introduced to German. Through oral activities, the children become familiar with the sounds of the German language.

After Primary 2 level, the children start on one of two programmes:

a) German as a Foreign Language (GFL) for non-German speaking children – more formal teaching of German through audio-visual materials, emphasizing the oral expression, or:

b) German Mother Tongue (GMT) for all children who speak German fluently. The lessons are entirely in German, with more emphasis on reading and writing.

From Primary 4 onwards the GFL programme is a continuation of the previous instruction, introducing reading and writing in German. For the GMT groups the aim is to bring the children up to the level taught in the local Austrian Schools, Volksschule and, in Primary 6, the first year of Gymnasium or Hauptschule."

The Secondary Curriculum

"Because of the international character of the school the place of languages is a very important one, especially at the secondary stage. There are three distinct needs: the language of instruction (English), *foreign* languages, and the student's mother tongue.

The Language of Instruction

The language of instruction at VIS is English for all students, both for those whose mother tongue is English (about one quarter of the school) and for others who will be led through the extensive "English as a Second Language" programme to a level of fluency which will enable them to join in all classes.

Other Languages

All languages are taught throughout using the language concerned (e.g.

German is taught in German, without using English).

Students are taught in sets, according to their experience and proficiency. Beginners classes are arranged each September whenever the number of students joining at a particular level justifies this. Students joining in mid-year are accommodated wherever possible.

a) English as a Second Language

Level 1: ESL Beginners. (Middle House only). Students who have little or no English are placed in a special ESL class where they study English for up to 31 periods a week out of 40. When their level of English is considered sufficient, they move (normally after 3 to 6 months) to Level 2. If not, they repeat Level 1. They do not start any other language. There is one course for all Middle House students. They join in Physical Education, Music and creative subjects with the other students when possible.

Level 2/3: ESL Intermediate. Students who have acquired enough command of English progressively join regular classes in other academic subjects, often starting with Mathematics followed by Science. During German, Arabic or French class time they return to the ESL intermediate class for special help in English for nine or ten lessons per week.

Level 4: ESL Advanced. Students sufficiently advanced in their command of English now start German, wherever possible, as well as following all other lessons in English. They are not able to take another language until they are secure in German, but this should be possible at the end of one year.

EAP: English for Academic Purposes. This is a bridging course to the content area skills; students are given specific instruction in the reading skills needed for the more academic nature of the material in the Secondary School. Emphasis is placed on English for Science, Geography and History. (Fluent command of written English is needed for success in Tutorial classes).

Following a demanding academic school course in English, when this is not the mother tongue, can be very challenging, but many students are in this position, and as much help as possible is given at all stages in the school career. An extra year is often needed.

b) German as a Foreign Language

All students are expected to study German as soon as they are fluent in English. They are taught in ability sets ranging from beginners to native speakers.

To take German in the International Baccalaureate course in T3 and T4, even for subsidiary level, two or three years' previous knowledge is normally required, or extra lessons. This applies especially to students who have not learnt by using the language in class, e.g. English students whose German classes may have been largely in English. For such students it is wiser to aim at subsidiary level rather than higher level studies.

c) German as Mother Tongue
German speaking students will follow their German language instruction, during the 4 – 5 German lessons per week, along the lines of the Austrian curriculum for German language and literature. The Social Studies curriculum (History/Geography) will include some units on Austrian History and Geography. The same depth of knowledge of German as in an Austrian Secondary School cannot be expected in an English-language school.

d) Other Languages
Once good progress is being made in German it is possible to add another language and this is usually expected unless the student is following a regular course outside the normal school day in another mother tongue.

e) French as a Foreign Language/Arabic as a Mother Tongue
French is available throughout the Secondary School, normally in ability groups. In classes M1 to M2, this will be for 5 periods a week, in M3, T1 and T2 for 4 periods a week. Tutorial 1 offers the last chance to start French: an intensive course (6 periods a week) brings the pupil to third year level by the end of T2. In T3, pupils having completed 4 or 5 years of French are offered the 2 year IB preparatory course. French language B (Subsidiary and Higher level). Students having completed only 3 years of French at the end of T2 may choose to attend the "T3 VIS course" (e.g. in order to meet the Austrian requirements for Matura equivalence, which are of 4 years of French for 2 foreign languages.[2]

g) Latin
A Latin course open to Middle 2 and above leads to the International General Certificate of Secondary Education examination: this course takes place in the afternoon after normal lessons."

Mother-tongue programmes

The sub-heading "Languages in the Secondary School", informs in para. *f) Other Mother Tongues*, (i.e. other than English, German, French or Arabic), that

> "Mother tongue instruction in other languages will normally have to be provided through private teachers engaged by parents. The teacher must be approved by the Head of Modern Languages, Dr. W.K. Kirk, who will be glad to supply information."

Parents are encouraged at every opportunity to enrol their children in the mother-tongue programme. At the beginning of the year new parents are addressed by those responsible for mother-tongue teaching at VIS, and information is distributed regularly.
The following is an example of the information sent out:

"VIS MOTHER TONGUE CLASSES

The VIS is keen to encourage all students to take lessons in their mother tongue.
VIS students in the secondary school currently speak about 60 languages as mother tongues. Apart from the obvious benefits of retaining spoken fluency in the mother tongue (e.g. contact with family and relations when returning to their country), there are now shown to be quite clear advantages to retaining and improving *written* ability in the mother tongue, summarized below.
In the past it was considered, when learning English, that the more of this language that the student was exposed to, then the more he or she would learn. However, many studies have now been made which show quite clearly that the better the student's literacy skills are in their mother tongue, the better they will be in English.
Thus it is important for all students to keep up classes in their mother tongue, but *especially* those who are still weak in literacy skills, and those who are in all levels of ESL classes, including beginners.
There is no doubt that developing written skills in the mother tongue will:
a. Help towards the student's future success in the IB programme.
b. Benefit the student when returning to his or her country (university, job).

c. Benefit those with weak literacy skills in English.

d. Give a solid base and support to those who are just beginning English.

Organization

Most mother tongue languages are taught after school. The school aims to put interested parents and mother tongue teachers in touch so that classes can be arranged. The school will provide classrooms; all financial matters are arranged privately between parents and teachers.

Our aim is to build up the teaching of mother tongue languages at VIS. We wish to establish clear curricula, collect a variety of materials (including video programmes, interesting texts), and motivate the students more."

German is taught to all students within the curriculum, and students are placed in sets according to ability, ranging from beginners to mother-tongue.

English is taught to all students within the curriculum, and students with very little English, or those at an intermediate level are taught a specifically ESL curriculum and also an adapted English curriculum.

Arabic is taught for any students who wish to take it; some Arabic parents prefer their children to do French instead of Arabic, and some students who are in ESL classes do Arabic after school (see again note 2).

Other mother-tongues can be taught during the French/Arabic slot if desired (but at the parents' expense), but the majority are taught after school or on Saturday mornings. Additional information on mother tongues is given to secondary school students and their parents (VIS 1993b)."

The main reasons for a pupil to "study courses in a mother-tongue language that cannot be offered as part of the regular school curriculum" are also detailed:

"1. It is a fact that instruction in a student's mother-tongue will *help* him or her become more proficient in English.

2. Many students who have been at VIS for some time can talk quite well in their mother tongue (if not English), but know nothing of their own culture, history, or literature, and have poor writing skills.

3. To begin mother-tongue classes just before the IB exam is often too late; it is continuity that counts – beginning in the Primary School. Students need to prepare for offering the language as one of the

subjects for the International Baccalaureate Diploma or Certificate at the end of the T3/4 courses.

4. Many students who have just arrived at VIS think they don't need classes in their mother-tongue as "they have only just left their country and are good at writing their own language". Maybe this is true, but they will quickly lose these skills if they do not practise them, and they should also keep in touch with their own culture, history, and literature.

5. They may need to meet entry requirements for universities in their home country.

   The Head of the ESL and mother-tongue languages department should be consulted before a private class is established, if school credit is to be sought for the work done. For this, the teacher and an outline syllabus must be approved, and an undertaking given by the teacher that school grades and reports will be provided at the usual times."

The approximate breakdown of the 58 languages and the number of students speaking them in the VIS Secondary School in September 1993 is given below. The mother tongues represented were, in ascending order (with the number of students for each language): Adagbe 1, Amharic 1, Armenian 1, Burmese 1, Czech 1, Georgian 1, Mongolian 1, Norwegian 1, Serbian 1, Somali 1, Tiv 1, Tswana 1, Ukrainian 1, Albanian 2, Bemba 2, Cantonese 2, Hausa 2, Hindi 2, Punjabi 2, Sesotho 2, Tonga 2, Turkish 2, Fante 3, Hebrew 3, Igbo 3, Malay 3, Malayalam 3, Sinhalese 3, Sundanese 3, Tamil 3, Mandarin 4, Finnish 4, Slovenian 4, Bulgarian 5, Croatian 5, Swahili 5, Thai 5, Danish 6, Serbo-croat 7, Swedish 7, French 8, Greek 8, Italian 8, Japanese 8, Bengali 9, Korean 9, Urdu 9, Hungarian 10, Pilipino 13, Yoruba 13, Portuguese 14, Polish 18, Russian 18, Dutch 22, Spanish 38, Arabic 65, English 144, German 167.

The mother-tongue timetable for 1992/93 shows that most "other mother tongues" are taught after school or on Saturdays, with the exception of Japanese which also has some other slots, including lunch breaks. Most languages are taught in the school, in classrooms or in the library, but some are taught in homes (Hungarian, Swedish, Thai), in churches (Italian, Armenian) or in special language schools (Polish, Korean, Swedish, Japanese). The time-table includes the following 15 (of the school's 58) mother tongues: Armenian, Bengali, Danish, Dutch, Hungarian, Italian, Japanese, Korean, Norwegian, Polish, Portuguese, Russian, Spanish, Swedish and Thai.

Language diversity is an important factor in a multi-faceted world, and increasing concern about the environment and preserving the richness of variety in all forms of nature should be extended to languages and cultures (it has been predicted that 100 years from now the 5,000 to 6,000 languages currently estimated to exist will have shrunk to some 600). Many students are shy about discussing their own language and culture, but an introduction of a mother tongue programme and related activities can do much to open up this area.

English as a Second Language Programmes

Given the preponderance of English as the language of instruction in International Schools (in 93% of schools offering the International Baccalaureate in 1989), and the large number of students who have either no English or a limited knowledge of the language, there is much demand for "the perfect ESL programme" to instantly solve the problem. Discussion of programme types centres largely around immersion[3], withdrawal, and content-area, sheltered teaching. There has been much research over recent years, mainly focusing on national systems, which often have different social objectives from international schools (i.e. the focus is frequently on the type of English which students will need to survive in the job market after leaving school, or on the language in the outside community – which of course is usually not English in international schools).

The focus for international school students must be first developing "survival" language, and then building up skills in written language in order to be able to perform successfully in the school curriculum. There are those who argue that this should be done strictly on a subject by subject basis, with the student learning the particular types of language needed in that subject (e.g. Widdowson 1968). Others, equally passionately, argue that English writing skills are learnt through the study of English language literature, and this milieu will give every student the tools they need for successful performance in all areas (Dr. E. Mace-Tessler, Head of English, International School of Düsseldorf, Germany – personal communication).

Given the lack of bilingual programmes in most international schools, the ESL conundrum is at the heart of the language issue and will undoubtedly continue to be hotly debated over the years.[4] Any school containing students from many language backgrounds, where there is *one* language of instruction (Language A), will have students with varying degrees of competence in that language:

- group 1, native speakers of language A;
- group 2, students who are not native speakers but who have a "native-like" competence in the language, and
- group 3, students who are at varying stages of development in learning the language.

The *first* group will have no intrinsic problems with the course. The *second* group are in a similar position and though they may not be naturally acquainted with the target language (A), they are in many ways advantaged as they have another language (their own mother tongue) and culture and are thus bilingual, with all the benefits this skill provides. The *third* group have a large task in front of them, and it is important that the immensity of this task be understood by all: teachers, administrators and parents. For some students, the switch to a new language, not only for day-to-day social discourse but for use in a sophisticated and complex written mode, comes quite easily; for many, however, the difference between their own language *and* culture and the target language, the pressures from home and shcool, and the amount of (or lack of) literacy in their own language are all key factors to be considered in developing a varied programme to suit their needs.

The students in group 1 will be in a strong position for Language A, but may have no knowledge of another language; thus from the point of view of number of languages known, they are the "poorest" students in the programme. Most international schools encourage the student body to take the host country language as Language B; or, if the language A is the same as the host country language, one of the generally accepted European languages. Students in group 2 already have two working language: the target language and their own mother tongue. For many of them, the language B at their school may be their own language – usually when it is the host country language and there are large numbers of host country students at the school; in this case they will be doubly advantaged, and well on the road to a high level of biliterate bilingualism. Those who are not in this situation, but who have a mother tongue which corresponds neither to the Language A or Language B of the school will be learning a third language when taking the Language B. This raises the important issue of which Language B a school should offer, and also the issue of supporting students' mother tongues, both discussed in other sections of this chapter.

Students in group 3 are those with the largest task in front of them; they have to tackle the whole school curriculum in a language which they either do not speak at all or which they have varying knowledge in. Schools need to instil an awareness of the need for patience and support in mainstream teachers. Many national systems are now used to the multicultural classroom, but teachers living in national systems are often surrounded by prejudice and bias which may not be relevant to the open-mindedness and tolerance needed for an international student body.

Long experience at the Vienna International School has shown that there is no single category of students in this last group (we are talking about ESL students in schools where English is the Language A). We do know that a student who comes to a school with no knowledge of the school language may take from 5-7 years to achieve the same level of competence and performance as his or her own fluent Language A peers; we know that achievement may depend very much on ability in the mother tongue; and we know that once competence in both languages is achieved, the student may well have cognitive benefits that monolingual students do not have. Experience also shows that some students at the Vienna International School can be well integrated in the regular school programme after three years (often arriving with no knowledge of the Language A) whatever the similarities or differences between this language and their mother tongue; some students require longer, but are good performers at a later age; and some students experience great difficulty and seem to have a history of never really getting on top of the language. For the first two categories mentioned, a specially-designed programme of language support is essential, providing students with all the language tools they need to be able to "catch up" with their peers; for the third category it is important to identify each individual and provide whatever back-up is deemed necessary – this may mean involving specially trained teachers. However, again experience shows that in the long-term such students are able to reach reasonable levels of achievement; identifying their needs is an important factor, and informing teachers of the specific characteristics of each individual; tolerance and patience over a number of years provide surprising benefits.

The Language B, foreign language chosen by the school, will often be the host country language, especially when this is a well-known language or one considered to be "useful" in the world. If this is the case, it is convenient as it encourages students (and possibly even staff!) to become more involved with the local community.

However, the Language B programme can also arrive at a similar situation to that of the Language A – there may be native speakers of the language, those who have been at the school a long time and who have a near-native knowledge, and genuine foreign learners (recent arrivals). In this case the second and third groups may contain students who have long-term language learning problems and who need careful monitoring and support.

Teachers and Staff

The following information applies to a whole range of International Schools, not only Vienna International School. Clearly, though, in such a diverse network as the international school no one statement can be made about teachers and staff which covers all situations. There are three factors, however, which determine that the majority are of the "Anglo-American" variety.

First, the fact that many, if not most, international schools developed from the Anglo-American heritage of education.

Second, the fact that English is the language of instruction in the majority of international schools.

Third, the fact that in many countries teachers are "civil servants" and are therefore not free to work in a different country.

> "International education is almost compelled to be independent education. Few teachers in international schools, particularly if they are making a lifelong career in international education, are from countries in which teachers are civil servants. The only regular exceptions are teachers in national schools abroad (the French Overseas Lycées, the German Auslandsschulen), whose international aspects are secondary to the national emphasis, and the schools of the European Community. The difficulties are the lack of freedom to move and respond to openings as they occur, the national career and pension structures, and the general bureaucracy. Most teachers on the international circuit are therefore either British or American. In a small but growing way, this trend is being strengthened by the wish of the IB schools in, for example, Holland and the Scandinavian countries, to recruit British teachers to teach their IB courses in the mother tongue English; and by schools too in Central and Eastern Europe which, among other things, are wishing hurriedly to make up for years of neglect of the English language. Nor do the United World Colleges find it easy to act otherwise as an examination of their teaching staffs, and above all the distribution of the responsibilities within their staff rooms, will show. The residential nature of the Colleges also requires residential school experience, again something more readily available from teachers from Britain and North America." (Sutcliffe, 1991, 36).

There are various regional organizations throughout the world which give back-up services. In Europe the main one is the ECIS (see above) which organizes a yearly conference in the autumn attended by well over 2,000 people. There are workshops, seminars, lectures, and meetings for school heads. Languages have their own sub-committees which have an open business meeting at this time, and many of them organize their own conferences later in the year. Individual schools allocate in-service budgets separately, so the amount available to attend courses or re-training sessions will depend on each school's financial situation. Some schools have departmental systems, others do not.

Parental involvement

The internal working language of international schools is usually English. Communications are therefore sent out in this language, special care being taken to present information clearly. Again, every school has its different approach, depending on whether it is more British, more American, or more "international", but schools usually have parents associations which centre around fund-raising and communication with the school authorities. There are frequent meetings and discussion of any matters that parents care to raise.

Each school will have its own policy on transportation or provision of meals – though these are usually areas that are included within the competence of the school.

Parent delegates attend certain school meetings, and there are regular information meetings on all matters pertaining to children's progress in school. This is a strong feature of international schools; teachers make themselves readily available to parents and are always willing to discuss any matters to do with students' academic or social performance in school.

In addition there are regular parent-teacher consultations throughout the year for parents to discuss progress with all their child's teachers.

Involving parents has proved to be easier at the Primary level when children are involved in activities (acting, singing) when parents come in large numbers.

Comparing with the European Schools: joint challenges

The linguistic heterogeneity: mother tongue, second language, foreign language, and anything in between

This is perhaps the right place to pause and take stock of the situation. It should by now be clear that there is no such thing as "the typical international school". On the other hand, there is quite clearly a move to support the children and parents who are internationally mobile by creating a universal curriculum, not prescribed precisely, but within a general framework, leading to a diploma which will be accepted by universities throughout the world.

This curriculum has at its centre a belief in "international humanism", and there is a desire to create a programme to meet the needs of schools "who are eager to promote the sense of responsibility gained through fostering intercultural understanding among their students, calling for strong cooperation between teachers and administrators, ... generating faith and enthusiasm".

> "International schools in particular enjoy a privileged position because of the presence of many cultures: they are pre-eminently the fields where the seeds of international understanding can germinate. 'International humanism' is an attitude at the root of which lies understanding and respect for other people's cultural backgrounds. This kind of attitude will be the only way that will lead to the progressive disappearance of prejudices and mistaken ideas about 'foreigners', prejudices which underlie intolerance and isolation." (Renaud, 1991, 14).

Developing a universal language programme for such a diverse network is therefore extremely challenging. The IB set out originally to respond to this challenge by stipulating that all students would have to take a Language A (the dominant language, or mother tongue) course and a Language B (a foreign language) course. As the IB realized,

> "The most complicated problem arises from the different linguistic background of the students. By choice or by necessity, many of them use a language of instruction which is not their mother tongue; at the same time their mother tongue may be taught to them as a foreign language or they may use it only at home or in private lessons. Consequently, instead of talking of 'mother-tongue' on the one hand and 'foreign languages' on the other, it seems more desirable to call the first means of expression (of which a pupil should have complete command at the end of his secondary school studies) Language A, and the second (of which he should have an adequate knowledge) Language B." (International Baccalaureate 1967; quoted in Tosi, 1991, 90).

Experience at the VIS has shown that characteristically many students develop better academic skills in the school language of instruction (English) than in their mother-tongue (where this is not English). They are thus in a position where they may take Language A in English and Language B (ostensibly a foreign language) in their mother-tongue. Even if they take Language A in their mother-tongue, they would then have a large advantage, doing English as Language B, over genuine learners of English as a "foreign" language.

The categorisation of languages as mother tongues and foreign languages is thus not enough. The languages are seen as falling into three, rather than two categories. This is a situation that International Schools share with the European Schools.

In his detailed analysis and comparison of the European Schools and the International Baccalaureate (in the World Yearbook of Education, 1991), Arturo Tosi summarizes the situation as follows (1991, 94):

> "In the IB schools as in European Schools, there are three different language learning processes at work with their multilingual population:
> 1. Mother tongue learning for the native as well as the non-native speakers of the school language;
> 2. Foreign language learning for the native speakers of the school language;
> 3. Second language learning for the non-native speakers of the school language.
>
> Unlike the European Schools, IB examination structure requires from every diploma candidate two instead of three languages, and these are examined respectively by one set of tests of mother tongue (Language A) and one set of tests of foreign language (Language B). The option of two Language A tests is also available, but this is taken up by virtually no students because it demands the study of an impossible literary load, and expects from each bilingual candidate standards of language competence comparable to those of two monolingual students.
>
> The lack of a special examination for bilingual students who have developed the academic use of two languages has consequences for the validity of the examination system as a whole. In one option, when those who are not native speakers of the school language choose to enter the examination of the language of instruction with its native speakers (Language A), they end up being examined in their mother tongue together with genuine foreign language learners. Naturally in a system operating with norm-referenced language tests, the top marks are awarded to native competence. In the other possible option, when those who are not native speakers of the school language choose that their native competence should be examined by a mother tongue programme (Language A), their second language achievement is examined by the

foreign language tests (Language B). In this case, the performance of students who have learnt another language within the most favourable curricular opportunity – that of using it as a medium of education – is allowed to set unrealistic standards against which is measured the achievement of those candidates who have studied it only as a foreign language, within the limited time-frame of a curriculum subject.

Either option introduces inconsistencies of standards, and the situation is further complicated as the majority of IB students who are not native speakers of the school language is almost evenly divided between the two options. Their decision to take one combination or another depends on a number of personal and contextual factors. For example, some schools have a policy whereby all students are free to choose the language they wish in the Language A and in the Language B programme. Others do not allow native speakers to enter a Language B programme. Some practically oblige native speakers to do so, since they offer only the Language A programme in the school medium of instruction. Moreover, there are language programmes which can be 'untaught', others which must be taught, and this is further complicated by the fact that all diploma candidates need a certain number of High and Subsidiary options: in the IB credit system a Language B High rates higher than a Language A Subsidiary, which is more challenging but less rewarding. This explains why the programmes of Language A and Language B, which have such different definitions in practice, include the same wide range of performances: from the ablest native speakers to those who struggle with a second foreign language having no exposure to that language outside the school (Tosi, 1989)."

This highlights the complexities of the system and also two crucial factors, i.e. the issue of what policy schools should take on allocating students to a particular course, which would involve the school in making a value judgement on each student's knowledge and competence in each language, and also the "lack of a special examination for bilingual students who have developed the academic use of two languages".

The first issue is one which may be partially resolved by the resolution of the second one, which has, fortunately, been taken on board by the IBO in the form of the new Language A2-exam and syllabus discussed above.

Élitism

Another issue raised in the context of international education is illustrated by Tosi (1991, 95, 97):

"A recent study summarizes the differences between the European Schools and the vast majority of what the writers describe as the 'so-called international schools' in this way:

(These) quite often are only international in pupil composition, occasionally provide bilingual education, but usually function as monolingual establishments. Moreover most international schools are fee-paying and élitist, and most are independent and not controlled by government organizations (Baetens Beardsmore and Kohls 1988)." (Tosi, 1991, 95).

However, he adds a little later:

"Though European Schools are not private, because of its high costtheir curriculum is offered only to communities of technologists and administrators working for the European Community institutions, and is not made available to communities of ordinary European families working outside their own countries. It is true that unlike in private international schools, education is free. This does not mean, however, that it is less exclusive: it simply means that children from non-civil servant families are admitted to schools in order to avoid social ghettos. Indeed the high cost of these schools has not prevented this privileged European education from being made accessible to a few powerful families; but so far, the high cost has been an obstacle in the spread of the same model to other areas of Europe where urban concentrations of non-nationals are made up of less fortunate and less powerful families.

The second strategy is adopted by the International Baccalaureate schools, most of which are private and need to be concerned primarily with resources and cost-effectiveness. Accordingly, they do not adopt expensive measures of bilingual education with two or more media of instruction, but they attribute to one international language, overwhelmingly English, the exclusive role of vehicular language and culture-carrying medium. Within the limited time-frame of another curriculum subject, some IB schools teach a foreign language to the native speakers of English and to its non-native speakers teach their mother tongue. The risk of falling into monolingualism or imbalanced bilingualism with cultural assimilation and cognitive operation predominantly in the English language is greater in IB than in European Schools, and this is proven by the functioning of the system if not by its pronouncements. Certainly, native speakers of English have no facilities to develop bilingualism with an academic use of another language in any English medium school. On the other hand, all those who are non-native speakers of English can study English as their native or adopted language and their mother tongue as a foreign language. If they feel inclined to maintain and develop the academic use of their mother tongue, they cannot find the appropriate facilities within the IB schools. Thus the IB curriculum works well as an immersion programme for those who have firm grounding in any language other than English, and wish to add the academic mastery of this language to their competence in the national language. But for those who have many years of education outside their own country, the IB curriculum speeds up the alienation from one's own cultural and linguistic origin, unless the family takes the appropriate precautions privately outside the school." (Tosi, 1991, 97).

The issues under discussion, then, are those of élitism or exclusivity, bilingualism (meaning equal academic mastery of two languages), and the lack of facilities for native speakers of English to develop bilingualism with an academic use of another language in any English medium school.

The first is not an issue that falls within the competence of an applied linguist; rather it is simply a fact of life that in the second half of the twentieth century there are many international bodies and individuals who are mobile and who need education for their children; a system has grown up to cater for their needs, largely in the English language, and most parents are more than willing to pay fees. As Tosi points out, the European Schools are not necessarily less exclusive; their bilingual structure makes them more expensive but they are also "exclusive" because their curriculum is offered only to those working for the EU institutions, well-funded by EU governments. He then points out that most IB schools are private and need to be concerned *primarily* with cost-effectiveness, so do not adopt expensive measures of bilingual education. This is no small matter; balancing the books is perhaps the major concern of many of the smaller international schools, and many of the larger ones; it is more important for them to be able to offer an international curriculum in the English language and stay open than take on an expensive bilingual programme that could well imply closure. (Though note J.J. Blaney's (1991, 203) comment: Strong financial aid programmes should be available to prevent the schools from being economically élitist.) The EU schools work in a limited area – there is nobody I know of that would subsidise international schools worldwide (and I wonder how EU schools will cope with the expansion of the community involving the addition of languages such as Swedish, Finnish, and maybe later Polish, Czech and Hungarian).

Bilingualism for all in International Schools?

There is no doubt that the whole area of language, languages, and bilingualism is one that many international educators take strong positions on. I am equally certain that there will be no agreement on what the "perfect" solution should be. Some quotes will add some background to the matter:

> "Of course, there were many other differences, I think, from national systems. One was our emphasis on all students doing at least one foreign language, with the emphasis on world literature as an important component of what we describe as Language 'A' – Language 'A' being broadly speaking the mother tongue of the student. The assumption being that if a student had been educated overseas for a number of years, very often in an English medium school – for example, a Swedish student in an English speaking school in Tanzania in East Africa – that student could often reach the stage where his or her English was often better than the mother tongue. Of course, this was a disadvantage if the student wished to return to higher education in Sweden. So both for cultural and practical reasons, we insisted and still do that the first requirement of the IB was a knowledge of their own mother tongue, language and literature. On the assumption, and this is an important matter, I think, in the philosophy of the IB about the nature of internationalism and international education. We would maintain, I think, that internationalism and international education does not mean a denial of one's own culture, one's own background, and one's own language. Indeed, that is a kind of substructure which must be found with internationalism as the top storey. Also there is a very practical reason with students going back to European universities, Scandinavia, France, Germany and so on, they really did need a knowledge of their own tongue and a particular qualification in it. There are some real differences from national programmes." (Blackburn 1991, 217-218).

Finally an extract from Dr. W.G. Mattern, former Executive Secretary of the ECIS and now ECIS Executive Secretary Emeritus.

"Consider bilingualism, for example, not a firm fixture in the credo of many schemes for international education. The underlying rationale seems to be the truism that a knowledge of the language of another culture provides the key to understanding and appreciating that culture. Perhaps so, but it is not a fact of much practical significance for those plotting school curricula. If bilingual education – and bicultural exposure – could start at the moment of participation, then there might be some relevance. But when the study of another language (even if integrated across the curriculum) is started at the early adolescent stage of formal education, as is usually the case, true bilingualism is hardly ever the result and biculturalism will surely be lagging far, far behind. Yet, it is the latter that is said to be the real point of the exercise. The acquisition of language skills in themselves, of no matter how high an order, may be impressive, good for business, excellent mental discipline, and a pleasant social emollient, but it is not per se the same thing as the acquisition of another culture.

We must not delude ourselves here. Those Asiatic businessmen, for example, whose skills in English so impress us do extraordinarily well in the passage of commerce – and it could be argued that commercial clout is an effective prelude to cultural influence. But bicultural they are surely not, nor would claim to be. Indeed, how many people with skills in a language other than their native tongue such as to be regarded as 'totally fluent', can say with hand on heart that they have thereby achieved true access to another culture? More so than they would have had without language fluency, yes; some measure of appreciation and understanding that they would probably not have acquired – or, more accurately, would not have been in a position to acquire – without language skills. But will anyone ever be able to stand wholly comfortably in the shoes of someone of a culture different from one's own? To claim so must surely be to misunderstand what culture really is!

Perhaps more to the point at issue, however, is the question of just what is so international about a bilingual or for that matter a bicultural person? If one is Anglo-French, that does not help much with understanding how Poles feel, or what life is like in Burma, or what is on the mind of the man in the street in Swaziland. Might there not in fact be a kind of anti-internationalist parochialism (not to mention a certain whiff of smug insular arrogance) in laying claim to an international perspective because one has mastered two Western European languages? Not one European plus Arabic or Urdu or Mandarin Chinese – any of the great regional languages and cultural repositories – but just, say Spanish and Portuguese? That would certainly make one bilingual – and would, by the way, satisfy the letter of the language requirement for the IB diploma and Cambridge's International Certificate of Education. But it must be obvious that it would scarcely satisfy the spirit of either. If we must – for practical reasons, let us say – talk about a student's acquiring a command (a more ambiguous, but probably for that reason a more apt word than 'fluency') of two languages only, then surely it must be the case that for the curriculum planner in the international school the choice of which two ought not to be resolved exclusively, as happens presently in many institutions, on such considerations as geographical proximity, literary values, ease of acquisition, or just good old current chic. Moreover, let us not lose sight of the fact that no matter what two languages we are talking about, a person would obviously be better off, better qualified as an internationalist, being trilingual or quadrilingual or as multilingual as a Danube riverboat captain: short of omnilingualism, we are still, it may be said, dealing with degrees of parochialism.

If bilingualism is not itself, then, the definitive hallmark of an international education, there are still some further things that need to be said about language in the international curriculum. If we accept a humbler role for foreign language – a key to the front door of another culture, or even just the servant's entrance, but surely not free passage to the entire structure; if our expectations are both less and fewer, then surely competence in another language is something to be desired, a beginning not an end. But the choice of which additional language remains important.

For those who are English-speakers, the alternative, the second language, must surely be one of the great regional tongues – or arguably the language of a student's future home, place of business, or spouse, though to choose any of such at ten is a fairly daunting responsibility. For those who are not English-speakers, however, the choice by this last decade of the century can only be English. I know any anglophone must be suspect in making that statement, and I shall not defend it here except to say that all considerations of demography and economics, politics and statistics, even linguistics and aesthetics, must lead the unbiased to that conclusion. Omnilingualism for all people is an impossibility; one language in common for all people (though never all people speaking but one language) might well be a goal to pin to the heart of every true internationalist." (Mattern 1991, 210-212).

These quotes, in addition to those at the beginning of this chapter, illustrate well the idealism of many international educators, and also what might be called a "supra-linguistic" (i.e. 'above' the whole area of language difficulty or national issues of 'bilingualism or not') approach to the matter.

"International Schools" are as much an ideal as a reality for many of those who work in them. There are also as many different models as there are schools, and it is thus not possible to isolate particular language programmes and generalize from them. To cover the area thoroughly would need several volumes; in this chapter I have aimed to give an overview of the field, and introduce not only the language issue but the broader educational philosophy of these schools which is often based on "international humanism".

Not many international schools would suffer from the rigours of the French national system in European schools implied by Baetens Beardsmore (1991, 46): "It is implied that the system in operation is overtly academic in philosophy, based on the French national system, and not sufficiently child-centred". The "Ideals of the Vienna International School" which are printed on the first page of every curriculum summary sent to parents and students, begins: *"Recognize all that is positive in the student and use your heart and wisdom to develop these attributes."*

The European Schools are set up by an institution (the European Union), in a limited number of languages and are for a particular group of people; they are entirely funded by the EU. (Baetens-Beardsmore mentions that "a factor that has not been gone into in this overview is the cost of running European Schools. This is evidently higher than monolingual education").[5]

International Schools are mostly private, usually have students from an unlimited number of language backgrounds, and are open for anyone who cares to send their children there; they are usually funded entirely by the fees paid by parents, and donations. It is no mean achievement, therefore, that they have managed to unite and achieve cohesive programmes to the degree so far reached.

In May 1990 the European Commission, the Council of Europe, the IBO and the European Schools jointly sponsored a conference attended by experts in bilingual and international education. One of the resolutions agreed proposes that:

"There should be closer cooperation between the various schools and institutions involved and in particular between IBO, the European schools, and ECIS. It was felt that there was a need to establish meeting of this group on a more formal basis." (Blackburn 1991, 22).

It seems obvious that, given the amount of organizational back-up available from the ECIS and the strong international curriculum, recognized in universities throughout the world, of the IB, the international schools will want to add to their sense of purpose and a shared goal by taking advantage of these organizations and benefiting from them as much as possible.

On the language issue, much will depend on the different composition of each school. The Vienna International School has a minority of mother-tongue English speakers, and this benefits the teaching model as a whole as it tends to avoid the situation where students who have weaker English language skills may have feelings of inadequacy and insecurity, thereby impeding the spontaneous arisal of input. There is no atmosphere of students who are in ESL classes feeling they are in a ghetto. Frequent discussions with such students reveal that on the whole friendship circles are quickly formed with groups of speakers from many different language backgrounds. Students of particular language backgrounds may speak their own language together in groups, but may equally well form cross-linguistic groups and converse in English. The constant mixing up of children for group activities is a key factor here.

The group chiefly disadvantaged are the speakers of English, who are potentially the only monolingual group in the school. However, the host-country, or environmental language, can play a useful role here, though much will depend on its importance as a language of "usefulness" in the world. Students living in Vienna usually reach high levels of competence in German; however, I can imagine that a less "useful" host-country language could prove less enticing; much will depend on the school's attitude to the language. The final destinations of leavers in the VIS in 1993 show that some 30% chose to go to universities in Vienna, involving study in the German language – this surely is a tribute to the German language programme and policy at the school.

As regards subjects taught in the first language and second language in order to reinforce grammatical accuracy and lexical precision, clearly International Schools are not able to do this in the first language, where up to 60 languages might be involved. The focus must be on ESL programmes, and this is the area where general teacher awareness of language issues is important. There is regular reinforcement of the view that adequate levels of conversational ability in English are obtained after about two years but that adequate levels of formal or academic language can take from five to seven years. Parents are also informed of this, and, following Krashen's advice to "read, read, read", are told of the benefits of much reading in the mother-tongue and also at the appropriate level in English (the library has a large selection of graded readers).

One factor that Baetens Beardsmore does not mention is that of students arriving or leaving in the middle of the programme. This is a regular feature of international schools as parents may be moved from one country to another, from a national to an international school system or vice-versa, at any time. This demands considerable flexibility on the part of the school; teachers can not say "there is no place for this student, we have now reached stage 'X' in the language programme". With only one language of instruction (English) the problem is not insurmountable but I wonder how it is dealt with in European schools.

There is no doubt that the fine-tuning being undertaken by the IB (with the introduction of the Language A2 programme), the development of the IB Middle Years Programme, and the ISCP (International Schools Curriculum Project) for a programme at the Primary level will bring a very sophisticated curriculum to all those seeking, or needing, international education. The programme is child-centred and flexible enough for each school to adapt to its particular needs. It does not demand continual testing at regular intervals, unlike public education in the United States, plagued by standardized tests, but focuses on teaching and learning, the main examination coming only at the end of the school cycle with the IB.

As more international schools around the world adopt the entire programme parents will feel more confident about moving to a new location; (significantly, many international organizations will not send personnel to a country unless they are confident about the educational programme available).

There must be a justification for bilingualism; it is not enough for linguists to be so smug about their own achievements that they believe others should therefore be encouraged to be the same. Of course being proficient in another language is an achievement in itself, but as an intellectual goal no more worthy than being proficient in Geography or Physics. To encourage the learning of a language as the gateway to understanding another culture does not really bring the desired rewards without living in the country where the language is spoken, and even then a long stay in the country, preferably working and being closely involved with the people there, is the only way to truly penetrate the culture. Bilingualism is, of course, a personal asset, along with many other aspects of personal development, and it should perhaps be modestly valued as just this.

International education aims to do more than simply equip students with languages, but to see what they have to say. As James Keson puts it:

> The students at international schools, because of limited contact with a large and pervasive youth culture, spend more time with their families. They are forced, often because they learn the local language before their parents, to interact with adults more than they probably did back home. People often feel that they seem more mature or sophisticated. Another difference, which is noticed by parents who are abroad even for a short period of time, is that their children's horizons expand noticeably. Not only do they begin to understand complex subjects which might have been difficult if they had not actually seen the Acropolis or a tropical rain forest, their own aspirations undergo a subtle change. 'If the person sitting next to me can study in Athens (or Anchorage or Aberdeen) then why can't I?' Or 'Since the medical profession doesn't seem to have such a bright future in my country at the moment, why not practise it in this country, or on the other side of the world?'

The effects of international schools

International schools, once a temporary solution to a fairly esoteric educational problem, now have a distinct philosophy and character, so much so that often local national families wish that their children could attend the local international school. Part of this is the prestige which seems to be inevitably associated with anything labelled "international", as well as the results that are possible from dedicated teachers and small classes. But more significant is the ability, partly trained and partly circumstantial, of international children to distinguish between what is superficial and what is essential. Having seen that students from any part of the world have similar pleasures and likes and fears, they come to appreciate the difference, for instance, between the people of a country and its government, between the way a person looks and the way he or she is, and between a person's ability to speak a language and what he or she has to say. Skills like these are of critical value in tomorrow's world, and they quite often come as a natural result of the experience of studying in an international school." (Keson 1991, 59).

Language is the very breath of our existence. The whole area of language and languages in International Schools is complex to a degree that leads many to find it annoying and therefore either to be "rationalised" or "ignored". It needs to be approached with patience and understanding; patience for those students who need more time to develop the many skills involved, and understanding for the staff who work in this area.

Many national systems are now becoming interested in the programme of International Baccalaureate; let us hope that this all-encompassing curriculum can help educators and students aim towards a community of mutual understanding, and steer us away from the ethnic divisions that are currently rippling around the world.

Notes:

1   Only English and German are compulsory. ESL is a priority in the sense that a pupil who takes ESL (which is compulsory if the teachers evaluate that the students need it), cannot take other languages, i.e. Arabic or French or Spanish, while attending ESL classes. In principle, mother tongue Arabic and Arabic as a foreign language should be taught separately, but in practice the classes are often so small that all pupils taking Arabic may be taught together.

2   M1-3 are the Middle School years, approximately ages 11-13, followed by T(utorial) 1-2 (ages 14-16) and T3-4.

3   Editor's note: "Immersion" in the sense used here is not immersion in the sense discussed in Cummins' and Artigal's articles, meaning classes where language majority pupils have chosen to be taught through the medium of a minority language, foreign to all the students, and where the teacher is bilingual. "Immersion" as it is used here refers to the fact that ESL students are "immersed" in content instruction through the medium of English, instead of being withdrawn. They may (as in most International Schools) or may not (as in ordinary submersion – see CDE 1984 and Skutnabb-Kangas 1990, chapter "Concept definitions", on details of this) get support (of the kind they need).

4   For more discussion of the area, see e.g. Murphy (1990) and Carder (1991).

5   Editor's note: see Baetens Beardsmore's chapter in this volume which discusses the cost – Maurice Carder did not have access to the detailed information on costs when finalising his chapter.

5

THE EUROPEAN SCHOOLS MODEL IN RELATION TO FRENCH IMMERSION PROGRAMS IN CANADA

Jim Cummins

I welcome the opportunity to respond to Hugo Baetens Beardsmore's comprehensive discussion of the European Schools Model and believe that it has considerable relevance in the North American context. I am going to direct my remarks to the implications of the European Schools Model for French immersion programs in Canada, partly because these programs are referred to frequently in Baetens Beardsmore's chapter and also because during the past 25 years French immersion programs have exerted considerable influence beyond Canada at both theoretical and applied levels.

The major point that I wish to make is that I believe the time has come to critically reassess the dominant model of early French immersion. Specifically, I will suggest that there is little justification for delaying English language arts instruction to grade 3 or 4 as is the case currently in early French immersion in Canada. This delay entails no long-term benefit with respect to students' French skills but carries considerable costs with respect to the likelihood and consequences of dropping out of the program in the early grades. It also reduces the possibility of parent involvement since a large majority of parents do not speak French. Finally, the delay in introducing English reading and writing limits the scope of two-way transfer between French and English conceptual and literacy development and potentially perpetuates teacher-centred transmission models of pedagogy that have tended to characterize early French immersion in the past.

The European Schools model has a much more gradual introduction of the L2 and is certainly one model that is worth serious consideration in the Canadian context. Another is to modify French immersion such that the Kindergarten year remains entirely through French but up to an hour of grades 1, 2 and 3 be devoted to promoting English languge arts and a more general awareness of language that would facilitate transfer between emerging French and English literacy skills. I would see a strong focus on children's literature and creative writing in both languages as central to this type of early French immersion program.

I will first briefly describe the dominant model of early French immersion and contrast some aspects of this model with the European Schools model, and then outline the major problems that have characterized this model during the past 25 years. Finally, I will consider the rationale and evidence for alterations to this model.

The dominant model of early French immersion was originally implemented in the St. Lambert school district near Montreal in the mid-sixties and evaluated by Wallace Lambert and Richard Tucker (1972). Children were instructed totally through French in Kindergarten and grade 1 and English language arts was introduced in grade 2 with content instruction through English increasing to about 50% by the end of elementary school (grade 6). The evaluation showed that students were behind the control group in English language arts in Kindergarten and grade 1 but began to close the gap in grade 2 and had caught up in virtually all aspects of English (except spelling) by the end of grade 3. By grade 4, their English spelling was equivalent to that of the control group. Students' French skills developed rapidly such that after a few years it was no longer possible to use the same test to compare them with peers who were taking core French taught as a second language.

All in all a resounding success story that has been replicated in virtually every city across Canada. Currently more than 300,000 students attend some form of early, middle or late immersion program. Middle immersion starts around grades 4 or 5 with between 50% and 100% of time through French. Late immersion generally starts around grade 7 with intensive exposure to French (usually at least 80%) for one or two years and then a reduction when students enter high school. However, by far the most common model is the early immersion model. Frequently the implementation of early immersion varies somewhat from the original St. Lambert model. For example, in the City of Toronto, English language arts is not introduced until grade 4 on the assumption that the more intensive early exposure to French will result in a better foundation in that language than if English were introduced at an earlier grade level.

The early immersion models in Canada are not that different from those implemented in Ireland (e.g. Cummins, 1978), the Basque Country (Sierra and Olaziregi, 1991) and Catalonia (Artigal, 1991). However, they differ considerably from the European Schools model in a number of respects which have been summarized by Baetens Beardsmore. The most obvious of these is the different status accorded to students' L1. In the European Schools model, L1 remains a major language of instruction throughout elementary school whereas in French immersion it is frequently not introduced until grade 4. Instructional philosophies in relation to teaching L2 also differ, with formal L2 instruction preceding content- or message-based instruction in the European Schools whereas in immersion formal L2 instruction is not a major focus until after several years of message-based instruction. The absence of peers who speak the target language as a L1 also distinguishes immersion from the European Schools and constitutes a limiting factor on the level of expressive French attained by students in immersion.

Problems in French Immersion

While I believe that immersion can justifiably be regarded as a major success story with respect to conception, implementation and evaluation, the research picture is not entirely positive. Two significant problems have emerged: first, students' expressive skills in French (both oral and written) are very far from native-speaker norms, although the gap is much less with respect to receptive skills (reading and listening). Differences are much greater in grammatical proficiency than in discourse or sociolinguistic proficiency (using the categories of the Canale/Swain [1980] framework) (Harley; et al., 1991; Swain and Lapkin, 1986). These grammatical difficulties reflect the influence of English (usually students' L1), and appear extremely resistant to eradication through formal instruction. The fact that pedagogy in immersion classrooms has tended to be considerably more teacher-centred than in regular English elementary school programs (Harley et al., 1991) probably contributes to students' problems in expressive language; if students have limited opportunities to use the target language in either oral or written modes it is hardly surprising that their expressive skills are limited.

A second major problem that has characterized early French immersion programs since its early days is the high rate of student drop-out from the program due to academic or behavioural problems. To illustrate the dimensions of this problem, consider some recent data from the province of Alberta (Keep, 1993). Between 1983-84 and 1990-91, attrition rates from immersion ranged from

43% to 68% by grade 6, 58% to 83% by grade 9, and 88% to 97% by grade 12. Clearly, not all drop-out from the program reflects academic difficulties, although Keep's review of the research suggests that academic and behavioural difficulties constitute major factors predicting transfer to the regular English program.

It is interesting to note in this regard that there is some evidence from the European Schools that they also succeed less well with students of lower ability levels than with higher ability students (Baetens Beardsmore, 1993).

The significant drop-out from immersion has been debated for about 20 years in Canada and considerable research has been conducted on this issue but without any definitive answer to the question of whether French immersion programs are suitable for all students. I am not going to review this research as extensive reviews already exist (e.g. Cummins, 1984a; Keep, 1993). However, I will add one emerging twist to the debate, namely, the increasing enrollment of students from non-English (and of course non-French) language backgrounds in immersion. Let me describe the demographic context in metropolitan Toronto to put the issue into perspective as I believe it respresents a central consideration in the future planning of immersion programs.

The Demographic Context

There have been dramatic increases in immigration to Canada in recent years. Immigrants numbered 84,302 in 1985 but the numbers have increased to a projected level of 250,000 annually from 1992 through 1996. These increases have been implemented as part of the federal government strategy to combat the combined effects of low birth rates and a rapidly aging population.

Within the schools of major urban centres, linguistic and cultural diversity have increased substantially in recent years. For example, in several Toronto boards and in the Vancouver school board, more than half the school population comes from a non-English-speaking background. Clearly, these proportions are likely to rise substantially in view of the fact that immigration levels in the 1990s will be three times greater than in the mid-1980s. In fact, it is projected that more than 300,000 children under age 15 from diverse countries will arrive in Canada between 1990 and 1995, almost double the 160,000 who arrived between 1984 and 1989. An estimated 55 percent of these children are expected to live in Ontario with 40 percent of all immigrant children living in the metropolitian Toronto area (Burke, 1992). Projections for the City of Toronto suggest that by the year 2000, 70 percent of its school population will come from an ESL backgound (Gerard, 1993).

These ESL students are instructed exclusively in English (with ESL support) although heritage language programs are funded by the Province and offered by school boards for 2.5 hours per week, usually outside the regular school day (see Cummins and Danesi, 1991). Research suggests rapid loss of L1 proficiency for students who enroll in Junior Kindergarten (Cummins, 1991) but anecdotal evidence suggests that L1 loss for these students is much less when they are enrolled in an early French immersion program. Recent data from the Montreal area (Fazio, 1993) also suggest that L1 maintenance for students from ethnocultural communities is much greater than in Toronto, a fact that might be explained in terms of the relatively greater ethnolinguistic vitality of the L1 when it is competing against two languages rather than when it is being overwhelmed by the pervasive presence of English.

The major point I want to make here is that in the past French immersion has tended to attract a relatively homogenous group of middle-class students primarily of English-speaking background. Although practice has varied, in some situations school principals have discouraged ESL students from enrolling in immersion on the grounds that they should get command of English before contemplating an additional language. However, the demographics of major Canadian cities are changing such that the ESL student is rapidly becoming the "mainstream". This means that if it is to stay viable, early immersion must adapt to take account of a much greater range of cultural, linguistic and class backgrounds than it has in the past.

In the next section, I will argue that part of this adaptation process involves the introduction of English language arts at the grade 1 level and a greater focus on integrating early literacy instruction (in both languages) with students' background experience. This will entail much more active oral and written language use by students than has been the case in the past in early immersion.

Adapting Immersion to Changing Realities

The major reason for considering the early introduction of English language arts derives from the fate of those who experience difficulty in immersion and are frequently transferred to regular English programs. About 75% of those who transfer will repeat a grade level (Cummins, 1984a); many experience a loss of self-esteem as a result of "failing" in immersion, and also frequently undergo the trauma of parting from friends and adjusting to a new classroom setting where teachers are not always welcoming since they resent getting the "cast-offs" of immersion. As indicated above, this has been a persistent problem and the numbers of students involved are not insignificant. An obvious reason why most students repeat a grade after they transfer is that they have acquired only minimal literacy in both English and French and are therefore very much behind their grade 2 or grade 3 peers in the regular program.

There are several ways in which the early introduction of English might alleviate this problem. First, if a particular student is not progressing in a satisfactory manner with respect to literacy acquisition, teachers and assess<evaluation>ment specialists can look at the other side of the coin; they can see whether students' difficulty is specific to French or is a more general problem that manifests itself in both languages. In the current model, educators can look only at one side of the coin (French progress) and are thus limited both in their assessment of the nature of the difficulty and in their strategies for intervention (since within the classroom only French is used).

Second, if a student is experiencing difficulty in early literacy development, it makes intuitive sense that concepts and strategies can be explained to the student more easily in their stronger language than in a language which is still very limited in its development. Thus, intervention is likely to be more successful when both linguistic channels can be mobilized than when only the more restricted channel is used. I would argue that, as a result, fewer students will drop out of immersion and transfer to the regular English program.

Third, if a student does drop out of immersion they will at least have had considerable instruction in English reading and writing and are likely to be less far behind their regular program peers in English literacy than if they had received no English instruction.

Fourth, in a multilingual context such as Toronto the early introduction of English would reassure many parents from heritage language backgrounds that French immersion is an appropriate program for them. There is no evidence that French immersion as it currently stands is inappropriate for students from ethnocultural backgrounds in comparison to those from English-speaking backgrounds, but the relatively low enrollments of these children in immersion would suggest that many parents, teachers and principals are not confident that immersion is appropriate for these children. Anecdotal evidence from both educators and community groups would support this assertion. Thus, if English language arts were introduced in grade 1, I believe that many more children from heritage language backgrounds would enroll in immersion and greatly add to the potential of the program to promote language awareness and multilingual/multicultural sensitivity. In addition, as I indicated earlier, there is evidence that maintenance of heritage language children's L1 would be increased if more of them enrolled in immersion rather than in the regular English program.

Finally, there are potential pedagogical benefits to be reaped from instruction in both languages in the early grades. Although this pattern has begun to change, for many years instruction in early immersion programs tended to be much more transmission-oriented than was typical in regular English programs. During the eighties, whole language strategies for promoting literacy were adopted in a significant number of regular elementary classrooms but to a much lesser extent in early immersion classrooms (Harley et al., 1991). The regular classroom has increasingly become characterized by strategies such as strong promotion of creative writing, classroom publishing of students' stories, encouragement of active involvement with children's literature, bringing books home on a regular basis to read with parents, cooperative learning, and individual and group project work. While some of these strategies are being adopted in immersion, the process has been slow and teachers continue to expend considerable effort trying to eradicate the deviant grammatical patterns internalized by immersion students. I would argue that the introduction of these strategies in the promotion of English literacy in the early grades would increase the likelihood that similar strategies would be adopted in the promotion of French literacy. Furthermore, I would argue that an increase in the amount of reading that students do in French (combined with a reduction in reliance on basal readers) and an increase in the amount of writing that students carry out in various genres, with appropriate corrective feedback, would increase the likelihood that students would internalize a more formally correct variety of French than is currently the case.

Would the introduction of English in the early grades reduce students' French proficiency? The research suggests that, over time, the achievement gap resulting from differences in the amount of French exposure that students experience tend to wash out. Swain and Lapkin (1986), for example, report a trend for early immersion students to outperform late immersion students at the high school level in listening, speaking, and reading but not in writing; however, the differences between groups are not large in view of the very much greater time that the early immersion students have spent through the medium of French. Thus, I would be very surprised if any differences were observed by the end of elementary school (grade 6) in the French proficiency of students exposed to English literacy from grade 1 in comparison to those whose early grades were spent totally through French.

In fact, a longitudial evaluation of the type of model that I am proposing was carried out by the Calgary Roman Catholic Separate School Board. Students who received an hour of English from grade 1 were compared to a regular immersion program and a regular English program over a three year period (Cummins, 1992). (It should be noted that both French language programs already had a half hour in oral English devoted to religion; thus the innovation consisted of adding an additional half hour devoted to English literacy).

The experimental group performed more poorly than the regular immersion group in French reading, writing and oral fluency at the end of grade 1 and, to a lesser extent, at the end of grade 2. However, by the end of grade 3 they had pulled ahead of the regular immersion students in French reading and writing and were performing equivalently on French oral skills. Their performance in English reading and writing was also superior to that of [both] comparison groups, particularly the regular French immersion group.

Parent observations throw some light on these trends. In general, parents of students in the experimental group reported a significantly higher level of reading and writing activities in the home than was the case for either of the other two groups. Parents also reported that the experimental group students enjoyed reading and writing activities in the home more than parents of either of the other groups. Thus, students who are becoming biliterate as a result of instruction through French and English in the early grades engage in considerably more voluntary literacy activities in English than the English comparison group and in French than the French comparison group. It is interesting to note that the regular French immersion group engages in far more literacy activities in English than in French; for example, 79% were reported to usually enjoy reading in English compared to only 25% in French.

These comparisons should not be given undue weight since they involved only one class at each grade level but they do suggest that concerns in regard to students' French are unfounded. They also suggest that the opportunity for parents to support literacy development in the home may have a significant positive impact on development of both languages.

In the proposed alternative model, I would envisage that the same teacher would teach both English and French language arts (as was the case in the Calgary example) and clearly this implies that the teacher be fluently bilingual.

In summary, I have argued that considerable advances could be made to address the persistent drop-out problem in French immersion by introducing one period of English language arts at the grade one level. This would potentially encourage greater parental involvement and a greater focus on active use of both written and oral language to permit students to integrate their experiences outside school with the literacy skills they are developing in school. The greater scope for validation of students' experience would be particularly significant for students from heritage language backgrounds who are currently very much underrepresented in early French immersion. I would also encourage consideration of the models based on the European Schools' experience and it is possible that the modifications I am suggesting might be a first step in that direction. There is nothing sacrosanct about the St. Lambert model of early French immersion. It does work reasonably well for most students who enroll but I believe that there are feasible alternatives that might work considerably better for [all] students who aspire to multilingual proficiencies.

6

MULTIWAYS TOWARDS MULTILINGUALISM: THE CATALAN IMMERSION PROGRAMME EXPERIENCE

Josep Maria Artigal

Introduction: does equal treatment lead to equity in situations of hierarchical power relations between languages?

Most (European) readers might agree with the thrust of the title of this book: multilingualism for all. Not only because our society is rapidly growing in linguistic diversity, cross-cultural cooperation, and economic interdependence, but also because we have accepted a principle which we might call the "additive bilingual enrichment principle". It assumes that additive bilingualism is enriching because it may enhance, for instance, linguistic and intellectual development and cognitive flexibility (Peal & Lambert, 1962; Leopold, 1970; Balkan, 1970; Ianco-Worral, 1972; Lambert & Tucker, 1972; Ben-Zeev, 1977a; Lambert, 1978; Cummins, 1979, 1980b, 1984b; Diaz, 1986; Diaz & Klinger, 1991; Bialystok, 1991; Malakoff & Hakuta, 1991; Mohanty, forthcoming).

However, once agreement on the beneficial effect of additive bilingualism has been established, a small but very important issue arises, reminding us of the fact that words are never neutral, and that a term may have different meanings and goals. It is one thing to agree that boys and girls are able to and have the right to learn as many languages as possible; but it is quite another issue to guarantee that every community has a choice so they can themselves decide which these languages will be, which one will be socially dominant, with its own territory, and what the most adequate ways might be to reach these goals in the context of each community. To build a multilingual Europe and multilingual World becomes a different process, depending on whether, as a speaker of English, French or German, you come from a dominant language background, or if you, as a Sard, Basc, or Catalan, come from a "minority" [1] language background. Thus, unless we are able to find *different* ways of building up the undoubtedly fascinating concept of "multilingualism" in the title of our book and the Symposium upon which it was based, the final result may well be a multiglossia, potentially as dangerous for minority languages as the present monolingualisms.

I was very pleased to read Hugo Baetens Beardsmore's chapter on European Schools (this volume). This model has met with great success, and it serves as a useful example of the fact that it is no more difficult to learn two, three or even more languages than to learn one. The crux of the matter is not the number of languages girls and boys are able to learn, but the way they, and we, build up a learning process, suited for the chosen number of languages. I know Baetens Beardsmore's intention is not to recommend that others take the model over and transplant it in its entirety to another context. He just wants to present a few reflections on some aspects of the European School model that could potentially be adapted to other multilingual settings.

Nevertheless, as a member of one linguistic minority community, Catalonia, I feel uneasy about one aspect of the European School model: the inalterable dominance of instruction through a child's family language for *all* language subsections, regardless of the social status of these languages in the out-of-school environment, their roles in wider society. One characteristic of trying *not* to privilege any child or any language in the European Schools is that "all pupils are put on an equal footing as far as (...) all are led through the same process of instruction through an L1 into that through an L1 and an L2" (Baetens Beardsmore, this volume, p. 64). In my view, equal treatment may in fact not suit situations where the starting point for the languages is unequal. I will provide examples to support this claim by drawing on the Catalan situation.

The Catalan immersion programmes

The following section deals with immersion programmes currently in operation in Catalonia. After a brief description of the social and political background against which these programmes have been implemented, general principles are defined and an overall description of the language distribution in the curriculum (L1, L2 and L3) is given. Once this background information has been presented, I will address some aspects of the issue raised above.

Historical and social background

Located in the northeastern corner of the Iberian peninsula, Catalonia covers a territory of 32,000 km² and has a population of over 6 million (all of whom do not speak Catalan). It is one of the most developed and industrialised parts of Spain. Catalan is the heritage language of Catalonia.

In terms of the number of people who speak it, about 6.000.000, Catalan ranks below languages such as Greek, Swedish or Portuguese, but above Danish, Finnish or Norwegian. The linguistic area in which the Catalan language is spoken also includes the Region of Valencia (3,800,000 inhabitants) and the Balearic Islands (680,000 inhabitants), both in Spain; the region of Roussillon in France (330,000 inhabitants); the Principality of Andorra (60,000 inhabitants) as well as the town of l'Alger (Alghero) in Sardinia, Italy. According to the latest data, about 6 million of that area's inhabitants speak Catalan and almost 9 million understand it.

For over 700 years, without a break, Catalan was the official language of Catalonia and the only language spoken throughout the country. However, after the War of Spanish Succession (1714), the official status of the language was annulled. Catalan was progressively limited to domestic and sporadic public usage (often clandestine), and Spanish gradually acquired the status of dominant language.

Though this diglossic process was set in motion over a long period, the major trend towards language substitution got underway during the dictatorship of General Franco (1939-1975) and was due to three main factors. The first was the massive influx of immigrants from Spanish-speaking areas of Spain seeking employment in the industrialised Catalan region. The second factor was the introduction of modern mass media in which the use of Catalan was forbidden, and which became a powerful social instrument exerting considerable pressure on a language already in a weak social position. The third factor was an all-out policy of cultural and linguistic homogenisation, implemented by successive Spanish governments under the Franco dictatorship, which carried out a systematic and brutal aggression towards all signs of Catalan identity.

At the end of the Franco regime, Catalan was facing a difficult situation of diglossia. While 100% of the inhabitants of Catalonia were fully competent in Spanish, the Catalan-speakers shrunk to 60% of the population. Whereas the Spanish language could be used in all registers, with all types of interlocutors and in all environments, the social scope of Catalan became very much more restricted.

Nevertheless, during the 1960s and 1970s an acute awareness and powerful social reaction had arisen in response to this severe repression. This large-scale social movement, as well as the democratic changes that took place in post-Franco Spain, established a solid political background from which it was possible, after the death of General Franco, to launch a widespread campaign aimed at restoring the Catalan language.

The first legal manifestation of this recovery was the approval of the Catalan Statute of Self-government (1979) proclaiming Catalan as Catalonia's "own language" and granting it co-official status with Spanish within its territory. The second legal manifestation was the promulgation of a special Law of Linguistic Normalisation (1983) designed to protect and encourage the social use of the language. From these two legal texts onwards, Catalan has managed to open up spaces and gain positions in the social life of the country. It has acquired prestige and currency, and is no longer a language limited to strictly domestic use. Nowadays, 93% of the population in Catalonia understand the language, and 68% are able to speak it (Municipal Census, 1990). However, Spanish continues to be the high or dominant language (as defined by Ferguson, 1959), and Catalan the weaker or minority one.

The Catalan language in education

Education has been both a cause and a consequence in this whole, complex, historical process. During the first part of the process, the Catalan language was banned from education. Schooling thus became a very powerful tool of Spanification in the hands of successive governments in Madrid. From the approval of the Catalan Statute of Self-government onwards, formal education became an important vehicle for the process of recovering knowledge and renewing the social presence of the Catalan language. At present, all children have to master both Catalan and Spanish by the end of compulsory education, at the age of 16.

The action of the Catalan Government in the pursuit of that objective can be divided into two major phases. During the first phase, which lasted from 1978 to 1983, the main goal was the enforcement of compulsory teaching of the Catalan language as a subject at least 4 hours per week. By the end of this first period, in 1983, over 90% of the pupils in Kindergarten (3-5 years) and Primary Education (6-13 years) received that minimum of instruction in Catalan (Arenas 1986, 88). However, on account of the social dominance of Spanish, this amount of time spent on Catalan instruction proved totally insufficient. The study published by the Catalan Teaching Service (SEDEC) in 1983, "Quatre anys de català a l'escola", showed that the learning of Catalan, the socially weaker language, could not be guaranteed by this minimum amount of schooling. The study accordingly concluded that "the language which is ill-treated in the environment ... is the one that must be granted most importance in school" (SEDEC 1983, 133).

During the second phase, from 1983 onwards, the Catalan Department of Education offered a school option giving priority to the socially weaker language. This was a political option unanimously approved by all political groups in the Catalan Parliament, even non-nationalistic.

Since 1983, three types of schools have existed in Catalonia. They are classified on the basis of the treatment they give to languages.

In the *first* type, which we will refer to as *"schools with predominantly Catalan-medium instruction"*, Catalan is used from the very beginning of Kindergarten as the sole vehicular language (i.e. medium of education) for the entire curriculum. In these schools, the children learn how to read and write through Catalan, with Spanish being introduced progressively later on, from Grades 1, 2 or 3 of Primary Education (at ages 6, 7 or 8).

In the *second* type, *"schools with bilingual instruction"*, basic learning - including learning how to read and write - takes place in Spanish. Four hours per week of Catalan Language Arts are introduced in Kindergarten and Grades 1 and 2 of Primary Education, followed by a progressive expansion of both Catalan language arts and Catalan as a medium of instruction.

The *third* type of school are *"schools with Spanish-medium instruction"*. In these schools, Spanish is used as the sole medium of instruction throughout schooling, and Catalan only taught as a subject.

To these three basic types, a *transitional fourth type* must be added, which we refer to as *"schools evolving towards predominantly Catalan-medium instruction"*. This comprises schools in which predominantly Catalan-medium instruction is offered from Kindergarten upwards, but bilingual or Spanish-medium instruction is still offered in certain higher grades.

The decade following 1983 saw rapid change over to Catalan becoming the main medium of communication and instruction in Kindergarten and Primary Education. The evolution can be seen in the figures for Catalan-medium schools: they increased from 3% of all schools in 1978, to 88% during the 1992-93 academic year.

In order to understand the extent of this change, virtually unthinkable under the repressive Franco dictatorship, we must bear in mind two contextual features of current education in Catalonia.

Firstly, in accordance with the afore-mentioned Law of Linguistic Normalisation, decisions are taken by the staff and parents of individual schools as to which language should be used as the main medium of instruction. Within the limits set by the Department of Education, and taking into account parental desires, the staff in every school is required to draw up a document detailing their choice of language policy in the school, in accordance with the pupils' specific socio-linguistic situation. This document, called "The Linguistic Project", must specify what role each language plays in the curriculum, establish a timetable for the introduction and teaching of these languages, and identify suitable strategies for achieving the objectives.

Secondly, according to the latest census figures, the family language of 53% of the students is Spanish. Catalan is the family language of 33% of the students, and 12% come from bilingual families (Bel, 1991).

As 88% of schools use Catalan as the main medium of instruction (i.e. they belong to the first and fourth types above), these schools must have a number of children with Spanish as the family language. Among the children who have chosen to attend schools which give priority to the socially weaker language these are the ones who have opted for what in Catalonia is classified as immersion programmes.

Features of the Catalan immersion programmes

The definition of what administratively counts as an immersion programme is quite detailed in Catalonia. In order to be classified as an immersion programme in Catalonia, a programme must exhibit the following features:

1. In a school with predominantly Catalan-medium instruction, or evolving towards predominantly Catalan-medium instruction, the majority of the pupils (between 70% and 100% of children in each classroom) must have Spanish, the socially dominant language, as their family language. All other situations involving a home-school language switch (including those in which the home language of the majority of the children is Spanish but over 30% of the children are members of the weaker language group, i.e. Catalan-speakers), are not considered immersion, or treated pedagogically as immersion.
2. The programme encompasses Kindergarten (3-5 years) and Primary Education (6-13 years).
3. Attending the programme is voluntary. Accordingly, positive parent and pupil attitudes towards the programme and the new school language is a primary feature for the success of the programme.
4. As a consequence of the abovementioned historical factors, many immersion pupils

come from a lower socio-economic background, that is, from immigrant families who arrived in Catalonia seeking employment during the 50's and 60's.

5. Teachers who introduce the L2 are bilingual: they have a thorough knowledge of the language in which they teach. They are also sufficiently proficient in the home language of the pupils to be able to understand them when they use it. Thus, even though the teachers only offer input in the new language (according to the "one person/one language" principle), their bilingualism enables the pupils to express themselves in their L1 at least during the initial stages of the programme.

6. Since 1983, the Catalan Department of Education has organised regular didactic advisory seminars for immersion teachers. The aim of these seminars is not only to orientate and help teachers but also to provide a place for them to exchange strategies, ideas and materials, and to offer them an opportunity for reflecting on and becoming aware of their own educational practices. At present, in-service seminars are being conducted in 476 locations all over Catalonia by 142 advisors. Hence, immersion teachers are proficient in specific methods and techniques, thus guaranteeing meaningful and effective interaction in the classroom at all times, even though the interaction occurs in a language which the teachers do not initially share with their pupils.

7. All instruction is conveyed and reading and writing learned exclusively in Catalan during an initial phase which varies from 2 to 5 years, according to how dominant Spanish is out-of-school. At the same time, the treatment of the family language, the socially dominant one, is not overlooked. It is introduced at a later stage, between the last Grade of Kindergarten and Grade 3 of Primary Education.

8. Conforming to the "New Education System" (1992), and in accordance with the situation of Catalonia within the current coordinates of united Europe, a third, foreign, language must be introduced no later than the 3rd grade of primary education, when the pupils are 8 years old.

Briefly, the Catalan immersion programme is a form of multilingual education designed for dominant language pupils who choose to attend a school where the minority language is prioritised.

Ten years after the establishment of immersion programmes, the number of classes and pupils enrolled in immersion schools has grown significantly. That is to say, 58% of all classes and 55% of all pupils, having the option to choose this kind of multilingual education (based on the above criteria), do so (Table 1). However, these figures may rise considerably higher in the future, considering that younger pupils show a marked trend towards choosing the immersion option even more often ((74% and 72%, respectively, for Kindergarten and first and second grade).

Table 1. Number of classes and pupils in immersion programmes (according to the criteria for immersion), 1992/93

	Classes	%	Pupils	%
K1-3 & Gr1-2 3-7 years	4,219	74	85,363	72
Gr3-5 8-10 years	2,152	51	47,717	49
Gr6-8 11-13 years	2,143	45	55,548	45
Total	8,514	58	188,628	55

Note: K1-3: Kindergarten (3, 4 and 5 years); Gr. 1-8 (6-13 years); Source: Vial (1994)

The results

Though not much research has yet been carried out to assess the linguistic and academic results of immersion programmes in Catalonia, the studies which have been conducted indicate that the Spanish-speaking children in the programmes attain significantly higher levels of Catalan than those reached by other Spanish-speaking children attending schools which were classified as bilingual or predominantly Spanish-medium (see above). At the same time, research shows that immersion pupils perform as well in the Spanish language as Hispanophone peers not enrolled in the programme (Bel 1989, 1990; Serra 1990; Arnau & Serra 1992; Guasch et al. 1992; Boixaderas, Canal & Fernández 1992; Vila 1993).

Furthermore, the studies show that there are in general no significant differences between immersion groups and Spanish control groups with regard to cognitive development and academic achievement (Arnau, Boada & Forns 1990). Serra (1990) and Serramona et al. (1990) show that the academic performance of immersion pupils in Grades 2 and 3 is at the same level or slightly higher than that of their Spanish controls. Only in Grade 3 (Boixaderas, Canal & Fernández 1992) and Grade 5 (Ribes 1993), do the immersion pupils perform at a lower level than their controls in some arithmetic skills (calculation). However, when mathematical knowledge is applied to problem solving, there are no significant differences. These researchers hypothesize that immersion teachers concentrate on L2 learning and may neglect some arithmetic skills.

Finally, according to two studies carried out at the end of Kindergarten, the development of communicative ability (Boada & Forns, in press) and social and emotional adaptation of the immersion children to the programme (Forns & Gomez, in press) is age-appropriate.

The children's third language

As mentioned before, a third language - a foreign one - must be introduced no later than in the 3rd grade of primary education when the students are 8 years old. Recently, however, several immersion programmes have started introducing a foreign language (L3) from the age of 6 or even 4.

One of these experiments introduces English (L3) from the age of 4 in Kindergarten 2. It has been implemented for the last three academic years (since 1991/92) in 10 schools in Catalonia, as well as in 23 schools in the Basque Country. Most of these schools have immersion programmes in Catalan/Basque, and the pupils' socio-economic background ranges from middle to lower class.

The experiment consists of four or five thirty-minute sessions of English weekly. During these sessions, the pupils and teacher collectively dramatise a set of stories in the new language. The stories have a simple plot and deal with topics akin to the experiences and fantasies of children in the target age group. They are narrated, from the very start, through collective dramatisation in which the whole class actively plays all the parts in the plot. Instead of focusing on formal L3 teaching, these situations of early multilingualism emphasize the communication of meaningful tasks through both target languages, i.e. English, their L3, and the immersion language (Catalan/Basque) from the very beginning (Artigal, 1994).

All teachers involved in the experiment have access to continuing in-service training. This ensure their possession of theoretical and practical knowledge needed to guarantee communicability and efficiency of the interactions conveyed through the new languages. Experience has proved this feature to be of vital importance.

Though the L3 teachers are trilingual, and therefore able to understand when their pupils use their first or second language, the teachers interact exclusively through the new language (L3) with their pupils, in this way respecting the "one person/one language" principle.

Although the implementation period of the experiment has been far too short, I would like to highlight three issues arising from the first evaluations (Bernaus, 1993, 1994; Cenoz, Lindsay & Espi, 1992, 1993).

Firstly, despite the short time of exposure to L3, gains made in that language are significant.

Secondly, pupils enrolled in the experimental programmes perform as well in their L1 and L2 as equivalent children in similar immersion schools which do not introduce the L3, and in some aspects better than these.

Thirdly, once a threshold level of teacher proficiency in the target language is guaranteed, the quality of pedagogic interaction is the most significant variable for the success of the pupils' L3 acquisition.

In summary, if quality instruction is provided, the partial (early) introduction of a foreign (L3) language in a minority (L2) language immersion programme, seems to benefit all the majority pupil's languages, even the mother tongue (L1).

Promoting proficiency in the family language: the maximum exposure fallacy

There is no doubt that, as claimed by UNESCO (1953), proficiency in the family language is a *sine qua non* prerequisite for any child's linguistic, cognitive and academic development. Hence, according to European Schools principles, promotion of the family language must be the foundation for any education model. However, it is a fallacy to assume that family language promotion may only be accomplished as a result of early instruction through the medium of that language. In light of many first language acquisition studies carried out in recent years, it seems possible to state that achievement in the family language is not always a direct consequence of the amount of instruction in this language. In order to substantiate this argument I briefly present four assumptions.

1. Boys and girls acquire a language - be it a first, second, third, etc - if their attitude towards that language is positive, if they have access to sufficient interaction through that language, and, above all, if the input and output mediating these interactions are comprehensible (i.e. can be recognized). In addition to positive attitudes and access to interaction, language acquisition is a process which necessarily requires the learner to perform certain semiotic operations enabling her to construct meaningful and efficient uses of the target language.

2. Instead of being learned first and used later, a language is acquired by being used as a medium for doing things with others. Language acquisition processes that the learner puts into action, in order to become a meaningful and efficient user/learner of the new language, are initially social and necessarily based on interaction with others. As Artigal (1991b, 1992, 1994) has pointed out, the possibility of use/acquisition of a language that the learner does not yet know is something that initially goes beyond her individual competence, something that inevitably implies the existence of semiotic operations which, if they were not collective, would disappear.

3. It is certainly difficult to make a clear distinction between dominant and minority languages. Despite this, we might argue that a dominant language is a language which has social guarantees of positive attitudes towards it, and which is widely used as a medium for interaction in all registers, in all contexts, with all types of interlocutors, and with all kinds of goals. Nonetheless, a minority language is not a smaller language, or a language with only few speakers, but a language which lacks these social guarantees of meeting with positive attitudes and having a wide range of opportunities of use as a medium of interaction.

4. As Cummins has argued (1979, 1980b, 1981, 1984a), if certain prerequisites are fulfilled, it is possible to hypothesize about the existence of an interdependency principle which accounts for successful transfer from language A to language B. That is to say, to the extent that a language use/acquisition strategies are mastered in language A, positive transfer of these strategies (as a tool for processing language B) occurs, provided that: 1. there is a positive attitude towards language B; 2. there is enough access to interaction through it, and 3. the type or level of input and output mediating the interaction in B can be processed by means of the transferred strategy.

In summary, and as a large number of studies have shown in recent years, family language development depends primarily on the status of the language in the wider environment, and the quality of educational interactions by which the interdependent language use/acquisition strategies discussed above are attained, not on the amount of L1 instruction children receive in school (Cummins, 1981, 1984a, 1984c, 1991; Swain, 1981; Swain & Lapkin, 1982; Vila 1983, 1993; Hernandez-Chavez, 1984; Sierra & Olaziregi, 1987, 1989, 1990; Sierra, 1991; Genesee, 1987; Artigal 1987, 1991a, 1992, 1993; Göncz and Kodžopeljić, 1991; Verhoeven, 1991a, 1991b; Siren, 1991; Wong Fillmore, 1991; Landry & Allard, 1991; Arnau, Comet, Serra & Vila, 1992). If certain prerequisites are fullfilled, the semiotic operations built through the L2 immersion interactions also enable pupils to construct meaningful and efficient uses for their family language.

If a pupil's family language is socially dominant, and the educational interactions are suited to the learners, instruction through the medium of a socially weaker second language for a substantial part of the school day entails no disadvantages to academic achievement in the family language. If, however, a pupil's family language is socially a minority language, promoting that language in school becomes the ineludible path to proficiency in that language, as well as the best way of providing support for the development of additional languages, including the socially dominant language. Similarly, given proper, rich pedagogy, dominant language development is relatively insensitive to school exposure, and instruction via the medium of a minority language does not impede the development of proficiency acquisition in the dominant language.

Final remarks

Maybe I am wrong, but when the European School model stresses the significance of instruction in the first language, regardless of its status and roles in the wider environment, or when it proposes that "In any adapted version it might well be that the majority out-of-school language should function as the lingua franca for the entire (school) population" (Baetens Beardsmore, this volume, p. 50), I as a member of one linguistic minority community hesitate to accept and transplant these arguments in their entirety to another context.

Multilingual education is not a purely educational phenomenon. It does not only stem from arguments about greater demand for competent multilingual citizens in industrialised societies, or arguments about the virtues of multilingualism. Also, such growth is based on consciousness of the need to maintain and develop minority languages and cultures. It is important to view multilingualism as not occurring in a vacuum. A central question is whether minority languages have any chance of survival, or if multilingualism will be a half-way house on the road to dominant language multiglossia. Multilingual education is not only a question of the number of languages to be learned. The value of considering one model of multilingual education rather than another, is, above all, to make us aware of the fact that choosing such a model is choosing one specific type of multilingual future. In that respect, the Catalan immersion experience tries to be a concrete step forward in regard to both goals which it has chosen: a World made up by multilingual citizens, and a World respectful of all its own languages.

If we agree with the notion that languages are learned as they are used in motivating and comprehensible interactions; if we assume that immersion programmes can be described, briefly, as great and meaningful settings for language use/acquisition, then the second languages which are most easily and rapidly acquired are those which offer learners a maximum of meaningful contexts for use. If we assume this to be so, then minority languages may be the best "second languages" for children from dominant language homes, in a context of languages in contact.

Sometimes offering an immersion programme in a minority language may be the best way of promoting the majority language, as well as a way of facilitating easier access to other languages later on. Sometimes it may be necessary to lead majority and minority children along different paths, in order not to treat them differently.

Notes:

1   As discussed later, in this paper the term "minority language" is used not as referring to smaller or less used languages, but language which became regarded as minor, inferior or unnecessary because of social reasons.

7

BILINGUALISM – A STEP TOWARDS MONOLINGUALISM OR MULTILINGUALISM?

Mart Rannut & Ülle Rannut

1. Introduction

In most cases bilingualism is a step towards acquiring more languages. However, there are cases when bilingualism leads to monolingualism. For example, there are immigrants, whose grandchildren or, even worse, children do not know the language of their (grand)parents (Wong Fillmore 1991). The same can apply to powerless linguistic minorities and other threatened groups (e.g. populations of occupied territories) who tend to lose their language one or two generations after the population becomes overwhelmingly bilingual. Education, especially language education, plays a major political role in homogenisation which is one step towards monolingualism (referred to by, [some] politicians, as national integrity), and multilingual diversification, one step towards multilingualism.

During the years of Soviet occupation (1940-1991), Estonia belonged to the former category. Due to significant demographic changes as well as compulsary one-way Estonian-Russian bilingualism (for Estonian-speakers), an immigrant Russian-speaking monolingual community was formed during the occupation. Thus, besides Estonian, also Russian was, and is still, widely used in unofficial communication.

Now that a normalisation process has started, the main task in educational language planning in Estonia is to create an educational system for all ethnic and age groups, providing language teaching which enables effective internal communication, by

- ensuring the effortless functioning of Estonian as the official language of the country;
- enabling international communication by ensuring high levels of competence in several foreign languages;
- ensuring linguistic rights for minorities, especially the maintenance and development of their mother tongues.

In order for these goals to be reached, it is necessary that the educational system provides a real opportunity for all children to become high-level multilinguals. The question is then how this can be done and here Estonia can look to other countries, with other experiences, in addition to drawing on the very different phases in its own past. In order to discuss and evaluate the alternatives, it is necessary to look at the present linguistic situation in Estonia and its historical background.

2. Demographic changes

Estonia, one of the three Baltic countries, has been under foreign rule for most of this millennium. Before the First World War, Estonia was *part of Tsarist Russia* for 200 years. Despite this, the language of administration during that time was mostly German, due to the existence of the privileged and powerful Baltic German minority, forming the upper class of the society. Estonia was independent between the two World Wars. During the Second World War, Estonia was occupied in 1940 by the Soviet Union, according to the Molotov-Ribbentrop Pact Secret Protocol. Estonia regained its independence in 1991.

During the period of *independence between the World Wars*, Estonia was mainly a mononational country. Nonetheless, its minorities (Russians, Germans, Swedes, Jews), though numerically small, enjoyed ample cultural autonomy, adopted in 1925. According to the 1934 census, the ethnic composition of the population of Estonia was as follows:

Table 1. Ethnic composition of the population of Estonia in 1934

	number	percentage of population
Estonians	992,000	88,0
Russians	92,000	8,0
Germans	16,300	1,5
Swedes	7,600	0,7
Jews	4,400	0,4
Others		1,4

Most of the *non-Estonians* were bilingual in their mother tongue and Estonian. The bulk of the largest minority group, Russians, lived in rural areas, the most "Russian" areas being the town of Narva (29.7%), the territories East of Narva, and the Petseri region. The percentage of Russians living in Tallinn, the capital, was 5.7%. As for the other major ethnic groups, the Germans and Jews lived in towns and the Swedes lived in the Estonian coastal region and on the islands.

In response to an appeal from Hitler, most Germans left Estonia in October 1939.

World War II and the *Soviet occupation* changed the linguistic composition drastically. Total immigration *into* Estonia during the Soviet occupation was 1.4 million, and emigration *from* Estonia 0.8 million, i.e. a net migration of 0.6 million. The number of Estonians during the occupation never reached pre-World War II levels. As a result, the Estonian-background population dropped from 97.3 in 1945 to 61.5 in 1989 (see Table 2).

At the same time as the functional domains as well as the number of regional areas where Estonian was used, decreased, a rapid rise in the status of Russian took place. It was caused by several factors, like Russian being mandated as the sole language of several functional spheres; the construction of a Russian-speaking network of plants, factories, offices, institutions and service bureaus as well as entertainment facilities and residential areas; the provision of full-scale education (including higher education, vocational schools, special shools for the disabled, Kindergartens etc) and services in Russian. These structures were filled with a regular, massive influx of Russian-speaking immigrants. As a result, a Russian-speaking immigrant environment was created in Estonia, in which contact was not made with Estonians and the Estonian language. This effectively prevented any possible integration.

The first years of renewed independence have witnessed a significant repatriation of Russian-speaking immigrants, making the restructuring of the educational system inevitable.

3. Language education up to 1991

3.1 Language education during independence 1918-1940
3.1.1 Education for Estonian-speakers. Owing to a long tradition of instruction at the home and a well-arranged network of public schools, the early 20th century witnessed a high standard of literacy among Estonians, even though the provision of Estonian-medium education was forbidden in public secondary schools. In the initial years of the Republic of Estonia (1918-1940), the effects of

Russification and Germanisation were quickly overcome, and a system developed which made education through the medium of Estonian available from Kindergarten up to higher education.

In the advent of the development of direct foreign relations with other western countries, the significance of Russian diminished, and the concept of the "three local languages" changed to some extent: instead of the Estonian, German and Russian combination at the beginning of the century, these were Estonian, Geman and English.

At that time, most of the educational institutions were Estonian-medium. Besides these, there were educational institutions in the minority languages, as well as in the more popular foreign languages. For example, the French-medium lycé and the English-medium college were popular among the elite.

3.1.2 Education for minority language speakers. The Law of Cultural Autonomy, adopted in 1925, granted the right to establish (state-financed) schools with their own language as the medium of education to all minorities numbering over 3,000. This right was widely used by local minorities. According to regulations by the Ministry of Education (passed on 17.12.1918), the Estonian language was required to be a compulsory subject in minority schools, with 4 lessons per week. To found a state-financed, minority language-medium school, a minimum enrollment of 20 pupils was necessary. If the number of minority children was less than 20, minority pupils could study their native language as a subject for 3 hours a week in an Estonian-medium school (e.g. Russian in Paldiski and Mustvee).

In 1929, Germans had 19 primary schools, Jews 3, Latvians 7, Russians 100, Swedes 15 and Ingrians 3. The Germans operated 14 secondary schools, Russians 9, Latvians 1, Jews 2 and the Swedes opened theirs in 1931. Founding native language schools was most difficult for heterogenous or "illiterate" (= orate) minorities. Jews, who had populated Estonia from the beginning of the 19th century used Russian mostly (sometimes German or Estonian) as their native language. Thus, the Jewish (primary and secondary) schools that were founded used Russian as the medium, gradually shifting to Jiddish. On 21.06.1926, the Jewish Cultural Council decided to transfer to Modern Hebrew.

Orthodox Ingrians *(inkeroiset)* spoke Ingrian, a Balto-Finnic language like Estonian and Finnish, but without an established literary form. It caused great difficulty to find a common literary language for the education of the minority. The three primary schools east of the Narva river used Russian up to 1922, when 2 of them shifted to Estonian, a closely related language. According to the Ministry of Education decision dating back to 1926, the medium of instruction was changed to Finnish, as the closest language, but oral use of Ingrian was also encouraged. Due to a petition from Ingrian parents who demanded Estonian, Estonian as well as Finnish-medium departments were opened in both schools in 1933, thus allowing a choice of medium of instruction.

Those non-Estonians who did not have schools in their native languages placed their children in German-medium schools. Besides Estonian-medium Kindergartens, German- and even French-medium Kindergartens existed. Several minorities organised nursery schools, operating on a half-day basis. Higher education was also available in minority languages. There was one German-medium institution for higher education: a private, theological-philosophical, Luther's Academy, and one Russian-medium institute: a private Polytechnic Institute.

3.1.2 The teaching of foreign languages. Estonian-medium secondary schools had two main streams of specialisation, a real and a humanitarian branch. In the real branch, a second foreign language (English in most cases) was added to German which was already taught as the first foreign language. In the humanitarian branch, Latin was also added. A classic branch also existed, featuring Latin and Greek in addition to the three local languages. The most frequently taught foreign language was German which was started in the 4th grade of primary school. Then came English, with French as the third language. Russian was sometimes taught as a second or third foreign language, in some commerce schools and in German minority schools. This was due to the fact that German did not need to be taught as the first foreign language.

3.2 Changes in language education during the Soviet occupation

3.2.1 Education for Estonian-speakers. The summer of 1940 marked the beginning of a new period of Russification. This was resumed at the end of World War II as an overt campaign, under the pretext of acquainting Estonians with Soviet culture. Estonian, as a "language with no future", was discriminated against in the curriculum of Estonian educational institutions. Russian was not seen as a foreign language for Estonians, but was labelled "the second mother tongue" of Estonian-speakers. In order to make Estonians bilingual in their two "mother tongues", the Russian language was taught in over 60% of the time allotted to mother tongue instruction. The number of hours reserved for the first foreign language (e.g. German or English) was gradually reduced (from 27 weekly hours in the total curriculum in 1945 to 16 in 1983).

In many other regions of the Soviet Union, mother tongue medium education was initially changed from being obligatory to being voluntary. In several minority areas, some parts of the obligatory education later became Russian-medium and the mother tongue was only studied as a subject (if at all).

In order to be able to retain the obligatory status of the Estonian language as a medium of education and the teaching of Estonian literature in Estonian schools, the Estonian Ministry of Education prolonged the duration of secondary education in Estonian-medium "national" schools by one year, as compared to Russian-medium schools. This was a bold step to take, and there were demands to remove the then Minister, Ferdinand Eisen.

The Russification process was based on several legal documents, like Decree No 835, issued by the USSR Council of Ministers on 13 October 1978. The document prescribed a considerable enhancement of the quantity as well as the quality of Russian taught in the "national schools" at the expense of other subjects. This decree was implemented according to a secret decree of the Bureau of the Central Committee of the Estonian Communist Party, of 19 December 1978 (Protocol 105, Article 1). That document legalised the priority of Russian over Estonian, declaring Russian the only means of active participation in social life, while teachers were obliged to "teach their pupils to love the Russian language". This was followed by Decree No 3, issued by the Estonian Socialist Soviet Republic Council of Ministers on 8 January 1979, and Orders 367-k (on the teaching of Russian at Kindergartens) and 713-k (on the further improvement of Russian teaching). According to these documents, the teaching of Russian received a considerable amount of additional material support. This enabled the authorities to raise the salaries of Russian language teachers and to reduce the number of students in Russian language classes, by dividing them into parallel groups. Publications promoting Russian, such as the new Russian methods journal *"Russkij jazyk v estonskoje skole"* ("The Russian Language in Estonian Schools"), as well as propagandist writings eulogising the Russian language (as Lenin's mother tongue and a language studied with great interest by Marx and Engels), received considerable support. A new curriculum was adopted that contained additional restrictions on the use and teaching of the Estonian language, adopted by the Council of the Estonian SSR Ministry of Education on April 28, 1983. This document presented a 5-year programme for preferential teaching of the Russian language in Estonian schools. The Estonian-medium schools were required to teach Russian as a "second native language", whereas the curricula of the Russian-medium schools contained little practical Estonian and no Estonian history or geography whatsoever.

Due to the unbalanced education system, two separate linguistic communities developed whose mutual understanding was deficient both linguistically and culturally.

3.2.2 Education for Russian-speakers. The number of foreign language lessons in Russian-medium schools of the Estonian SSR was smaller than in Estonian-medium schools. Estonian language lessons in the Russian-medium schools were lesser in number than foreign language lessons, or Estonian was made so optional that the 1956 curriculum lacked it as a subject altogether and from 1965 to 1972, no Estonian was taught at the secondary level. This kind of language policy was characteristic of the Estonian SSR education system until 1988.

3.2.3 Education for (other) minority language speakers. For other linguistic groups, using one's native language in education was not allowed. Their education was mostly in Russian (or, in exceptional cases, in Estonian).

3.2.4 Teaching of foreign languages. During the years of the Soviet occupation, foreign language teaching was considered unimportant, as non-knowledge of other languages was considered a virtue. Russian was regarded as the second mother tongue of Estonians, though basic knowledge of Russian, according to the census, was 33%. The official foreign languages in the curriculum were English and German (to a minor extent). French was taught in 2-3 schools.

4. Prerequisites for present education

4.1 Current ethnolinguistic situation
According to the 1989 census, Estonia's population was 1,565,000. This included people of 121 different nationalities. The ethnic composition in 1989 is shown in Table 2.

In 1993, *citizens* of Estonia (who could belong to any ethnic group) comprised 74% of the population; 40,000 inhabitants had Russian citizenship; the

Table 2. Ethnic composition of the population of Estonia in 1989

	number	percentage of population
Estonians	963,000	61,5
Russians	475,000	30,3
Ukrainians	48,000	3,1
Belorussians	28,000	1,8
Finns	17.000	1,1
Other nationalities		2,13

proportion of other nationals was marginal. The rest of the population, ca 350.000, were non-citizens.

The naturalisation rate is ca 20 000 new Estonian citizens a year. It is expected to increase in the near future.

Nowadays ethnic Estonians account for two-thirds of the population. Of non-ethnic Estonians, 61% are first generation immigrants, ca 20% second generation immigrants and ca 15% third generation immigrants; 4% are Estonian citizens from the indigenous ethnic groups (Russians, Jews, Swedes, etc.) and are mostly bilingual.

About 18% of non-ethnic Estonians could speak Estonian in 1989. The knowledge of the language is increasing rapidly. Half the non-Estonian population is already able to speak Estonian at least at an elementary level. The main constraint hindering the process is the high status Russian still holds in their esteem.

According to the 1989 census, Russian was a language known by 922,000 people (59% of the population of Estonia). Russian is still used in several functional spheres like rail and sea transportation, communication, and the corrections system. For this reason, Russian was, and is up till now, considered by a major part of the Russian-speaking population to be the language with the highest status in Estonia, while Estonian is regarded by them as a minority language which it is of no use to learn. Fortunately, noticeable positive changes have taken place during the last few years, and the number of learners of Estonian has been increasing.

4.2 Present Estonian governmental policy

After the failure of the August 1991 coup in Moscow, and the restitution of Estonian independence after more than 50 years of occupation, the Estonian Government introduced a normalisation programme to overcome deep deformations in the social structure containing two main, isolated communities with entirely different interests. The situation for Russian-speaking immigrants was especially hard, since the status of their language fell drastically with Estonians, with "new" state borders between them and their families and relatives in Russia and other parts of the former Soviet Union, and an insecure future. The new governmental policy tries to overcome these difficulties by introducing three main principles:

1. Financial and know-how help for those wanting to repatriate (according to opinion polls, up to 15% of non-Estonians).
2. Governmental funding for activities promoting integration, e.g. Estonian language

learning (two thirds of the non-Estonian population has shown a willingness to learn Estonian).

3. Financial help for minorities in order to preserve their language and culture.

Repatriation has been significant. The main factors hindering it are Russia's indifference towards newcomers (having refugee flows from Central Asia) and the devastating economic situation in the Commonwealth of Independent States. Net migration in Estonia (+ immigration – emigration) is strongly negative: 1990: – 4000; 1991: – 8000; 1992: – 35,000; 1993: – 14,000. The annual repatriation rate is forecasted to lie between 10-20,000 during the next years. Reasons for emigration are different: one being rapid changes in the social environment and restructuration of the economy, which make maintaining the previous living standard in Estonia difficult. The other factor, noticable among Ukrainians and Belorussians, is the search for their ethnic roots and national identity. As obtaining the corresponding citizenship requires residence in the state concerned, repatriation becomes the sole option. The government as well as the international community are providing considerable funds for Estonian and minority language courses, minority language radio programmes, producing and obtaining language teaching materials, etc.

4.3 The basis for language planning and implementation: laws and administrative structures

The Estonian Language Law was passed on 18 January 1989. The Language Law was a provisional one in its content, matching the needs of the transformation process going on in Estonia. Though it described Estonian as the sole official language, due to political expediency as well as the reality of a situation in which most of the Soviet-period immigrants had not got acquainted with the Estonian culture or language, the main principle was the requirement of Estonian-Russian bilingualism. The law demanded holders of certain jobs to have a certain proficiency level in both Estonian and Russian (in most cases 800 words were sufficient). To reach the required level, a 4-year delay was introduced in the law, making the requirements effective from February 1, 1993. In order to coordinate the teaching of Estonian to Russian adults a special office was founded on 13 March 1989, namely the Estonian Language Center.

On 23 November 1990 a National Language Board was established. It is the main body responsible for implementing language planning in Estonia, for monitoring the usage of Estonian, the official language, as a native and second language of the population, but also for supporting and regulating minority language usage among the adult population.

The Board's work is based on relevant articles of the Constitution, the Language Law, the Law on Education, and the Law on Cultural Autonomy, as well as on the European Charter on Regional or Minority Languages.

Primary functions are the elaboration of language policy and language planning strategies, including the organisation, supervision, and analysis of the implementation of the Language Law, the improvement of language teaching methods, the supervision of normative terminological and onomastic work, and the pursuit of sociolinguistic studies. Thanks to positive political developments, a change has taken place in the consciousness of the Estonian people: the socio-psychological status of Estonian has risen, and its use has widened in various functional spheres. To improve corpus planning, a language panel was (re)established at the Mother Tongue Society (affiliated with the Estonian Academy of Sciences) in 1993. It was given a wider function in the normalising of the language corpus.

4.4 The two "linguistic filters"

4.4.1 *Competence in Estonian required for employment.* Nowadays, there are two linguistic filters on the path towards integration into Estonian society: one when obtaining citizenship, the other one for employment. For the latter, the official guidelines for implementing the Language Act, issued in 1989, establish six categories of language abilities, from A to F. Category A requires a language proficiency corresponding to basic listening comprehension of 800 of the most common words and expressions. B requires both listening comprehension and oral production, based on the 800 words, and C also requires reading comprehension and a basic, limited competence in written production. D is based on a more advanced lexicon of 1500 words, with both receptive and productive oral and (basic) written skills. Category E corresponds to an ability to use the language of one's own profession, both orally and in written form, at a level which corresponds to the use of a vocabulary of some 2500 words. Category F is defined as full proficiency in the language. The guidelines prescribe in great detail for which jobs a knowledge of Estonian is necessary. Level C is prescribed for most retail sales and service jobs, levels D or E for persons in top-management positions. Fluent knowledge of Estonian is expected from the President, members of the Government, Ombudsman, judges, psychiatrists and a few other professionals.

4.4.2 *Competence in Estonian required for citizenship.* According to the Law on Estonian Language Requirements for Citizenship Applicants (adopted in 1993), one must have a basic listening comprehension in Estonian, be able to hold a conversation on everyday topics, read and provide a short summary of news and reports; be able to complete simple written exercises, such as filling out personal applications, compose a curriculum vitae, writing an address on an envelope, writing an application for study or employment, writing a letter of authorisation and filling out standard forms. It also provides special examination guidelines for persons born before January 1, 1930, and disabled persons. Both groups are exempted from the written test and are expected to show only the basic oral proficiency in Estonian (with the exception of the deaf who take a written test).

5. Present language teaching

5.1 Education for Russian speakers

Today, Estonia's most acute language problem is connected with the approximately 300,000 residents of the country, who do not know any Estonian. To solve the problem, a special adult language learning network has been established by the state and is run by the local government. It consists of 24 language centres which provide Estonian language lessons, consultations and assessments of language skills. They also organise and administer language examinations for citizenship and employment. Most of their costs are covered by the state. Also other countries provide financial support.

In addition to these centres, numerous privately-owned language centres are in operation, providing a wide range of various language learning options.

Changes are taking place in the numbers of pupils in schools. In the 1992/1993 school year, there were (in addition to 553 Estonian-medium schools) 108 Russian-medium schools and 28 mixed schools. Currently, there are 70,000 pupils in Russian-medium schools, a figure which decreases by 4-5% every year. The main reason for this drop is the repatriation connected with withdrawing Russian troops by September 1994, consequently resulting in a shortage of pupils. Due to this, several Russian schools near the Russian military bases have been closed. The second, highly visible reason is Russian parents' desire to place their children in Estonian Kindergartens and schools in order to immerse them in the language in a natural way. This has resulted in a lower proficiency level in Estonian as well as in other disciplines for all pupils. To avoid these negative effects, the number of Russians in the Estonian-medium educational institutions has been limited. Simultaneously alternative programs for Russian children are being started.

The most challenging areas in Estonia are migrant towns which were closed for Estonians previously and where Russian only is used. In these areas, Estonian language learning stimuli are scarce and the number of teachers insufficient. For example, in the border town of Narva, where the Russian speaking population makes up 95%, 5 out of the 79 teachers of Estonian have had their training through correspondence courses, and 28 of the posts are vacant. This can partly be explained by highly hostile policies of past municipal governments, effectively blocking any initiatives to introduce Estonian in the schools of Narva. Similar situations may be observed in the town of Sillamäe (96% Russian speakers), and in Paldiski, with 98% Russian speakers. These situations are in sharp contrast to those of core Russian minority areas like the town of Mustvee (56% Russian), or Kallaste (88% Russian) on the shore of Lake Peipsi. The populations here are overwhelmingly bilingual and there is no basis for ethnic or linguistic conflicts.

The Law on Basic and Secondary Schools, approved in September 1993, forecasts the transfer to Estonian-medium instruction in all state and municipal secondary schools by the year 2000 or, alternatively, students must enroll in minority schools. Education in Russian minority secondary schools continues to be offered in the native language. Russian-medium basic schools must give their students sufficient knowledge of Estonian to continue their studies in Estonian, if they so choose.

The curriculum envisages 3 Estonian language lessons per week, beginning in the 3rd grade. Starting in 1996, Estonian will already be taught from the 1st grade onwards. Some Russian-medium schools use Estonian as a medium for teaching certain subjects (history, geography), as in partial immersion.

Nevertheless, the general level of Estonian teaching is unsatisfactory. Of all Russian-medium secondary school graduates, only 1/6 were able to pass the language exam for citizenship, requiring basic knowledge of Estonian. Moreover, there are still schools where Estonian is not taught. The monitoring and expert aid from the Ministry of Education is not apparent. No tests are carried out to evaluate success nor proposals for improvement drawn up. One of the reasons is definitely the number and quality of teachers.

Due to the Soviet-time bans and limits on educating teachers of Estonian as a Second Language (the first 25 teachers graduated in 1990!), the teacher shortage is still felt and the competence of those now working is sometimes unsatisfactory. In order to support them, a new generation of Estonian language teaching materials has been produced, including language videos for children and adults.

5.2 Education for (other) minority language speakers

The Law on Cultural Autonomy for Ethnic Minorities, approved in 1993, grants all minority groups the right to establish private (but state-financed) schools, including secondary schools in which a minority's own language serves as the language of instruction and where additional instruction in their cultural heritage is provided.

Today there are 2 non-Russian, full-scale minority language schools (Swedish and Jewish) in Estonia. Belorussians, Finns, Ukrainians and Armenians have some primary school classes where their languages are used as media of education. In addition to these, several ethnic minority groups arrange lessons in their native language and culture in the form of Sunday schools, as a first step towards opening schools in their native languages. The main constraint with regard to using the right to establish minority schools, the dissociation from the minority's native culture, can thus be overcome by "artificially" creating native language environments.

As ethnic Russians account for three-quarters of the population of non-Estonian ethnicity, schools with Russian-medium instruction may still face the additional task of integrating other language speakers (like Belorussians, Tatars and Ukrainians) into the Estonian-speaking society. Thus, in several cases, Russian-medium schools offer optional lessons in other minority languages for the purpose of accomodating these groups.

5.3 Teaching of foreign languages

In 1992, a new foreign language curriculum was adopted in Estonian schools, taking into account the pattern of needs for languages in society. The new curriculum is being introduced step by step, according to the availability of teachers and language teaching materials. The current foreign language teaching policy in education foresees two obligatory foreign languages (and a third optional one to be learned in the humanities stream at the secondary level). The main foreign languages from which 2 compulsory languages are chosen are English, Russian, German and French. English is rapidly gaining popularity nowadays, at the cost of Russian, with Russian and German sharing a second place. Other languages learned in state schools are Finnish, Swedish, Classical Greek, Latin, Spanish, Italian, Esperanto and Japanese.

6. Various multilingual teaching options in the Estonian context

In Estonia, there is an apparent need for multilingual teaching policies. The transformation process has been started, even though the theoretical foundations are vague. In Estonia, several specific characteristics must be taken into account.

Firstly, the proposed solutions must cover the whole society, not only some part of it. It presupposes a variety of models, as appropriate for the region as well as the age and linguistic or social status of the target group concerned. As the population is linguistically very heterogeneous, the main task is to ensure the effortless functioning of the Estonian language. Due to the small number of inhabitants, effective foreign language teaching is a high priority as well.

Minority language maintenance should be achieved by using the cultural resources of the minority itself and with the state providing financial aid for education. Educational planning must take into account the different language histories and present sociolinguistic situations of the three groups mentioned: Estonians, Russians and (other) minorities.

The Estonian-speakers, who have earlier been treated as a minority, with transitional bilingual education which they have tried to resist, need language shelter types of programmes (i.e. Estonian-medium education, with good foreign language teaching), at least until they become a secure majority population. This is especially important in the Russian monolingual areas with a marginal Estonian community.

The Russian-speakers, who earlier had a typical monolingual mainstream majority type education, with very little if any second or foreign language teaching, now need to become the real minority that they in fact are. As long as they feel like a majority (partly also because their language is very strong internationally, in terms of numbers and in terms of being spoken by many non-Russians), Estonian-medium immersion programmes might be suitable for them. When the Russian-speakers become a "real" minority later on, immersion should be replaced by language shelter programmes, with good teaching of Estonian as a second language, provided by bilingual teachers.

To smooth out ethnic stereotypes and support positive cross-cultural attitudes, joint educational systems are of vital importance. Russian and Estonian speakers could be in two-way dual language programmes (two-way bilingual immersion programmes) together, with Estonian as the main medium of education, with good mother-tongue teaching for the Russian-speaking children throughout the school, and, maybe, a transition to more Russian-medium instruction for Russian-speakers in secondary school.[1]

A European School model could also be an option. In the case of Tallinn, the Estonian capital, a European School model might be functional. During the last few years, Tallinn, with a population which is 2/3 Estonian and 1/3 other ethnicities, has become considerably more international, (an international school has even been opened). The multilingual education provided by European Schools has several markers that fit the local conditions. The languages of instruction should be the ones used by the larger communities in Tallinn: Estonian, Russian, English, German and the neighbouring language Finnish.

The third group, namely the minorities who have experienced the worst educational conditions, with little or no mother tongue support, must be provided with know-how and enough financial support to enable them to start their own minority schools where the main emphasis will be on language maintenance and Estonian as a second language.

Notes:

1   Editor's remark: Later on, when native Estonian-speakers have a secure linguistic majority situation, one might also envisage a programme where both Estonian and Russian speakers, after having studied both each other's languages and a common foreign language as subjects for some years, together participate in a partial or late immersion programme through the medium of that common language, foreign to both groups, e.g. French or German. Trilingual education of this kind does not seem to be harmful to minorities, as experience from Canada shows.

8

MULTILINGUALISM FOR ALL – RUSSIANS?

Alexei A. Leontiev

Introduction: the need for Russians to become multilingual

If *España* with its four languages is *plurilingüe* (Siguan 1992), Russia with officially 123 ethnoses, almost all of them with their own languages, is almost unimaginable. And there are more than 123 languages in Russia. We do not know in any definite way how many there are. I have myself listed 163 languages (compare this with the official number of 130) in my latest book (Leontiev, in press). Many of them are spoken mostly only on the territory of Russia.

According to the official census data from 1989, there are some 120 million Russians in the Russian Federation. Only 726,450 (0,637%) of them know another language of the former USSR. 11,802,537 Russians live in formerly autonomous Republics, now mostly called "Republics" or Soviet Socialist Republics. Only 84,427 (0,7153%!) of them fluently speak the official language of the Republic where they live[1]. This should be compared to the number of Bashkirs, Buryats, etc who speak Russian fluently. We can compare this by looking at the data on the second language proficiency of the other "majorities": native speakers of languages of the "title nations", e.g. the Chuvash in the Chuvashian Republic or the Yakuts in Saha-Yakutia. The total number of native speakers of "title nations"' languages is 9,708,632. Of these, 7,766,761, i.e. 79,99%, speak Russian fluently.

This makes it clear why so many Russians are leaving the new national Republics which are a part of the Russian Federation. Because of their monolingualism, they are excluded from the cultural life of the state. They cannot even understand the media or official documents, unless Russian is the second official language of the new state.

Many of them do not want to learn a "new" language; they have no real experience of being bilingual or multilingual, as for instance citizens of Switzerland have. Psychologically, they have no other choice except to return to the Russian regions of Russia: only this opens the lost possibilities to them.

But in these regions of Russia they are alien too. They can hardly find a place for themselves in Russian society, and finding work is difficult unless they are peasants.

On the other hand, there are many highly qualified specialists among the Russian-speakers of the Republics. The industrial potential of the new Republics depends to a large extent on these specialists. If they leave the country, industry will diminish if not crash completely. So the Republics are not interested in having the Russians emigrate.

But the Russian regions also have no interest in Russians emigrating from the new Republics! The number of technical specialists and highly qualified workers in Russia is already more than Russia needs. There are also enough workers with low formal qualifications.

Accordingly, both sides would be happy if the Russian population of the Republics became an integral part of the multinational societies where they reside, and if most of them did not leave the Republics.

How can their emigration be prevented. Let us not discuss here the factors connected with economics or domestic policies. It is clear that the Russian-speaking populations must not become second class citizens – there are some such tendencies in some Republics now. Russians must be able to feel themselves full-scale citizens of the new Republics.

In order for this to be possible, a special educational language policy is needed for the adults and for the children. If the Yakut Republic is interested in Russians in the Republic learning the Yakut language, the state has to elaborate sets of teaching materials, manuals, dictionaries etc. It must create language schools and other institutions. The television in Yakutia has to send Yakut language lessons for Russians, etc.

There are very few materials of this kind. There are some books in Tatar, Finnish, Mari etc for Russians, but even these are difficult to buy. The language schools do not yet exist at all in practice.

The schools play a central role in this educational language policy. If only a small number of Russians now know the official language of the Republic in which they live, the only reasonable place which can change the situation within the next decade is the schools. The languages of the different Republics must have a reasonable place in the school curricula of all schools in the Republics.

It is with these background facts in mind that I now proceed to analysing the question of multilingualism for all. Is it possible for Russians, and how?

Missing data

Without having full and correct data on the present linguistic situation, it seems impossible to elaborate on any conceptions or hypotheses concerning educational language policy in Russia or the Republics. The information available to Western readers on the present linguistic situation in Russia is definitely insufficient if not incorrect.

First of all, even the best works on the problem do not reflect the real troubles and the real diversity of languages and their functions or language contacts, with the notable exception of the three-volume book by Harald Haarmann (1979-1984). The book by E.Glyn Lewis (1972), based on Soviet sources, does not take into consideration a number of languages of numerically smaller ethnoses and ethnic groups. The article "Redéfinition du statut des langues en Union Soviétique" (1992) by Jacques Maurais does not describe one of the most interesting language laws, the one of the Russian Federation, nor any of the new documents on the status and functions of minor languages of Russia. Even the latest census data (1989) have not been analysed in any fundamental way so far. Secondly, it is almost impossible for anybody outside Russia to evaluate the reliability of statistical and other data on languages published in Russia and other newly independent countries. If we, for instance, are told that only half of the Russian Germans speak their mother tongue, it has to be added that the other tongue for most of them is not literary German (*Hochdeutsch*) but a dialect or mixture of dialects, and that practically all "Germans" emigrating from Russia to Germany need special German language courses. Data from earlier censuses have to be corrected because many people (Talyshes, Crimean Tatars, etc) have not given their real mother tongue but have – of course under psychological if not legal pressure – presented themselves as members of the relevant "great" ethnoses, here e.g. Azerbaydzanis and Uzbeks.

Thirdly, the situation changes practically every month, if not every week; therefore e.g. Haarmann's book has more historical than actual interest.

This is why we begin with a brief description of the linguistic situation in contemporary Russia, and how it is reflected in Russian legislation.

Languages

Description of the Russian sociolinguistic situation

The languages of Russia can be divided into the following groups:

a. *The official language of the Russian Federation* (RF): Russian.

b. *Official languages of the Republics* which are part of the RF, e.g. Bashkir, Buryat, Kabardinian. In some Republics Russian is a second official language of the Republic. A very unusual case is that of Altai Republic: the official language is Russian, and there are two "working languages: Altai and... English. It is important to note that many of these languages have spread to other regions too. Many Tatars, for instance, live outside Tataria, in different units which do not have any autonomous administrative status.

c. *Languages of inter-ethnic communication.* In some publications, even professional ones, only Russian is erroneously called a "language of inter-ethnic communication". In practice, there are some 20 such languages in the Russian Federation. Here I am only thinking of languages which have additional social functions, in addition to functioning as normal, "common" mother tongues ("common" languages). But other kinds of target languages for inter-ethnic communication also exist: "contact" languages, typical for communities living in frontier zones. For instance in Daghestan, a small, multilingual Republic in the northeastern part of the Caucasus, there are 4 common languages (Russian, Azerbaydzanian, Avar and Kumyk) and no less than 7 contact languages (Lak, Dargin, Lezgin, Tabasaran, Tsakhur, Chechen and Georgian). These cannot be ignored when we try to define educational policy.

d. *Languages of peoples who have no local, administrative autonomy* – they only have cultural autonomy, most importantly expressed by the fact that their language has been reduced to writing. Some languages from this group are Vepsi (the language of a small Finno-Ugric ethnos near St.Petersburg), Itelmen in Kamtchatka and Ket in the centre of Siberia.

e. *Languages without literacy.* Some interethnic language (e.g. Russian, Avar, Tatar) serves as the group's language of literacy. This is of course possible only when practically all members of the group are bilingual. Some examples are Akhvakh (Daghestan), Kerek (Chukotka) and Ulchi (Far East of the RF).

f. *Languages spoken mostly in other Republics of the former USSR.* In Russia there is e.g. a small group of Turkmens ("Trukhmen") in the Stavropol region, many Armenians in the Rostov region, not to speak of Ukrainians and Belorussians. Some of these languages are "frontier languages": Abkhaz in the Sochi region near Abkhazia, Kazakh in the Astrakhan region.

g. *Languages spoken mostly in other countries.* These differ from the languages under f.)

above, not politically but in practise: ethnic groups speaking these languages have fewer relations with the corresponding countries. Often they use a dialect of their own which does not coincide with the standard language. The Germans in Russia have been mentioned. Another interesting example is the Greeks. One part of the Greeks in Russia who live in Caucasus call themselves "Rumei" or "Pontiytsy" and their Greek dialect the Pontian language. There is no H(igh) variety.

h. *Diaspora languages*, spread in different countries. One example is the Roma (in reality no Roma language exists, there are only different Roma dialects). Another example is Yiddish (one of the languages of the European Jews; the official language of Israel is Ivrit, not Yiddish). Formally Jews have their autonomy in the Far East of Russia (the Jewish autonomous region with Birobidjan as its centre), but of its 190,000 inhabitants only 10,000 are ethnic Jews and only 14% of them speak Yiddish as their mother tongue. The third example are the Assyrians.

Present tendencies in the development of languages and their status

Next I will supplement this very brief survey of the sociolinguistic status of the different languages of the Russian Federation with a description of the most important present tendencies, as I see them.

By analysing census data, we can see groups of languages developing in opposite directions. Some languages are *decreasing*: most speakers are beginning to be bilingual, and the revival of the national culture seems a bit artificial. This is true for the Vod' near St.Petersburg, the Kamasin in Siberia (in the 1980s', only one woman spoke the Kamasin language), and the Kerek in Chukotka. Several languages from this group are taught in elementary schools, e.g. Nivkh and Aleut in the Far East of Russia, but most persons who call themselves Nivkh or Aleut no longer speak these languages as their mother tongues (77 and 66 per cent, respectively); if they do, they also speak Russian fluently as their second language (78 and 80 percent, respectively, of those who speak Nivkh or Aleut as their mother tongues).

Another group consists of languages where the number of speakers is on the *increase*. The number of social functions for these languages is widening and the number of bilingual persons is either stable or is diminishing.

Another tendency could be called the *autonomization of dialects*. It can be seen e.g. with the Altai language, where Teleut and Kumandin, usually treated as dialects, have started to be called separate languages (and their speakers consider their communities to be separate nationalities [or ethnic groups]). Dolgan was, in the 1920s and 1930s described as a dialect of Yakut. Now practically everybody thinks of it as an independent language.

But at the same time, an opposite tendency also exists: a *consolidation of different*

dialects, even of genetically related small languages, *around the "main" language.*
This is, for example, the situation of the Tatar language, of Avar, etc.

The last tendency is connected with the current political situation and it could
be called the *internationalization of the sociolinguistic situation.* An example would
be the plan to teach Finnish in the schools of Fenno-Ugric Republics, e.g. Komi
or Udmurtia. In another case, Korean dialects in Russia are beginning to model
themselves after the standard language of the Republic of Korea. A third
example is that of different Turkic Republics discussing the possibility of a
latinization or even Arabization of the present Cyrillic alphabet (see also
Rannut & Rannut, in this volume).

Laws

The first two documents, on Declaration and one Law, containing modern and
reasonable positions towards linguistic human rights were adopted by the
Supreme Soviet of the USSR in October 1991. The history of problems in the
USSR ends in September 1991 when the "Declaration of Human Rights and
Freedoms" was adopted by the USSR peoples' Deputies Congress (Declaration
1991). The Declaration is extremely brief (only one page), but contains very
important thoughts. The most important aspect is that real guarantees are
given: "Every person is guaranteed the right to use the mother tongue, to have
education through the medium of the mother tongue, and the protection and
growth of the national culture...". This position contrasts sharply with some
recent documents of European origin which contain absolutely empty
formulations like "everyone has the right of expression in any language" (from
FIPLV, 1993). The formulations in this "Declaration of Human Rights and
Freedoms" are developed in detail in Russian language legislation.

The second, the all-union Law "On Languages of the Peoples of the Russian
Federation" is, in my opinion, one of the most brilliant documents of this kind
in the contemporary world. Having participated in its drafting as an official
expert, I consider it to be on a par with international requirements, though it
contains a lot of undefined expressions with several possible interpretations.
What is meant, for instance, by "the language of the Republic"? Why is it
equated with "the language of the people"? Even key notions such as
"languages of the peoples of the USSR" were not defined.[2] In any case, this law
is not presently in force.

I will summarize the main ideas of these two documents. One of the important
breakthroughs in the preamble of the first document, the Declaration, is

"acknowledging the linguistic sovereignty of every people and every person irrespective of parentage, social or financial status ..." etc. The Declaration also declares

> "The right of everybody to free choice of the language of instruction, the language of education, the language of intellectual creativity;
> the right of everybody to free choice of the language of communication;
> equal possibilities for the maintenance, study and development of all languages of the peoples of the Russian Federation;
> equal social, economic and juridical defence of all languages of the peoples of the Russian Federation by the State;
> special care and attention by the State towards the languages of minorities and of peoples who do not have their own national states or national administrative territories;
> the desirability and necessity of (mutual) mastering of the languages of interethnic communication and of the languages of other peoples of the Russian Federation inhabiting the same territory."

Let me fully quote the last paragraph, too:

> "The Supreme Soviet of the Russian Federation calls on the citizens of Russia to contribute to the fostering of a respectful and careful treatment of the languages of all the peoples of our motherland, to develop the culture of language communication in every possible way, to protect the purity of the mother tongue. The importance of language for the historical destiny of every ethnos defines it as a unique phenomenon of the culture common to all humankind."

Even the style of this document is quite alien to previous Soviet legislation and reminds one much more of international United Nations or European documents. A European will probably not find anything new in the text.[3] But for us Russians, this Declaration opens a new age. For instance, the idea of the linguistic sovereignty of the person, though it stands in second place after the sovereignty of the nation, is extremely important. It contradicts not only the practise of Soviet language policy, but also recent tendencies in public opinions held by some ethnoses and national states in the Federation. An example was a recent, sharp discussion during an educational conference in Moscow. The topic was the possibility of opening Tatar schools in Moscow. The position of the Tatar Cultural Society was: "Give us a list of the addresses of all the Tatar families in Moscow and we will force them (!) to send their children to the Tatar school." Here one can see very clearly the priority of the ethnos in comparison to the rights of the person. There were similar discussions during an International Seminar on Linguistic Human Rights in Tallinn, Estonia, in November 1991.

It is also interesting that the State practically considers it as its duty to defend all languages socially, economically and juridically. The idea of the "desirability" and "necessity" of mastering languages other than the mother tongue (including the languages of interethnic communication in the same territorium), seems very progressive. This is, of course, made optional. But even mentioning languages of interethnic communication, and not only official languages, is a great advantage over previous legislation.

For the first time, problems of languages *and* culture are seen to be issues at the state level. And I like the formulation about the interdependence between *ethnic languages* and *the culture of all humankind*.

The key notion in the second document, the Law, is the "linguistic sovereignty" (paragraph 2), seen as the totality of linguistic rights, belonging to both peoples and persons, a sovereignty that the State has to *guarantee* to both.

Naturally, *all* languages in Russia have equal rights and *all* languages enjoy State support.[4]

Paragraph 3.4 guarantees the possibility of using the language of any people without territorial autonomy (or languages mostly spoken in other countries, group g above), in official functions. If this were to be applied in practice in contemporary western Europe, it would mean the right of Turks in Germany or Slovenians in Italy to use their languages for official functions.

Paragraph 4 has hardly any Western analogies and is extremely important. The State has the duty to defend all languages socially, economically and juridically. The *social* defence of all languages is about a scientifically based language policy directed towards the maintenance, study and development of *all* languages spoken by the peoples of the Russian Federation. Secondly, the *economic* defence is the purposeful financial support of the state's own programmes and of research programmes for the maintenance and development of these languages, and – last but not least – the application of a preferential fiscal policy towards them. Thirdly, the *juridical* defence bears on the responsibility of the state to prosecute violations of the relevant legislation.

Paragraph 5 guarantees the enactment of fundamental political, economic, social and cultural rights to all citizens of the Russian Federation, irrespective of their knowledge of any specific language. Such knowledge, or its absence, must not be the reason for any restriction of the linguistic (or other) rights of citizens.

As far as I know, this is the first official Russian document which mentions the notion of "linguistic rights". These rights include the right of free choice of the language of communication (para. 8) and of instruction and education (para. 9). The State ensures the right to learn, and the teaching of, every mother tongue and other languages of the peoples of Russia. Every people whose language has not been reduced to literacy has the right to create this literacy for its mother tongue, and this must be supported by the State (para 10).

Further paragraphs regulate the official use of languages and their functioning in mass communication, industry, business, etc. The all-Russian newspapers are, for instance, to be published not only in Russian but also in other languages (here not only in the languages of the peoples of the Russian Federation [para. 20]). In practice, all-Russian newspapers exist in German, Yiddish and English.

The last paragraph (28) states that any violation of the legislation on languages must be punished.

Let us also note that para. 15.6. introduces the notion of "linguistic qualification requirements".

The enactment of the Law is regulated by a special order of the Supreme Soviet, undersigned by Ruslan Khazbulatov. It mandates the creation of a special institution, the Institute of Languages of the Peoples of the Russian Federation, whose principal aim it is to elaborate and implement the State Programme for the maintenance and development of these languages. It has recently been established at the State Committee of National Policy of the Russian Federation, with Prof. Vladimir P. Neroznak as its head. The State Programme has been written, mandated by an order signed by Egor Gaidar.

A special document, a Statute on linguistic qualification requirements, has likewise been elaborated. In its two appendices it establishes a system of levels of linguistic proficiency which are coordinated with levels adopted by the experts of the Council of Europe (e.g. van Ek and Trim 1991). A modified Russian version of the Threshold levels will be applied to the teaching of Russian as a foreign language. A Russian State Service for interpretation and translation is likewise supposed to be created. But all these documents are, so far (August 1994), unofficial.

Education

The present situation

In May 1992, the Council of Experts on Language Policy in the Educational Institutions of the Russian Federation was established at the Russian Ministry of Education. The Law of the Russian Federation "On Education" was adopted by the Supreme Soviet in July 1992. Its special paragraph on "Languages of instruction" grants citizens of the Russian Federation the right to have a basic general education in their mother tongue or another language of instruction, i.e. they can choose the language of instruction among the possibilities offered by the educational system. This right has been guaranteed by establishing special educational institutions. Every concrete institution determines its language of instruction. The State supports the members of ethnic diasporas (e.g. Russians and other people from Russia who live abroad) in getting basic education in their mother tongue.

In the autumn of 1991, I published a small working document, with no official status, called *A Conception of the Language Policy Applied to the Schools of the Russian Federation*.[5] Some of its ideas will be discussed below. But first I will give a short summary of the present educational situation.

Of the more than 120 languages of Russia, about half are used in some capacity in education, e.g. 66 languages in 1991. Only Russian is used in higher education.[6] Of the languages used as *media of instruction*, only Bashkir, Georgian, Russian and Tatar are used in all forms, from the 1st to the 11th. Yakut is used in forms 1-9, Estonian, Kazakh and Tuvinian are used in forms 1-7. All other languages which function as media of instruction are used only in elementary school, forms 1-4: Altaic, Avar, Azerbaydzanian, Buryat, Chuvashian, Dargin, Kalmyk, Kumyk, Lakian, Lezgin, Mari, Mordovian, Nogai, Ossetinian and Tabarasan.

The following languages are taught as *subjects* from the 1st to the 11th forms: Abazin, Adyghean, Altaic, Avar, Azerbaydzanian, Balkarian, Bashkir, Buryat, Chechenian, Chuvashian, Dargin, Estonian, Finnish, Georgian, German, Kabardian, Kalmyk, Kazakh, Khakassian, Komi-Zyryan, Kumyk, Lakian, Lezgin, Mari[7], Mordovian[8], Nogai, Ossetinian, Russian, Tabarasan, Tatar, Turkmen, Tuvinian, Udmurtian and Yakut.

The following languages are taught as *subjects* in forms 1-7 or 1-8: Chukotian, Evenkian, Komi-Permyak and Nenets.

The following languages are only taught as *subjects* in elementary school, forms 1-4: Armenian, Dolgan, Eskimo, Evenian, (modern) Greek, Ingush, Itelmen, Karelian, Ket, Khanty, Korean, Koryak, Lithuanian, Mansi, Nanai, Nivkh, Sámi, Selkupian, Shorian, Crimean Tatar, Tatian, Tofalarian, Udegeyan, Vepsi, Yiddish, and Yukagirian.

All these languages can be divided into two groups, though. One consists of languages which are taught in schools *practically* (i.e. not only symbolically, more than 1,000 students in the Federation are studying them), e.g. Abazin,

Avar, Chukotian, Evenian etc.

The other group includes languages taught only *symbolically* (fewer than 200 students in the whole Federation). These include Estonian, Itelmen, Ket, Lithuanian, Sámi, Shorian, Crimean Tatar, Tatian, Tofalarian, Turkmen, Yiddish[9], and Yukagirian.

Some languages fall between these two groups, e.g. Eskimo, Georgian, Karelian, Khanty, Korean, Koryak, Mansi, Nanai and Nivkh.

Unfortunately, viewing these languages in historical perspective shows that the number of languages used in education has decreased. In 1934, there were 104 languages used as media for instruction in the USSR; in 1988-89, only 44. In 1926, there were 14 languages of instruction in Uzbekistan; in 1961, only 5. In 1927-28, there were 32 languages of instruction in Russia; now 23. Development was not only determined by the conscious process of Russification, but much more by the quite insufficient quality in teaching "national" languages, as compared with Russian, and, in general, by the poor quality of education in "national" schools.[10] In order to learn to speak Russian fluently, and become really well educated, one was supposed to go to a Russian medium school – and many people did so...

There are now approximately 58,000 monolingual Russian medium schools, where Russian is taught in mother tongue language arts lessons. There are 4,300 "bilingual schools", schools with Russian as the medium of education but with another language taught as the mother tongue. There are also some 1,500 "mixed" schools with a multiethnic population and different mother tongues as subjects, but also with Russian as the medium of instruction. Finally, there are 6,200 monolingual schools with other languages as media of instruction and Russian taught as a subject (Russian as a second language).

Problems encountered in the planning process

As can be seen from the description above, the linguistic and linguodidactic situation in the Russian Federation seems to be more complicated than is the case in any other European country. It could make the Russian Federation a kind of practical model for sociolinguistic problems presently growing in every country or region of Europe. Most problems encountered in Russia can also be found in the rest of Europe, either in the history of educational language policy and language teaching, or in contemporary language teaching practice. I will mention some of our problems, before finally relating the situation to the European Schools model and general principles.

Our main problem in educational language policy planning has two sides. On the one hand, it has to do with the *"linguistic ignorance" of ethnic Russians*, as discussed in the introduction to this article. This ignorance is not only typical of Russians living in national Republics – it is, regrettably, typical of the Russian ethnos in general. If we can speak of any kind of general "Russian mentality", it definitely includes what Tove Skutnabb-Kangas (e.g. 1990, in press) has named "monolingual stupidity" or "monolingual naivety/reductionism".

It is, of course, not a recent phenomenon with the Russians. It is connected with many factors related to the Soviet period in Russian history. A large percentage of those Russians who were multilingual were part of the White Army (and emigrated or were killed) or the "old intelligentia" (and perished during the 1930s), or they belonged to the "third wave" of emigration. The new generation of the intelligentia never went abroad, never met foreigners, and had no real need (or opportunity) to read foreign books. Such reading was sometimes even dangerous, for instance in the late 1940s, when reading something in foreign – i.e. not national or second – languages was enough to lead to accusations and imprisonment. Conversely, learning and speaking certain national languages sometimes also meant being labelled a "bourgeois nationalist"...

On the other hand, the educational language policy in the USSR which began by proclaiming a completely free choice as to language of instruction and creating a literary language for some dozens of minor languages (in the 1920s and still in the early 1930s), was fairly soon changed so that the number of languages in educational practice was reduced to fairly small numbers. As mentioned above, it was not a result of some conscious "Russification" policy, though there are many examples of attempts to exclude non-Russian languages from the school system, mostly at local levels. Rather, the language policy was to make Russian a "second mother tongue" for everybody – a senseless idea which allowed Russian to become the dominating language in all the schools of the USSR. Under those circumstances, it seems quite "natural" that most non-Russian and half-Russian families allowed their children to have Russian as the language of instruction in school, because they were aware of the restricted social functions of "minor languages". Moreover, Russian was the language of instruction in secondary and tertiary education. Many more text books and manuals of Russian (for non-Russians) than of other languages (for Russians) were published. Most teachers of non-Russian languages had either no professional training as language teachers, or were badly trained. Finally, Russian was presented ideologically as the main language of the whole country. It became more prestigious both to be Russian and to speak Russian than to be, for instance, Chuvash and to speak the Chuvash language.

All these factors led to a decrease in the number of people studying the non-Russian languages of Russia, either as mother tongues or as national, second or foreign languages. It also led to the "monolingual stupidity" of Russians, not only on the national level but also in the purely Russian regions. Why on earth should I learn any of the USSR's other languages if I am Russian, and most people surrounding me are Russian, too, or at least speak Russian? *My* language – Russian – is "great, potent, truthful and free" (according to Turgenev), and "it is impossible that such a language was not given to a great nation" (Turgenev). A person who feels he belongs to a great nation must definitely be happy...

To conclude: Planning future educational language policy

We badly need a reasonable linguistic policy in education. Step by step, one is presently being elaborated by experts in collaboration with the Russian Ministry of Education officials. Let me summarize main principles of such a policy, as I see them (see also Leontiev 1994).

1. The authorities must guarantee the teaching of
     a. all mother tongues used in the relevant region;
     b. the official language(s) of the Republic;
     c. Russian as the official language of the Russian Federation;
     d. the most widely used languages of interethnic communication in the region;
     e. at least one foreign language.
2. Nobody should force students to be educated through the medium of a particular language.
3. Besides "linguistic rights", individuals must have "linguistic duties".
4. The mother tongue must be a compulsory subject in school. Of course the *choice* of mother tongue is a personal matter.
5. The second compulsory language to be taught is an official language of the Russian Federation, or the particular Republic, or a language of interethnic communication. Naturally, a language of interethnic communication is only compulsory if it becomes the language of instruction, after some years of teaching through the medium of the mother tongue. An example of this would be a Nogai student receiving Nogai-medium instruction in the first 4 forms, and Tatar-medium instruction from form 5 onwards.
6. The third compulsory language is a foreign language.
7. In any case, the number of languages *offered* the student must be higher than the number of languages a student is obliged to choose.

8. The student is obliged to learn only *one* language in addition to her/his mother tongue and a foreign language. If more than three compulsory languages are taught in school, the student must choose which ones are compulsory for her and which (if any) she wants to study as optional. In a "Russian" school in the Yakut Republic, for instance, Russian as the mother tongue, Yakut as the official language, and one foreign language must be taught. For Yukagirs in the same Republic, Yukagir must be taught as the mother tongue, and a foreign language must be taught, but the student must choose between Yakut (as the official language of the Republic) or Russian (as the official language of the Federation) as compulsory subjects. Of course the student can still take the other one as an optional subject if s/he so chooses.

9. A principle of parity must be established: the total number of school hours dedicated to compulsory mother tongue instruction must be identical for all students, regardless of which mother tongue they study. Likewise, the number of hours spent studying obligatory second languages and foreign languages, respectively, must be identical, regardless of which specific language is being studied.

Tove Skutnabb-Kangas is definitely right when she claims that monolingualism as a social construction is unmodern, underdeveloped and primitive; that it is an illness which should be eradicated as soon as possible; that it is even dangerous for world peace (1988). This is all true, and we in the former USSR have some experience supporting these thoughts. But I cannot imagine how monolingualism can be eradicated in purely Russian-speaking areas of Russia. To be honest, the only way to do this would be what I have sketched above, to introduce not only a foreign language, but also a non-Russian language of Russia (or of a country which formerly belonged to the USSR), such as Georgian, Armenian, Ukrainian, into Russian schools, as compulsory subjects. Of course, the students and their parents should be free to choose which language to study. Regrettably, this seems unrealistic at the present time.

Perhaps the most realistic step we can take to overcome Russia's present "monolingual stupidity" is to improve the quality of teaching foreign languages – they are badly taught in most schools in Russia right now.

Multilingualism for all Russians? Definitely it would be good. But in Russian-speaking regions, we must begin with bilingualism based on Russian and a foreign language, not with Russian and a second language – yet.

Notes:

1 We disregard here the non-Russian populations in these republics, groups like Tatars, Mari and Ukrainians in Bashkortostan, Kazakhs, Belorussians or Germans in Kalmykia, or Armenians in Adygea, who give Russian as their mother tongue (about half of them) or who speak it fluently.

2 Are, for instance, Greek or Hungarian "languages of the peoples of the USSR"? Definitely they are, or were. Naturally, Greeks and Hungarians are not aborigines of the USSR if we neglect the Ugric origin of the Hungarians. But is it important for their legal status? No.

3 Editor's remark: Alexei Leontiev's appreciation of "European" (i.e. Western European) language policies seems to be a bit rosy...

4 In practice, the State does not have enough money to realize this principle.

5 For a summary of the main content, see Leontiev 1994.

6 This situation (1994) may have changed when this article reaches the readers.

7 In the two literary languages of Mari.

8 In the two literary languages of Mordva.

9 The situation for Yiddish is rapidly changing, but the new data are not yet available in June 1994.

10 Since 1988, the term "national schools" is no longer used, at least not officially, in Russia. The former Institute of National School Studies under the supervision of the Russian Ministry of Education has changed its name into "Institute of National Problems in Education". This is a matter of principle. Russian schools must also be national ones, but traditionally the term "national school" did not include Russian schools.

9

MULTILINGUALISM FOR ALL – AN INDIAN PERSPECTIVE

E. Annamalai

Universalization of bilingual education: goals and principles and features

It is well documented (Fishman 1976) that there are a number of models of bilingual education throughout the world and the models keep changing based on community perception, research findings and demographic changes in the school population. It is obvious that there is no universal model and there cannot be one, because of the different sociopolitical policies of the countries regarding education. The search for universals then is for shared goals, principles and features of bilingual education practised in different parts of the world. Baetens Beardsmore (in this volume) states explicitly that the European School model may not be applicable in other situations. It should be accepted that the success of a particular model does not give it a universal appeal because the success may be due to the local conditions, as in the case of St.Lambert experiment in Montreal, rather than to the model itself. The question of the applicability of the European School model to other places is then really a question of examining the goals, principles and features of it which are universally applicable independent of the local conditions. With their identification, one can look for – to use a Chomskyan phrase – parametric variations to account for the differences in individual models.

We may ideally postulate that the *universal goals of bilingual education* are

1. bilingualism (or multilingualism) for all, including minority and majority language speakers;
2. to achieve bilingualism of equal performance in the sense that both languages are

usable for their intended purposes, with the same fluency and correctness;

3. to have better education in all subjects in the sense that the competence in the languages is not achieved at the expense of competence in other subjects.

The *first goal* is to ensure that the entire population gets the benefit of bilingual education.

The *second goal* is to ensure that the minority language is not used merely as a prop to gain competence in the majority language.

The *third goal* is to ensure that the medium does not become the content.

Bilingual education serves to give effect to certain *social and educational principles*. They are:

1. everyone has the right to education which does not put him or her at a disadvantage;
2. the language of education aids social mobility of the learner;
3. education contributes to societal harmony through language.

The *first principle* is to ensure that no-one is denied and disadvantaged by education because of his or her language.

The *second principle* is to ensure the same with regard to one's social and economic development.

The *third principle* asserts that multilingualism which grants pedagogical recognition to all languages brings societal harmony and not disharmony.

The *features* of bilingual education are the educational strategies used to achieve the specified goals as above and to satisfy the principles mentioned above. The defining feature of bilingual education is that the two languages are used as medium of instruction concurrently or successively. Another feature is that both languages have specified curricular objectives for achievement, which may be the same or different.

Europe and India

Europe and India are comparable in their linguistic diversity, but they are different in their linguistic tradition. Europe, from the time of the Renaissance, promoted monolingualism as part of nation-formation and many mother tongues were lost or marginalized. In India, during the colonial period, though the Indian languages were marginalized with regard to power, they were not lost, and contact with English triggered renaissance in the major Indian languages and set in process ther modernisation.

The current concern for multilingualism in Europe is a consequence of labour migration from other countries and of promoting a common economic space. The promotion of multilingualism in schools through bilingual education conflicts with the national ethos of many European countries. In India, on the other hand, multilingualism is part of the national ethos and the current preference for English at the risk of marginalizing the Indian languages is part of the exercise for economic development. This causes concern. Bilingual education in some élite schools, as reported by Baetens Beardsmore (in this volume), will not be enough in India as a corrective measure. Bilingual education with the universal properties mentioned above should become part of mass education in India.

Education in India

India is a multilingual country not only demographically, with about 200 distinct languages, but also functionally, with many languages used in education, administration and the mass media. The multilingualism of the country is reflected naturally in its educational system. In the education policy of the country the language policy has been to teach a minimum of three languages, known by the name the "Three Language Formula".

The three languages are basically the two official languages of the Union, viz. Hindi and English and the official languages of the state, which could be any language spoken in the state. It is mostly the numerically and politically dominant language of the state. When two of these languages happen to be the same, any other modern Indian language in included in the Formula.

The policy does not provide for the mother tongue when it is different from the dominant language of the state nor for a classical language like Sanskrit, preferred for its religious importance. Nevertheless, in practice these languages are learnt in place of the dominant language of the state, called the regional language.

In recent years the states have been making the learning of the regional language compulsory. The provision for the linguistic minorities to learn their mother tongue continues. This requires switching over to the regional language at some stage. Thus switching over is not gradual but abrupt, usually at the end of the primary level of four or five years of education. The languages are taught as subjects independent of each other.

The options offered for medium of instruction are reduced at the subsequent stages of education. This makes a switch-over of medium necessary for those who go through higher levels of education. But since the drop-out rate is as high as 70% after the primary stage, the majority of the students end up with a single medium of instruction. Though the English medium schools are not in general supported by the governments, they are run in the private sector and they are in demand from parents. The students who join the English medium schools at the primary stage have the same medium throughout their education. Nevertheless, they are not monolinguals because they learn two other languages, according to the Three Language Formula mentioned above.

The students who pass through the secondary stage of education with ten years of schooling will have learnt three languages, whichever medium they follow. Their competence in the three languages varies. This is particularly so for the students in the Hindi-speaking states with regard to another Indian language, which they study as the third language.

With regard to the minority languages, one must distinguish between the minority languages which are major and are majority dominant languages in another state, and minority languages which are minor and are spoken only in a particular state by the tribal and other such disadvantaged peole. The students of the former group may have their mother tongue as the medium at the primary stage, but many of them prefer the medium of the regional language or the medium of English because of the poor quality of their mother tongue medium schools. For the students of the latter group, the new Education Policy of the Central Government, promulgated in 1986, recommends the use of the tribal and other minor languages as medium at the primary stage if the population of their speakers is more than 100,000. But this has not been implemented effectively by the states.

The above is a global picture for the whole country, with about six million schools at the primary level. In these schools, bilingual education is not followed with the goals mentioned earlier. Nevertheless, the students who go beyond the primary stage will be trilingual, because of the Three Language Formula, though not with equal proficiency in the three languages. Thus the educational policy in India is to promote multilingualism, though not through a method of bilingual education following the universal properties given above.

There are, however, special sets of schools which follow bilingual education. One set of such schools is central schools under the auspices of the Central Government, meant primarily for the transient people who are employed by the Central Government and who move from state to state in the course of their career. In these schools, the science subjects are taught through the medium of English and the humanities subjects through the medium of Hindi. The mother tongues of the students are taught as subjects at the post-primary level in a cursory fashion.

The Central Institute of Indian Languages has run, on an experimental basis, bilingual education schools in some tribal areas, using the tribal languages as the medium at the primary stage.

There are some prestigious private schools like the Sardar Patel Vidyalaya in Delhi which follow bilingual education in a planned manner (Sahgal 1992).

To conclude

India is known for its grassroots multilingualism. The education system is also committed to preserving and promoting multilingualism. There is, however, a crucial difference between multilingualism through formal education, as part of secondary socialization and through informal learning in the community, as part of primary socialization.

Multilingualism through schooling gives primacy to proficiency in the languages of power – the official languages of the state and the Union, i.e. the regional languages, Hindi and English (Annamalai 1986). With increasing preference for English, bilingualism involving English may have an edge over other languages and it may even lead to imbalanced multilingualism with mother tongues restricted to the home domain. This needs a corrective measure. Bilingual education with the properties outlined earlier is the instrument for such corrective action.

10

MULTILINGUALISM FOR ALL – GENERAL PRINCIPLES?

Tove Skutnabb-Kangas and Ofelia García [1]

"... a multicultural and monolingual curriculum is a useless palliative in a society that claims to promote cultural pluralism ... multiculturalism cannot be genuinely achieved without an adequate policy of multilingualism." (Tosi 1984, 175)

"The dominant monolingual orientation is cultivated in the developed world and consequently two languages are considered a nuisance, three languages uneconomic and many languages absurd. In multilingual countries, many languages are facts of life; any restriction in the choice of language is a nuisance; and one language is not only uneconomic, it is absurd." (Pattanayak 1984, 82)

"Many of my contemporaries have only learned Spanish in school, but they never learn it perfectly. At the same time they stop speaking their own language which in my case is Aymara. They end up as people without identity, people who belong nowhere." (Vice-president Victor Hugo Cárdenas, Bolivia, in an interview by Steffen Knudsen, in *Zig Zag – en verden i bevægelse*, 26, 1994, p. 9.; our translation from Danish).

"Berlin of 1884 [when Africa was divided between the European empires, our remark] was effected through the sword and the bullet. But the night of the sword and the bullet was followed by the morning of the chalk and the blackboard. The physical violence of the battlefield was followed by the psychological violence of the classroom. But where the former was visibly brutal, the latter was visibly gentle ... The bullet was the means of the physical subjugation. Language was the means of the spiritual subjugation. (Ngũgĩ, 1987, 9).

"... attempts to artificially suppress minority languages through policies of assimilation, devaluation, reduction to a state of illiteracy, expulsion or genocide are not only degrading of human dignity and morally unacceptable, but they are also an invitation to separatism and an incitement to fragmentation into mini-states." (Smolicz 1986, 96)

"The real issue, therefore, is not whether, how or under what forces does an individual or a group become bilingual; it is whether and at what cost does one become a monolingual..." "If social integration is taken to be a psychological state characterized by positive self/ingroup identity along with positive other/outgroup identification (Mohanty 1987), then bilingualism, both at the individual and at the social levels, seems to promote social integration." (Mohanty, forthcoming, 163; 158)

"I am really worried about those children who do not have a strong mother tongue. Of course, as a parent, you do not need to ensure that the children learn their mother tongue up to a really high level, if you can be hundred percent sure of a few things. If you KNOW that you are never going to move house or school or country, that the parents' relationship is VERY stable, and that the child is NEVER going to have ANY emotional or learning problems in her life, then you can take risks with your child and not send them to mother tongue classes." (Joanna Sancha, teacher in the English subsection in The European School of Brussels, in an interview 8 June 1994)

Introduction: multilingualism for all[2]

The first challenge of multilingual education in the 21st Century will be how to combine the two trends that have dominated bi/multilingual education in the past, one for the rich or majorities or dominant groups, with an emphasis on increased knowledge, scholastic achievement and benefits, and one for the poor or minorities or dominated/subordinated groups, with a focus on increased educational access, linguistic human rights, and self-determination. More and more, as the world becomes increasingly interdependent, it is important for *all* its citizens, not just privileged elites or poor minorities, to be fluent and literate in at least two languages.

The second challenge will be to be able to offer *all* citizens of the 21st Century a multilingual education that would increase the global knowledge and scholastic achievement of all, while providing greater social equity (between different regions of the world, between classes/social groups, racial, religious and age groups, the genders) and participating in the elimination of prejudice, racism and antagonism labelled "ethnic"".[3]

For multilingual education to become this integrated alternative for the education of all citizens, it also has to move beyond its focus on only two languages (as in bilingual education), and beyond the nice phrases about the equality and worth of all cultures (as in much of multicultural education which treats racism and classism as information problems and many mother tongues as a nuisance), and to recognize the linguistic human rights of all groups.[4] But multilingualism and multiculturalism must rest on bilingualism and biculturalism, as a first step. This also means that two opposite types of understandable but still irrational fear have to be overcome. One, typical of many Western countries – and the U.S.A. is one of the "best" representatives for it – could be labelled the "majority group misperception of bilingualism". It sees bilingualism as dangerous for national unity, as a factor which can lead to "ethnic unrest" or "ghettoization" or "separatism", and in the last end to the disintegration of the "nation state".[5] The other one, which we could label the "minority group misperception of bilingualism", sees bilingualism as something that a powerful majority forces on an unwilling powerless minority in order to be able to assimilate them. A recognition of this fear (which apparently was real under the Soviet rule) can be seen in the title of Mart and Ülle Rannut's chapter in this book and in Alexei Leontiev's chapter where his criteria for whether linguistic groups are decreasing or increasing includes the number of bilingual speakers: if most speakers are bilingual, the group is decreasing; if the number of bilinguals is stable or diminishing, the group is increasing. But this fear is also felt by some representatives of stable national linguistic minorities with maximal legal protection (see e.g. Thomas Rosenberg's (1994) book on Swedish speakers in Finland).

In this chapter, however, we do not touch upon the complex issues of how overcoming the fear of bilingualism might be attempted. It is inextricably mingled with the larger societal power issues (which we will not discuss in this chapter, having done it often and extensively elsewhere) which form a basis for any educational policy. Instead, the rest of this chapter outlines the progressive steps that can be taken so that additive multilingualism and multiliteracy (and, to some extent, multiculturalism) would result. It then discusses general principles that schools can follow in order to enable students to become both multilingual and multiliterate. Both the progressive steps and the general principles for multilingualism and multiliteracy are derived from the strong forms of multilingual education (Baker 1993, see below) discussed in the book.

Multiplying and using the lenses

The global WHY

Our global changed consciousness has made evident not only our commonalities, but also our differences. As we try to capture the world's diversity with one of the instruments we have for communication, language, we have come to understand how limited and limiting having only our mother tongue, without extensive access to other languages, is, in making sense of the cultural and linguistic pluralism of the world and, indeed, creating this world (García 1992, Khubchandani 1983, Pattanayak 1991, Skutnabb-Kangas 1988).

An accomplished photographer knows that to capture the essence of multiple images, a variety of lenses are needed. Even the most far-reaching wide-angle lens cannot seize the complexity of reality. In the same way, a monolingual person, even if speaking a Language of Wider Communication[6] such as English, can never make complete sense and have full understanding and knowledge of other ethnolinguistic groups – or even their own group. One has to be able to see one's own group both from the inside, from the point of view of Self, and from the outside, as different Others see it, in order to fully appreciate and know it.

To include the world's diversity in a picture, a variety of lenses are needed. But it is not enough to inherit or be able to buy many lenses. An accomplished photographer also needs proper instruction: opportunities to use varied lenses to create multiple images and a balanced and focused vision, and to learn when to use one lens or the other, or both or all.

The purpose of this chapter is to identify principles used in educational systems to enable students to become expert "linguistic photographers", with a variety of lenses, able to use their multilingualism to get more focused and complete pictures of our heterogeneous world, to make others see what they see, to understand that others may be using different lenses – and to create new worlds. As the world recognizes its own multilingualism, multilingual education has been increasingly recognized as a means to provide the world's citizenry with the varied lenses needed to capture, understand and create our global reality.

The differentiated WHYS

But the reasons for adding a second or third lens are often very different for diverse groups. Acknowledging this also implies that we do not see ourselves as romantic Whorfians. Some groups have recognized multilingual education as a means to make their own children bilingual, thereby improving opportunities of doing business with and getting ahead in an increasingly interdependent world. Immersion programmes, the European Schools and International Schools[7] are examples of this approach of enrichment and extra benefits. For others, multilingual education represents a means to better understanding of other ethnolinguistic groups with which they are in contact. Both immersion programmes and two-way programmes may have an element of this "integrative" motivation. Still others, often threatened ethnolinguistic groups have adopted multilingual education as a means of linguistic survival. Maintenance/language shelter or revitalisation programmes for minorities, e.g. the Frisian schools in the Netherlands or the Finnish schools in Sweden or Kōhanga Reo programmes in New Zealand, are of this type. And yet another use of bilingual education has been to educate in the mother tongue ethnolinguistic groups which had previously been excluded from equal educational opportunity and, especially, equality of outcome. Again, both maintenance and two-way programmes may belong to this group. Likewise, many educational programmes in African countries could be counted under maintenance programmes.[8] The reasons and goals in using two or more languages in the educational system thus vary greatly, ranging then from increased knowledge and economic gain, to increased mutual understanding, to ethnolinguistic survival, to improved educational opportunity and outcome. Many programmes are multipurpose and combine several of the goals.[9]

"Strong" models of multilingual education

As the practice of multilingual education has expanded, different models have been developed to respond to the purposes outlined above. This book treats in depth several models of multilingual education which can be considered *"strong"*: their linguistic aim is to promote multilingualism (or, minimally, bilingualism) and multiliteracy.[10] Other educational models can be considered *"weak"*: their linguistic aim is not multilingualism and multiliteracy, but rather monolingualism or limited bilingualism. Some of them do belong to the category of *bilingual education* in the classic sense of the term[11], though, because they use two languages as media of instruction, e.g. all transitional models. Others use one language only as a medium but teach foreign languages as subjects, i.e. they are not properly to be considered "bilingual education". Only one of the models discussed in depth in this book could, with some considerable modification, be called "weak", namely the International Schools. Among the strong models, we can identify the following four, which will be described (see also Skutnabb-Kangas 1988 and 1990b for definitions):

1. *Plural multilingual model* (also called mainstream bilingual/multilingual);
2. *Immersion model*;
3. *Two-way dual language model* (also called two-way bilingual immersion, as in Dolson & Lindholm's chapter in this book);
4. *Maintenance model* (also called language shelter or heritage language model).

1. *Plural Multilingual model*: The European Schools studied by Baetens Beardsmore are a prototype for this model. These schools are controlled by the education authorities of the member states of the European Union and the languages of the different subsections are official languages of the member states. In that sense, then, all children are considered "language majority students" and all languages are "majority" ones. The students are of different nationality and language background – therefore "plural" – and several languages are used as media for instruction and the goal is that all students become not only bilingual but multilingual – therefore "multilingual".
   The societal aim[12] is clearly one of enrichment and pluralism, while the linguistic aim is to make students high level multilinguals and multiliterates, able to function in the European Union and beyond.
2. *Immersion model*: This originally Canadian model, discussed in this book by Cummins and Artigal, has spread to many countries[13]. Immersion programmes typically involve ethnolinguistic majority children, although there are some exceptions.[14] Two languages are used as media of instruction, initially the students' second language.[15] This model aims to make students bilingual (or, in Europe, multilingual) and biliterate so that they can function in (and draw benefit from) pluralistic societies. The societal goals have so far to a large extent been more about maintaining old or gaining new benefits or privileges for middle class populations than general equity.
3. *Two-way Dual Language model*: The bilingual immersion schools in California and elsewhere in the United States, discussed in this book by Dolson and Lindholm, are the prototype. Here, there are both majority and minority students, and both

languages (in most cases English and Spanish[16]) are used as media of instruction with both groups, with a strict separation of languages. Again, the objective of this type of bilingual education model is enrichment and pluralism, and bilingualism and biliteracy, for both the majority and the minority group. Alternate days programmes could be seen as a sub-category under two-way programmes.[17]

4. *Maintenance model*: These schools are most often organized by an ethnolinguistic minority community, and most typically educate minority children using both the minority and the majority language, with strict separation. Initially, the students' native language is used for most of the content matter education, especially in cognitively demanding, decontextualised subjects, while the majority language is taught as a subject only. Later on, some (but by no means all) maintenance programmes use the majority language as a medium of education for part of the time, but in proper maintenance programmes the minority language continues as a medium of education in several (or most, or all) subjects throughout the school. For a few national minorities, maintenance programmes are a self-evident, "normal" way of educating their children, a natural human right. It is indicative that most minorities of this type, e.g. the Swedish-speakers in Finland, Afrikaans- and English-speakers in South Africa, or Russian-speakers in Estonia, Latvia and Lithuania, are either former power minorities or in a transitional phase where they have to accept the fact that they no longer have the power to impose their will on a numerical majority but where they still do have the power to organise their own children's education through the medium of their own language. Of course, it should be a fundamental, self-evident linguistic and educational human right for *any* ethnolinguistic minority to use its own language as the main medium of education, but in fact most minorities in the world do not have this basic right.[18] A few indigenous peoples (who are numerically a minority in most of their own countries) have maintenance programmes (see e.g. Black 1990, Harris 1990, Kretu 1994, Magga 1994, McLaughlin 1992, McLaughlin & Tierney (eds.) 1993, Stairs 1988, for examples); most of them do not (see e.g. Jordan 1988, Hamel 1994a, b). Most immigrant and refugee minority children do not have access to maintenance programmes either, even if it can be shown that they result in high levels of bi/multilingualism, enhanced school achievement and more societal equity.[19]

The purpose of this type of multilingual programme is to ensure that language minority children continue to maintain and develop their mother tongue up to a native (national minorities, indigenous peoples) or at least near-native (immigrant minorities) level, learn the majority language at a native level, and become biliterate. In a European context, they typically also learn further foreign languages. This type of multilingual programme enriches society at large by promoting pluralism and mutual understanding and by ensuring that minorities gain access to linguistic and educational prerequisites for social, economic and political integration (see also Mohanty, forthcoming).

Although the strong forms of multilingual education outlined above have different sociolinguistic realities with regard to the linguistic background of the students and the language(s) of the classroom, and different sociopolitical realities with regard to the power relations between the groups attending and the rest of society, they all share an aim of cultural and linguistic pluralism, with the bi/multilingualism and bi/multiliteracy of students as an avowed minimum aim.

"Weak" models of multilingual education

For purposes of comparison when we discuss educational principles for multilingualism, we also mention two other models of education which are classified as "weak" in Baker's typology (1993). One of them, the Transitional model, uses two languages as media of instruction, whereas the Mainstream Monolingual, with Foreign Language Teaching only uses one language as the medium of instruction. These models are presented only because the principles for education leading towards high levels of multilingualism can be seen in a clearer way by comparing them with these two models which do not have multilingualism as their goal.

5. *Transitional model*: This model is strictly for (immigrant or refugee) minority students who do not know the majority language well enough for using it initially as a medium of instruction. It is thus based on defining the students negatively, as deficient, in relation to their (lack of) knowledge of the majority language, (see Skutnabb-Kangas 1990a, 1991b, Wink 1994). Initially, the minority language is used as a medium of instruction until the child becomes orally fluent in the majority language, at which time instruction continues first mainly and very soon only through the medium of the majority language. There may (often in Europe) or may not (mostly in the USA) be a mother-tongue-as-a-subject component after the transition. Sometimes there is some auxiliary teaching through the medium of the mother tongue even after the transition during a limited time.

Teaching through the medium of the mother tongue is not seen as a right that the child is entitled to; the mother tongue is seen as useful only so far as its auxiliary use enhances the knowledge of the dominant language (see e.g. Baker & de Kanter 1981 for clear statements on this; in the U.S.A. context even reports like Ramirez et al

(1991) clearly embody this type of principles in their design and presentation, seen from a "European" point of view. It is often, especially in the higher grades, more the attitude towards the minority mother tongue, the rationale legitimating its use (a self-evident right, or an instrument towards better proficiency in the majority language) than the number of hours devoted to the minority language that is decisive for how a model should be classified.

There is often no clear language policy for this model, with both languages used as the teacher sees fit. This model is, after ordinary submersion models (where minority children are instructed through the medium of the dominant language only), the most prevalent education type in most European and Europeanized countries[20] for immigrant minorities (and indigenous peoples) and certainly the most prevalent type using more than one language as media of education. Transitional bilingual education encourages shift to monolingualism in the majority language.[21]

6. *Mainstream Monolingual with Foreign Language Teaching*: This model teaches one or several foreign languages as subjects in separate classes, for a few hours per week. All students are treated as if they were language majority students or dominant language speakers, and the majority or dominant language is used for instruction (except maybe in the foreign language classroom). This is still the preferred mode of foreign language instruction in the world, leading most often not to high levels of multilingualism, even if it can give a solid basis for multilingualism later, if the students continue to develop and have opportunities for using their foreign languages. With some considerable modifications, the International Schools discussed here by Carder can also be considered under this model. In the International Schools, students of different ethnolinguistic backgrounds are taught through the medium of English (or another "international" language) only, with a strong ESL program. The language of the host country is often taught as a second language in primary school. Although students in these schools gain full literacy in English, their use of another language (either their mother tongue or the language of the host country), is often limited, especially in one of the modes; either in writing (for the mother tongue – which is not often taught), or orally (which is often the case for the language of the host country if the students do not have extensive active contact with host country peers during their leisure time). Full bilingualism and biliteracy are rarely achieved in these schools.[22]

We will refer to these models below in our comparisons. Next we move to a pragmatic "guided tour" through the progressive steps which schools may take when planning for multilingualism.

Progressive stages toward multilingualism/multiliteracy through schooling

Full additive multilingualism and multiliteracy just doesn't happen accidentally. Instead, it is planned and organized by different agents. Parents, communities, school administrators and educators, and students themselves must actively commit themselves to multilingualism and multiliteracy on a long-term basis. So must the politicians. Although all agents in the educational process must remain actively involved throughout the stages leading to full multilingualism, different agents take on more active roles in each of the stages. We have identified four stages through which students move toward full multilingualism and multiliteracy. These stages, and the steps taken by the different agents, are displayed in Table 1 and discussed below:

Table 1. Progressive stages toward full multilingualism and multiliteracy

FIRST STAGE: PRE-MULTILINGUALISM STAGE

Time Frame:	Before school starts
Principal Agents:	Parents; Politicians

SECOND STAGE: EMERGING MULTILINGUALISM STAGE

Time Frame:	The initial school years (K-3)
Principal Agents:	The Administrators & Staff; The Teachers

THIRD STAGE: DEVELOPING MULTILINGUALISM STAGE

Time Frame:	The middle years in school (grades 4-10)
Principal Agents:	The Teachers; The Administrators and Staff

FOURTH STAGE: FULL MULTILINGUALISM/MULTILITERACY STAGE

Time Frame:	The final school years (grades 11-12)
Principal Agents:	The Students

FIRST STAGE: PRE-MULTILINGUALISM STAGE

Time Frame:	Before school starts
Principal Agents:	Parents; Politicians

Step one is that the parents commit. Parents, either monolingual or multilingual, decide to send their children to a multilingual school (see again note 2). These parents are well informed, interested in multilingualism and multiculturalism as important societal aims, and willing to become active participants in their child's multilingual education. Many times they become involved in establishing the multilingual school. In order for the school to be able to start, at least local but often also regional and national politicians need to at least accept but preferably actively support education leading towards multilingualism. Often this is the main hurdle to be overcome (and hundreds of books have been written analysing the sociopolitical reasons).

SECOND STAGE: EMERGING MULTILINGUALISM STAGE
Time Frame:	The initial school years (K-3)
Principal Agents:	The Administrators & Staff; The Teachers

Firstly, schools, the administrators and staff, support multilingualism by establishing and continuing to keep a *multilingual* language surround: a social context in which the different languages are used orally and in written form *outside* of classrooms.

Secondly, the teachers establish a *monolingual* language surround *in* the classrooms where the students' *first* language is used, and a *more bilingual* or multilingual language surround in classrooms where the students' *second* language is used (whether as a medium or as a subject). While the L1 classroom always functions as a monolingual language surround, the L2 classroom *initially* functions as a multilingual language surround, using the students' L1 to contextualize input. This is so even in the Canadian immersion schools, where students frequently use their L1 initially to make sense of the linguistic input given to them by the teacher in their L2.

Students with different language backgrounds are taught separately. They are *not mixed* for INSTRUCTION at this stage (and at least never for instruction in cognitively and linguistically demanding, decontextualized subjects). But when possible, they are *mixed* for highly contextualized school ACTIVITIES, such as lunch, recess, gymnastics, music, "European Hours" or equivalent.

This emerging multilingualism stage could take the first three or four years of formal education, depending on at what age this starts.[23]

THIRD STAGE: DEVELOPING MULTILINGUALISM STAGE
Time Frame:	The middle years in school (grades 4-10)
Principal Agents:	The Teachers; The Administrators and Staff

Firstly, the classroom teachers support the development of multilingualism and multiliteracy of students by creating *monolingual* language contexts in terms of the *input from teacher to students*, in the classrooms in which content is taught in either language, L1 or L2, and in the language arts classrooms. The students thus receive a wealth of *input in one language at a time*, and they are themselves expected to produce rich *output in either of the two languages involved*, L1 or L2.

Students with different language backgrounds can now be *mixed* for progressively more *content instruction* through the medium of their L2, provided four conditions are present.

1. *All* students in the school have equal opportunity to experience instruction both in their first language, as well as in their second language.
2. The subjects taught through the medium of L2 are in the beginning of the more context-embedded kind, and become more cognitively demanding and decontextualized only towards the end of this stage.
3. Teachers maximize their use of context-embedded language, especially in the beginning.
4. Appropriate instructional material in the language of instruction, as well as appropriate supplementary instructional material in the languages of the students, are readily available. For example, all classrooms should be equipped with bilingual dictionaries and multilingual reference books.
5. Instruction through the medium of the students' L1 continues in several subjects, according to a carefully monitored plan.

Secondly, the administrators and staff continue to support multilingualism and multiliteracy by keeping a *multilingual* language surround in the school: all the languages are used orally and in written form *outside* of classrooms.

This stage is the longest one: it could last between five to seven years. It is in this stage that what CumminsCummins (1980a, 1981) has called CALP (Cognitive-Academic Language Proficiency) or context-reduced language is fully developed. Thus, the ability to fully use the second language in context-reduced ways has eight to ten years to develop.

A third and even fourth language can be introduced after the first three years of this stage, i.e. in grade 7 or 8.

FOURTH STAGE: FULL MULTILINGUALISM/MULTILITERACY STAGE

Time Frame:	The final school years (grades 11-12)
Principal Agents:	The Students

Fully multilingual/multiliterate students now contribute to the *multilingual* language surround of the *school and* the *classrooms* and use their multilingualism as an instrument for further inquiry, knowledge, expression and analysis.

Students at this stage choose their instructional language in voluntary subjects, and it can be their L1, L2, L3 or even L4. The language of instruction in some of the core subjects is prescribed and in some of them it continues to be the student's mother tongue. The students also choose the language/s in which they will be assessed. The classroom language surround now resembles that used for initial L2 instruction, with *teacher input* to students being *monolingual*, but *student input and output* being frequently *multilingual*. That is, although monolingual instruction in all of the languages continues during this stage, students are now freer to use their many languages in getting information and in creative expression. Thus, in practice, classrooms become a more multilingual language surround than formerly.

It is instructive again to remind ourselves of the fact that full multilingualism and multiliteracy takes a *long* time to develop, as most authors in this book confirm. It is generally achieved only in the last couple of years of secondary education, that is, after ten years of a carefully orchestrated multilingual education.

In each of the four stages toward full multilingualism, different agents have the main role, and different modes of expression, ranging from monolingualism to multilingualism, are used, although, of course, all agents and all modes of expression are present during all the stages. To get to a full additive biligual/biliterate stage, students must be given practice in using one or the other lens, and using both or all. In this process, they must be guided sometimes by parents who make the decision to give them a second lens, sometimes by experts who know all the lenses that are available and their full range of possibilities, sometimes by instructors who know how to use a particular lens or how to use them in combination. But beyond all this guidance, students must be allowed to create their own images by using their lenses freely and without constrictions. This then is the challenge of every multilingual educational context, how to control the functions of the two languages in their midst and to allow their development and expansion, while potentializing for the students the power of the languages at their disposal.

To do this, good multilingual educational contexts must follow certain principles, and it is to those principles that we now turn.

The guiding principles for education for multilingualism, multiliteracy and multiculturalism

It is important to first underline that a sound multilingual educational policy is in several ways not too different from a sound educational policy in general.

Despite the fact that both teachers and students develop high levels of metalinguistic awareness, the focus is often not on language per se, but rather the education of students, with multilingualism and multiliteracy being both a means to enhance good schooling[24], and one more product of good schooling.

Informed parents, enlightened politicians and school administrators, and well-educated and committed teachers are important for the education of any child. Likewise, well-structured schools, progressive and inclusive educational policies and teaching strategies, rich and diverse materials, and fair educational assessment are principles of effective education for all. All this is most important in multilingual education too.

But to achieve the full multilingualism and multiliteracy of students, certain additional principles have to be followed by the *agents* involved, developed by the *educational context* in which the action takes place, and supported by the surrounding *society*.

Planning for multilingualism, multiliteracy and pluralism through schooling requires the active involvement of *agents* from the community, as well as the school. Furthermore, these agents must be engaged in developing a *school context/culture* that supports multilingualism, multiliteracy, and pluralism, beyond that which exists in the societal culture.

But this school culture must also be supported by society at large. A multilingual and pluralist school culture cannot exist in opposition to that of the *societal context* in which the school has life. True, the school culture can be different and attempt to alter the community. But in order for a school culture to have long-lasting impact on a societal context by truly transforming citizens, it must be nurtured by societal aspirations. Thus, a multilingual and pluralist school culture can only ultimately be effective if it responds to the needs of its societal context. It is then important, whenever possible, to plan for multilingualism, multiliteracy, and pluralism, as resources of the entire community, both minority and majority, as e.g. Joshua Fishman saw already in 1976. As we have said earlier, the focus of this chapter is on the within-school conditions for multilingualism, not the societal prerequisites.[25]

If multilingualism, multiliteracy and pluralism are to be a goal of schooling, it is most important to have a fair amount of control over the nature of the educational agents and the educational culture. One can also, within the educational system, plan the sociolinguistic characteristics of incoming students into a school to some extent through cooperation between schools and school districts. It is clear that one single school cannot use, say, fifty languages as media of instruction, in a community with fifty linguistic groups present. But the European Schools, for instance, use 8 or 9, without much difficulty. If different schools have partly different, partly overlapping sets of languages of instruction, and inform about it properly, parents soon learn where "their" language is used. In that way different schools can "specialize" in different languages and to some extent "plan" or at least entice the intake.

It is, of course, impossible and would be pretentious to come with a list of principles for multilingual education which is claimed to be exhaustive. We know that many points could be added or deleted. Also, our points have not been weighted in here in any way, so we would not recommend assessing a programme by simply counting on how many characteristics it would get a plus. In addition, we have, as mentioned earlier in this chapter, omitted the larger societal context/culture which is basic for educational agents and the educational context to function in a way conducive to multilingualism. But with many reservations, we venture to suggest that among the important characteristics that we see as desirable or required of the educational agents and the educational culture (i.e. the guiding principles for multilingual education), are the following (and a shorter list is given in the Introduction to this book):

Table 2. Characteristics desirable for education leading to multilingualism and multiliteracy

I. Educational Agents

A. Multilingual administration & staff.
B. Bi- or multilingual teachers.
C. Committed parents (bi- or multilingual or monolingual).
D. Progressively multilingual students.

II. Educational Culture/Context

A. Multilingual educational context.
B. Multilingual language policy.
C. Multilingual educational strategies.
D. Multilingual materials.
E. Multilingual fair assessment.

These principles, presented as characteristics of educational agents and the educational culture, are discussed in the next section. The last section then shows how the principles could be applied to characterise the six models of education (multilingual or not) discussed previously.

I. Educational Agents
A. A completely multilingual (or minimally bilingual) administration and staff.

1. The administrators, teachers, counselors, paraprofessionals and clerical and custodial staff must be *multilingual* or minimally bilingual. Preferably they should be productively fluent in more than one language, but at a minimum they should all have receptive bi/multilingual ability (or be willing to work toward it within a specified time limit).

2. The bi/multilingual administrators, teachers, counselors, paraprofessionals and clerical and custodial staff should be of *different ethnicities* and/or nationalities. Cultural and linguistic pluralism is then always obtained within the school community. No child should be put in a situation where there is no adult in the school speaking the child's language.

3. All languages should have *native* language *speakers, as well as second language speakers,* among the staff. In this way, different ways of speaking languages will be acceptable, including different accents and varieties.

4. The ethnolinguistically diverse staff of the multilingual school should be *committed to* (and be economically rewarded for) *developing their own bi/multilingual proficiency,* as well as that of their students.

5. The career patterns in the school should reflect appreciation of diversity. It is especially important to plan both short-term and long-term solutions to ensure that competent *minority members occupy high status positions* in the school, both in administration and among other staff.

B. *Highly qualified teachers of all languages present in the school who are bi/multilingual.*

1. Teachers who are multilingual should, whenever possible, actively *teach only through the medium of one language* and/or teach only one language (even if, as we said before, the teacher receptively uses also the other language, especially during the emerging multilingualism stage, and gives translation equivalents when needed). When a bi/multilingual person functions as a teacher of *one* language, the "one language-one person" relationship is clearly demarcated, establishing distinct language boundaries, both for the teacher and for the student. This encourages students to respond to the teacher in the language in which input is received. At the same time, bi/multilingual teachers are important identity role models, also in terms of showing (outside the classroom, or in class, for translations, etc) that is is NOT necessary to choose either/or, but a both/and; and that this latter choice is both possible and preferable.

2. Multilingual teachers should have *native or very high levels of linguistic competence* in the language in which they teach or that they teach. Balanced multilingual individuals are a theoretical ideal since multilinguals most often use one language for one purpose, and the other for another. It may in some countries be difficult to find multilingual individuals who have full range of competence in the two

languages for *all* topics and subjects (e.g. Fishman 1971). But bi- or multilingual teachers who have high levels of linguistic competence in *one* language and a bit lower in the other(s) can be relatively easy to find in most countries. Besides ensuring a rich linguistic input for students, these multilingual teachers, though functioning as teachers in one language only, also stimulate a richer linguistic output from the students since the students know that the teachers understand several languages.

3. These multilingual teachers differ from monolingual ones not only in linguistic capacity, but also in their formal education and knowledge. Just like monolingual teachers, multilingual teachers are knowledgeable of:

    a. the subject matter taught;
    b. pedagogical principles and teaching strategies; and
    c. the language, history and culture of the ethnolinguistic group whose language is used in instruction or is taught.

    In addition to the above, multilingual teachers need to be also knowledgeable of:

    d. theories of mother tongue and second language acquisition and bilingual language development;
    e. strategies for teaching second and foreign languages as subjects and using them as media of instruction;
    f. sociolinguistic and psycholinguistic principles of multilingualism and language contact; and
    g. theories and practices of bilingual and multilingual education.

    Thus, the training of multilingual teachers should go beyond that given to monolingual teachers, including more specialized courses.

4. The ethnolinguistically diverse competent teachers of the multilingual school should be *committed to and be economically rewarded for developing their own bi/multilingual proficiency*, as well as that of their students.

C. *Active parental participation and support.*

1. Parents must have made the *choice* of multilingual schooling for their children.
2. Parents should be well *informed* at all times.
3. Parents must be *committed* to the multilingualism and multiliteracy of their children.
4. Parents should be encouraged to *participate* in the multilingual school, bringing not only their language/s, but also their history, culture and values into the school.
5. Parents should be interested in the *development of their own bi/multilingual proficiency*. Whenever possible, opportunities for the development of the multilingual proficiency of the parents should be provided within the school setting.
6. Parents must be *organized to direct the school's* educational and language *policy*. They should hold administrators and staff responsible to carry out their wishes on ways in which their children are educated.

D. *A student body that is (expected to become) progressively multilingual and multiliterate.*

1. Depending on the sociolinguistic context of the community from which the school draws its student body, initially students could have different language ability, from all being totally monolingual in one language or the other, to some having different degrees of multilingual proficiency. Progressively, however, *all* students will be *expected to become fully multilingual* and multiliterate.

2. Students should be well *informed* at all times. They should know enough about the long-term goals of their schooling, the strategies for how to get there, and the benefits of high levels of multilingualism, as well as how to cope with possible negative outsider attitudes. They should be progressively more *responsible for the development of their own multilingualism.*

3. Students should be sufficiently *organized* so that their needs are met and their educational wishes and aspirations respected.

II. *Educational Culture*

A. *A completely multilingual educational context. The multilingual language surround outside the classroom.*

1. The *entire* school system must be designed to promote *(minimally) bilingualism for all*, multilingualism for most (or, initially, for some, in traditionally monolingually oriented countries), *monolingualism for none*. A multilingual programme in a monolingual school or classroom where multilingualism is the goal for only *some* students (e.g. minority students are to become bilingual whereas the majority students can stay monolingual), does *not* provide the appropriate support for multilingual proficiency.

2. The bilingual/multilingual school system must *encompass the whole of primary and secondary education*. Full bi/multilingualism needs a LONG time to develop.[26] Both the main languages need to be developed throughout the entire schooling, starting in primary education and continuing throughout secondary education, as will be discussed below. This is especially so for minority languages. A third and fourth language can be added after students have reached the later phases of the developing multilingual stage.

3. The multilingual school system should encourage a *multilingual language surround* in the entire school, also outside the classrooms, *in practice* and not only as a nice vague recommendation about equal value of all languages and cultures. Some recommendations follow:

    a. Staff should be encouraged to use *all the languages everywhere*, in the hallways, offices, lunchroom, playground, restrooms, and in announcements. If of the two or more languages in the school one or several have minority status or are less used in the societal context outside school, conscious effort must be made to use that/those language/s as much as possible in the school. That is, the lesser used language should have a life of its own in the school *beyond* the classroom.

b. *Correspondence* and notices should always be written *in all the languages* represented in the school. When this is not possible, the administration should differentiate, on the basis of an evaluation of the purpose of the communication. For parents, letters and notices should be written in the language they know best. For staff and students, letters and notices should be written in (one of) the lesser used language(s). This maximizes the opportunity to use the lesser used language(s) for meaningful and authentic communication.

c. *School signs* should be posted *in* both or *all languages*.

d. There should be some *bulletin boards* devoted to *each of the languages* used as media of instruction, other boards should be designated as multilingual and focus on awareness of, and familiarity with, (the) other languages.

e. In general, the different languages of the school *assemblies*, dealing with general school matters, should be chosen, depending on the topic of the assembly and the needs of the school, according to a careful plan. Some schools may alternate languages for school assemblies by term, month, week or even time of day.

B. *A Multilingual Language Policy. Progression in relation to the languages as subjects and as media of instruction.*

1. *The Mother Tongue (MT)*[27]

The students' mother tongue (from now on, MT) is expanded and developed, and students are made to feel linguistically secure in their MT by the following:

a. Giving *everybody's MT* important functions in the school curriculum and using (proficiency in) it as one of the measures of school success (i.e as *one of the core subjects* in the curriculum).

b. Securing the role of the students' MT as a link to their ethnolinguistic identity, by making sure that those teaching it are members of the *same ethnolinguistic group* and/or have native-like or near-native proficiency in it, in addition to being extremely knowledgeable of the history and culture of the ethnolinguistic group.

c. Using the *MT as a medium of instruction throughout the whole educational process, from K-12*, at least in some subjects, so as to expand the functions for which that language is used at home, especially initially. This is important for all students, but especially crucial if the MT has a limited societal role.

d. Teaching the *MT as a subject, throughout the whole educational process, from K-12*, ensuring that this complements its use as a medium of instruction and in the school at large.

e. Students must be in *linguistically homogeneous groups for MT language arts* instruction.

f. Ensuring that the students' *MT*, especially if of minority status, is *protected* from the encroachment of the majority language by maintaining a non-hierarchical functional differentiation in which the MT has clearly defined functions and spaces. In addition to having a specific teacher for teaching the MT, separation can be accomplished through the following:

 – Specific *spaces* where the MT is always used;
 – Specific *contents* taught in the MT;
 – A specific *time of day* using (only) the MT;
 – Specific *days* when (only) the MT is used

g. Exposing students to the *different* social, regional, age and gender *varieties* of the MT beyond the home context, those spoken and written by different monolingual communities, as well as those spoken and written by different multilingual communities[28].

2. *The Second Language (SL)*

The students' second language (from now on, SL) is expanded and developed, and students are made to feel linguistically secure in their SL by the following:

a. Giving the *SL* important functions in the school curriculum and using (proficiency in) it as one of the measures of school success (i.e as *one of the core subjects* in the curriculum).

b. Securing a positive identification with the SL as a link to another ethnolinguistic community, by making sure that those teaching it are bilingual *members of the SL ethnolinguistic group* and/or have native-like or near-native proficiency in it, in addition to being extremely knowledgeable of the history and culture of the ethnolinguistic group, that the students are not forced to use the SL productively before they feel ready for it, and that they can always switch to their MT when they feel the need for it.

c. Using the *SL as a medium of instruction*, in carefully monitored situations, with a well-thought-through progress plan (see below) and with supportive methods (see below).

d. *Teaching the SL as a subject, throughout the whole educational process, from K-12*, ensuring that this complements its use as medium of instruction and in the school at large. The SL should be *taught as a second language* (i.e. *not* as a mother tongue, and not together with native speakers), by bi/multilingual teachers, during the whole educational process, from K-12. Students must for the first many years be in *linguistically homogenous groups for SL language arts* instruction. During the later phases of developing bilingualism and during the full bi/multilingualism phase the groups need not be linguistically homogenous, but still they should not contain native speakers of the SL.

Special *L2 intensive classes* should be available to students who want or need them (e.g. when coming from another school/country).

e. Students must for the first many years be in *linguistically homogeneous groups when using a SL as a medium of instruction* (as in immersion), except when in specifically designed context-embedded situations. During the later phases of developing bilingualism and during the full bi/multilingualism phase the groups need not be linguistically homogenous.

f. During the emerging multilingualism stage the *silent period* in the students' L2 should be *respected*. The emphasis should be on the wealth of L2 input from the teacher, from guests, materials, etc. Students should be *allowed to answer in their L1*. However, progressively students must be encouraged to produce output in the L2, both orally and in written form.

g. Exposing students to the *different* social, regional, age and gender *varieties* of the SL beyond the school context, those spoken and written by different monolingual communities, as well as those spoken and written by different multilingual communities.

3. *The progression*

The students' MT is the basis for the acquisition and development of the students' second and further languages and for developing full bilingualism/multilingualism. Each stage of bilingualism requires different educational language policies with regard to both languages. Therefore, the progress in relation to both will be presented in relation to the three school stages discussed above. However, we have not included the progression part in our Table 3, applying the principles to the six models discussed, because of the amount of detail needed. Several of the other characteristics in table 3 could (and some should) also be differentiated according to the stages, as we have done here.

During the *emerging multilingualism stage*, MT is the medium of instruction and L2 is being taught as a second language. During this stage, the students' MT may be used to make input given in students' L2 comprehensible, even if the teacher uses L2 only (as in the immersion model).

Free activity, playtime, recess, and lunchtime should be planned so that students of different language background interact freely from the very beginning, but in supportive environments, counteracting hierarchisation that would value one language over others.

L2 should only be used as a medium after minimally a couple of years of studying it as a subject, and then only in specifically designed context-embedded activities. These activities might be similar to those that take place during European Hours in the schools here described by Baetens Beardsmore, where students and teacher work together on a collaborative project to be shared with other students. Other context-embedded activities might later on include lessons in Art, Music and Physical Education. When using the L2 in these context-embedded activities, linguistically heterogeneous groups can be arranged, but they should always contain more than one child from each language group, in order to make support in the MT and translations possible when needed. In that way, both input and output, in the first as well as the second language, can be realistically and authentically produced.

Progressively, during the *developing multilingualism stage* (after approximately the first 6-7 years), the time devoted to using the MT as medium of instruction can be decreased and the SL can be increasingly used as a medium. In the beginning, the use of context-embedded language in teaching through the medium of L2 should be maximized, even when the content is cognitively undemanding. The subjects to be taught through the medium of L2 should move toward the more cognitively demanding end (history, biology, etc) during the seventh to ninth year of multilingual education, and the language use may necessarily become more context-reduced.

During the later phases of the developing multilingualism stage, students of different language backgrounds can be grouped for instruction using a language that is a second language for *all* of them. In core subjects, however, these heterogenous groups should not contain native speakers of the language of instruction, whereas any combinations can be used in voluntary subjects, and some of them can be taken through the medium of a language which may for some students be their L1 and for others their L3 or even L4 (e.g. studying photography in grade 9 through the medium of Greek, with both Greek and other students, in a European School). This heterogeneous grouping works as long as *all* students are *required* to receive instruction through the medium of at least their first and second language.

During the *full multilingualism and multiliteracy phase*, most students move, in terms of competence, beyond mother tongue and second language, to full multilingualism and multiliteracy. During the two final school years all groups in voluntary subjects can include students of all language backgrounds. It is important, though, that some of the most linguistically demanding core subjects are studied through the medium of the students' MT, in order to ensure full linguistic and cognitive proficiency at a native level.

During the full multilingualism stage students should also follow a course on sociolinguistic and psycholinguistic aspects of multilingualism, so that they can reflect on their own linguistic experience. This should also include discussing political aspects of language policies worldwide.

During the full multilingualism stage students are encouraged to use both languages actively as instrument for inquiry, knowledge and creativity. Practice in doing some of this has occurred throughout the school years, spontaneously, because of the multilingual language surround of the school, as well as in organized ways, as a result of the educational strategies used, even in classrooms that functioned in one specified language only. Some of them will be discussed below.

C. *Inclusive educational/pedagogical strategies that support multilingualism and multiliteracy.*

1. An *inquiry-based, problem-oriented approach to learning* uses both or all the languages as instruments for knowledge.[29] Students are encouraged to use the languages of their choice during the process of inquiry, both to inquire and to multiply the sources of knowledge and in finding solutions to problems which they pose. However, products in a specified language, either orally or in writing, are required at times, especially in the different language classrooms.

2. A *student-centered and interactive pedagogy* allows for student to student, as well as student to teacher and teacher to student collaboration. However, during the emerging multilingualism stage and the first stage of the developing multilingualism stage the teacher should plan some teacher-directed activities for L2 learners in order to provide the instructional scaffolding they need.

3. *Whole language strategies*[30] are used, including reading of authentic literature in all languages and, when it exists, of literature written by other multilinguals, and reflecting the dynamic use of two or more languages by multilingual communities. Newspapers and magazines from different monolingual contexts, as well as multilingual ones, should be used as reading material.

4. *Use of the writing process*, including the keeping of personal journals where students are encouraged to use all their languages as a means of expression, either separately or in combination, reflecting the bi/multilingual literature they read. The students should be encouraged to be responsible for their own portfolios, also used for assessment (see below).

5. *Authentic communication in all languages.* This should include talking and writing to officials, friends and relatives in monolingual communities, as well as in bilingual and multilingual communities, using the appropriate language(s) for communication.

D. *Varied teaching materials*

1. Teaching materials in all languages should be *rich and highly varied*, reflecting both the language(s) and the culture(s) of the home community and language as used in different societal contexts, including bilingual and multilingual ones. When the language is spoken in many national contexts, the material chosen should be written by authors of different nationalities.[31]

2. When teaching materials do not exist in a "lesser used language," teachers must make every effort to produce their own. For this purpose, members of the community, including parents, community elders, and students themselves, must be recruited. The preparation of *teaching materials* should be a joint community venture. *Student products* can also be used as teaching materials.
3. Multilingual materials are also needed to encourage students to make *contrastive analyses* of texts and to become aware of language differences and similarities.
4. Materials from oracy-oriented cultures should be used on an equal basis with more literacy-oriented cultures. Both *orature* and *literature* should be equally valued.

E. Authentic and fair multilingual assessment

1. Language assessment should *never compare native speakers of a language with speakers of that language as a second language.* If students *want* to sit for final exams<examination>, intended for native speakers, in their SL, in addition to or instead of exams intended for second language speakers, they should naturally be allowed to do so. Both types of exam results (in a language as a MT or as a SL) should be of equal value, e.g. for university entrance.
2. Assessment should be criterion-referenced or performance-based, with different (but equal) measures expected of native speakers and second language learners, respectively. Portfolio-based assessments should be used extensively.[32]
3. Content assessment should be conducted in the language in which the student has received the instruction or in the language which the student chooses.

Applying the principles to the models

It might be impossible for an educational context that promotes multilingualism and multiliteracy to have all these features. But maximizing these characteristics would ensure that students travel the full distance required to become multilingual and multiliterate.

Table 3 applies (most of) these principles to the different models of multilingual education discussed previously. We are fully aware of the fact that it is obviously a gross oversimplification to try and capture complex processes in a plus/minus dichotomy. Much more differentiation would be needed in the characteristics themselves, in relation to both the content of several characteristics and to how they rate during the 3 or 4 stages. How would a school be placed on IA3 ("Native and second language speakers among the administrators and staff"), for instance, if it has both native and second language speakers of the majority language, but only native speakers of the minority languages (a common situation for almost all minority groups except Spanish-speakers in the U.S.A.)? Many of the characteristics should also be differentiated according to stage as we did for the Progression in Multilingual languages policy above. The rating is often different for different students in the same class, depending on the students mother tongue. The Mainstream Monolingual with Foreign Language Teaching Model (6) looks completely different from an American or Russian angle (a good start for majority populations), as compared to a European or Indian angle (the regular absolute minimum, hardly worth including, except as something we have to get rid of). A more finely tuned scale than a dichotomy would also be necessary. Still, we think that the results of our rating excercise are worth including, because the rating process (which we ask all the readers to repeat for themselves and to agree and disagree with our ratings[33]) may make one realise the enormous complexity and variation.

As can be seen in the Table, each model responds to its societal situation and none of them are completely perfect or ideal. However, it is clear that the models applying the greatest number of principles also have the most success in promoting the multilingualism and multiliteracy of students. The Plural Multilingual Model will thus be most successful. We will not discuss any of the details in the table – most of them have been discussed, directly or indirectly, in other articles in this book. But we invite the reader to reflect over their own educational context by trying to place it in the table and by seeing what they might want to change.

It is also obvious from Table 3, that an integrated model for the multilingual education of majorities and minorities is yet to be developed. Whereas the Plural Multilingual Model of the European Schools works well for the selected population of these schools, we do not yet know whether it would function equally well with *all* students, given its traditional educational strategies.[34] The same is to some extent true for the Immersion Model, despite its more varied intake (see e.g. Genesee 1976, 1985, 1987). Whereas the Maintenance Model works well with minority populations, it makes no room for the majority. More hopeful in this regard is the Two-Way Dual Language Model discussed by Dolson and Lindholm. However, its inability to structure a distinct educational language policy for the minority and the majority population, especially in the beginning, may lead to a partial failure in promoting the *full* multilingualism and multiliteracy of many students, both majority and minority, later on. Despite the positive early results in the two-way dual language programs of the kinds presently initiated in the US, it seems to us that it is a weakness that they

Table 3. Characteristics of multilingual education

Name of programme	European Schools	Immersion	2-way biling.	Mainte-nance		Interna-tional	Transi-tional
TYPES	strong	strong	strong	strong		weak	weak
TYPICAL CHILD	Heter Maj	Homog Maj	Maj.& Min	Homog. Min		Heter. Ma&Mi	Min
MEDIUM OF INSTRUCTION							
Initially	L1	L2	Min L1 Maj L2	L1		L2 for most	L1
Subsequently	Both or all	Both	Both	L1 or both		L2&FL	L2
				F	S		
I EDUCATIONAL AGENTS							
A. Multilingual admin. & staff							
1. All multilingual	+	+	–	+	+	–	–
2. Different ethnicities	+	+	+	+	+	+?	+?
3. Native & second language speakers	+	+?	–?	+?	+	–?	–?
4. Committed to own multilingualism	+	+	–?	+	+	–	–
5. Minority members in high status positions	+	+	–?	+	+	–	–
B. Multilingual teachers							
1. Teach only (through) one language	+	+?	+?	+	+	+	–
2. High levels of linguistic competence	+	+	+	+	+	+	–
3. Specialised education & knowledge	–	+	+	+	+	–	+
4. Committed to own multilingualism	+	+	+?	+	+	–	–
C. Committed active parents							
1. Choice	+	+	+	+	+	+	–
2. Informed	+	+	+	+	+	+	–
3. Committed	+	+	+	+	+	+?	–?
4. Participants	–	–?	+	+	+	–?	–?
5. Develop own bilingualism	+	–	–?	+?	+?	–?	+?
6. Organised to direct policy	–	+?	+?	+	+	–	–

Name of programme	European Schools	Immer-sion	2-way biling.	Mainte-nance		Interna-tional	Transi-tional
TYPES	strong	strong	strong	strong		weak	weak
TYPICAL CHILD	Heter Maj	Homog Maj	Maj.& Min	Homog. Min		Heter. Ma&Mi	Min
MEDIUM OF INSTRUCTION							
Initially	L1	L2	Min L1 Maj L2	L1		L2 for most	L1
Subsequently	Both or all	Both	Both	L1 or both		L2&FL	L2
				F	S		
D. Progressively multilingual students							
1. Expect to become multilingual	+	+	+	+	+	+?	−
2. Informed, responsible for own learning	+?	+	+	+	+	+?	−
3. Organised for real influence	+?	+	+	+	+	−	−
II EDUCATIONAL CULTURE							
A. Multilingual surround outside classroom							
1. Goal bi/multilingualism for all	+	+	+?	+	+	+?	−
2. Goal encompasses 1-12 grades	+	−	−	+?	+?	+	−
3. All languages used							
3a. - in all spaces in school	+	+?	−	+	+	−	−
3b. - in correspondence	+	−?	+	−	−	−	+
3c. - in signs	+	−?	+?	+?	+?	−	−
3d. - on bulletin boards	+	+?	+?	+	+	−	−
3d. - in assemblies	+	−	−?	+	+	−	−
B. Multilingual languages policy							
1a. L1 has important core subject functions	+	+	+	+	+	−?	−?
1b. link to identity: same group	+	−	+?	+	+	−?	−?
1c. L1 used as medium 1-12	+	−?	−?	+?	+?	−	−?

Name of programme	European Schools	Immer-sion	2-way biling.	Mainte-nance		Interna-tional	Transi-tional
TYPES	strong	strong	strong	strong		weak	weak
TYPICAL CHILD	Heter Maj	Homog Maj	Maj.& Min	Homog. Min		Heter. Ma&Mi	Min
MEDIUM OF INSTRUCTION							
Initially	L1	L2	Min L1 Maj L2	L1		L2 for most	L1
Subsequently	Both or all	Both	Both	L1 or both		L2&FL	L2
				F	S		
1d. L1 taught as a subject 1-12	+	+?	–?	+	+	–	–
1e. linguistically homogeneous groups for L1 language arts	+	+	–	+	+	+	+
1f. Expose students to different varieties of L1	+?	–	+	+	+	–	+
1g. Protect L1 from majority language encroachment	+	+	+	+	+	–	–
2a. L2 has important core subject functions	+	+	+	+	+	+	+
2b. link to identity: same group	+	–?	+?	+	+	+?	+?
2c. L2 used as (one of the) media 3/4-12, according to monitored plan	+	+	+	+	+	+?	+?
2d. L2 taught as a subject 1-12	+	–	–	+	+	+	+?
2e. linguistically homogeneous groups for L2 language arts, and, for many years, for L2-medium instruction	+	+	–	+	+	–	–?
2f. Expose students to different varieties of L2	+?	–	–?	+	+	+?	+
2g. Silent period allowed	+	+	–	+	+	–	–
C. Inclusive pedagogical strategies							
1. Inquiry-based, problem-oriented	–	–?	+	+	+	–	–
2. Student-centred, interactive	–	–?	+	+	+	–?	–

Name of programme	European Schools	Immersion	2-way biling.	Maintenance		International	Transitional
TYPES	strong	strong	strong	strong		weak	weak
TYPICAL CHILD	Heter Maj	Homog Maj	Maj.& Min	Homog. Min		Heter. Ma&Mi	Min
MEDIUM OF INSTRUCTION							
Initially	L1	L2	Min L1 Maj L2	L1		L2 for most	L1
Subsequently	Both or all	Both	Both	L1 or both		L2&FL	L2
				F	S		
3. Whole language strategies	–	–?	+	+	+	–	–
4. Use of writing processes	–	–	+	+?	+	–	–
5. Authentic communication	+	+	+	+	+	–	+
D. Varied teaching materials							
1. Rich and varied materials	+	+	+	+	+	+?	+
2. Produce own materials with community & students	+?	+?	+	+	+	–	+?
3. Materials bi/multilingual	+?	+?	+	+	+	–	+?
4. Orature & literature equally valued	–	–	+?	+?	+	–	+?
E. Authentic & fair multilingual assessment							
1. Not compare native and L2-speakers	+	+	–	+	+	–?	–
2. Criterion-referenced/ performance- based; use portfolios	–?	–?	+?	+?	+	–?	–
3. Language of assessment same as medium of instruction, or chosen by student	+	–?	–	+?	+?	+?	–

+ Model generally has this feature

– Model does not generally have this feature

F = A Finnish School in Sweden (Upplands Väsby)

S = A Spanish School in the U.S.A. (La Luz, Dade County, Florida) mix language minority and majority students in the beginning and make no differentiation in instruction or assessment, always comparing them in ways which might disregard their linguistic prerequisites and needs. US two-way dual language models that truly aim to develop high levels of multilingualism of language majoritites and minorities will have to undergo a series of transformations in the future. Firstly, it seems clear to us from the above that a different educational treatment is needed initially for majorities and minorities. Integration can come about during especially designated context-embedded activities and instruction. But initially effective instruction for majorities and minorities must segregate them for some instruction during some part of the school day. Secondly, assessment for the majority and the minority should never compare their achievement in one or the other language. Mother tongue development and second language development follow different patterns and progressions, and these must be recognized. Finally, two-way dual language models must be expanded beyond elementary school, recognizing the slow development of multilingualism and multiliteracy both for majorities and minorities.[35]

Where the International Schools have tried to solve the "problem" of having speakers with several different mother tongues in the same class, by starting from what a language is *for the educational system* rather than for the student (Language A, Language B), and using one common language of instruction (which can be the student's mother tongue, her/his second language, or, at least at the beginning, a foreign language), the European Schools have tried to solve the problem by starting from what the language is (or is supposed to be) *for the student*, and using each of them as languages of instruction. The International Schools then get into problems of mother tongue loss, enormous heterogeneity in initial linguistic proficiency, and unfair assessment – and the introduction of Language A1 and Language A2 is trying to alleviate the latter – whereas the European Schools get into problems of either a less "clean" model (where the students in many subsections in reality do not have the language of the subsection as their mother tongue) or impossible logistics (if they try to maintain the principle of teaching students through the medium of their mother tongues). It seems to us that the problems facing the European Schools may be easier to solve.

Multilingual education must come to grips with the knowledge, gained from the European Schools, that full integration of multilingual and multicultural citizens may be based INITIALLY on partial physical separation, within a context of psychological and partially physical unity and collectivity. ALL ethnolinguistic groups must be given an opportunity for growth and development in and of themselves, while gaining knowledge of the language(s) and culture(s) of others. They must be given opportunity for linguistic and cultural autonomy, as well as integration and participation in the lives of others. They must learn to use the lens to which they were born, the one they acquired later, and others, and all in combination, as experienced participants in a world that needs the multiple images that only multilingual multicultural citizens could produce.

To conclude

Multilingual citizens hold the key to global understanding and improvement. To achieve that, humanity must be aided by an educational context able to expand our ethnolinguistic roots downwardly as well as upwardly, enabling us to move laterally to encompass other ethnolinguistic identities, and to contract into our own, enabling us to be different and the same, connected to others and to ourselves. In a diverse and increasingly interdependent world, we can expect that only the plurality of lenses offered by a multilingual and multicultural education will bring the harmony, balance stability and quiescence of the rapidly spinning top. The motionless illusion of the spinning top holds a lesson for all of us. Serenity, in a rapidly spinning world, can only be gained if we move along with it, with its multilingualism and its multiculturalism, and not if we remain captives of our monolingual, monocultural identity.

Does it sound idealistic? Romantic, naive? Academic poetry? The interesting thing is that some of the most exciting critics of the whole development paradigm we know, analysing political and economic power relations, come to very similar conclusions about the necessity of diversity (see e.g. *The Development Dictionary. A Guide to Knowledge as Power*, edited by Wolfgang Sachs, especially the entries on Equality by C.Douglas Lummis, Helping (Marianne Gronemeyer), Needs (Ivan Illich) and One World (Wolfgang Sachs). Multilingualism may give more access to Knowledge as Power – and the knowledge of both Self and Other that may come with it, might guide the "user" of that Power in a direction which does not harm the planet as much as the present power élites.

Notes:

1   This article builds on several of our earlier publications and typologies, mentioned in the bibliography. We have here concentrated on the educational context *in* the schools, and only mentioned societal and political prerequisites for schooling in passing. Those who are interested in seeing how we situate education in general and the education of minorities in particular, should consult our other publications. We thank Hugo Baetens Beardsmore, Alex Housen and teachers in the Brussels European School, especially Joanna Sancha and Julia Leigh, for a wealth of background information and for organising a most informative and delightful visit to the school. Likewise, thanks to Markku Peura, Head of the Sweden Finnish School in Upplands Väsby. One of us (TSK) also wants to thank Raquel Otheguy for so patiently waiting for the one page on Einstein's relativity theory, the writing of which this article and this book have delayed for too many months.

2   Hereinafter we shall use *"multilingual"* to mean both bilingual and multilingual. Debi Prásanna Pattanayak, the former Director of the Central Institute for Indian Languages, used to complain about reductionism, every time one of us used the term "bilingual", and ask which five of his seven languages he was supposed to discard in order to become bilingual only.

    "Multilingual schools" and *"multilingual education"* is used to mean schools/education where the *aim* is high levels of multilingualism for all. Using two or more languages as media of education (see also note 11, the classic definition of "bilingual education") is a necessary but not sufficient prerequisite for multilingual education in this sense.

3   It is "simplistic and dangerous to give too much currency to the phrase 'ethnic conflict'", says Alan Phillips (1994, 5), in his introduction to Asbjørn Eide's report *New approaches to minority protection* (1994). Eide, a member of the UN Sub-Commission on the Prevention of Discrimination and the Protection of Minorities, summarizes in the report his 3-year study for the Sub-Commission. Eide and Phillips (1994, 5-6) quote the NGO World Congress on Human Rights, New Delhi, 1991, where the phrase 'ethnic conflict' is labelled a misnomer which leads to false perception. Other prominent peace and conflict researchers who have critisized the labelling of conflicts and antagonisms as 'ethnic' as soon as ethnic lines happen to coincide with class lines, economic, geographical, religious, linguistic or other power-related lines in a conflict include Björn Hettne (e.g. 1987, 1990) and Rodolfo Stavenhagen (e.g. 1988, 1990). There may in some cases be a *correlational* relationship between conflict and language/ethnicity, but this should not be interpreted as a *causal* relationship (see Phillipson, Rannut & Skutnabb-Kangas, 1994; see also Fishman, 1989 and Pattanayak, 1988).

4   For more on linguistic human rights, see especially Skutnabb-Kangas and Phillipson 1989, 1994 and de Varennes (forthcoming).

5   Related to this is also the belief that bilingualism is causally connected to (other) psychological, educational or economic deficiencies and disasters. For refuting this type of claim, see, e.g. references to Corson, Cummins, Fishman, García, Hakuta, Nieto, Pattanayak, Skutnabb-Kangas, in the bibliography.

6   Or Language of Wider Colonization, as we prefer to call it.

7   Most International Schools are not part of bilingual/multilingual education in the classic sense of the term, though, because they only use one language of instruction.

8   See e.g. Obura 1986, Rubagumya 1991, Rubagumya (Ed.) 1990, for some examples. As Birgit Brock-Utne observes, "[I]n many of the African countries the majority language is treated in a way that minority languages are treated in the industrialized world" (1993, 39).

9   For more on different aims of multilingual education, see, e.g. Baker 1993; Ferguson, Houghton and Wells 1977; Fishman 1976; Hornberger 1991; Lo Bianco 1990; Mohanty, forthcoming).

10 For more on the distinction between strong and weak models of multilingual education and a typology, see especially Baker 1993, 153). See also the typologies in Skutnabb-Kangas 1984, chapter 6, which Baker has developed further.

11 They use two languages as media of education in subjects other than language arts in the languages themselves (Andersson & Boyer 1978).

12 For the concepts of linguistic & societal goals, especially when these do not tally with the officially expressed goals which sometimes function as a smokescreen, in the best doubletalk way, see Skutnabb-Kangas 1988, 1991b, and the introduction and final comments by the editors in Skutnabb-Kangas & Cummins (eds.) 1988.

13 Early, late or partial immersion programmes which have been studied and reported exist in many countries, e.g. Australia, Canada, Catalunya, Finland (e.g. Helle, in press) , Hungary (e.g. Duff, 1991), USA. Many countries are trying them out but without much research follow-up, others are planning them (e.g. Switzerland, or Estonia; see (Ülle) Rannut 1992). For studies on immersion programmes in other countries, see the references in Artigal's and Cummins' articles in this volume and Genesee 1987.

14 See e.g. Taylor, in press, on indigenous Mi'kmaq children in Canadian French immersion. See also Swain et al., 1990.

15 Unless something else is clearly indicated, we use "L2" or "second language" to mean the language which is the second in the order of learning for the student (as opposed to the first language or a third or fourth language). A second language in this sense may or may not be a language which the student can hear and use in the

immediate environment (one of the other common ways of defining a second language, *as opposed to* a *foreign* language which one does not use daily in the environment).

16 We thank Donna Christian for providing us the latest country-wide information which is included in the Dolson & Lindholm chapter.

17 See Curtis 1988 for a description of an alternate days programme, from its inception to its preliminary but temporary death – it functions in Calistoga again. See also Tucker et al. 1970 for an early description of this type of programme, in the Philippines.

18 See articles in Skutnabb-Kangas & Phillipson (Eds.) 1994, for analyses and examples; see also Minority Rights Group (Ed.) 1994.

19 See e.g. Skutnabb-Kangas 1987 and articles in Peura & Skutnabb-Kangas (Eds.) 1994, for examples of Finnish migrant minority children in maintenance programmes in Sweden; see also Eriksson 1993. Although not discussed in this book, ethnic mother-tongue schools in the United States are of this type; see Fishman 1980, García 1988, García and Otheguy 1988.

20 See note 9 in the Introduction to this volume for the concept of "Europeanized countries".

21 For more on how this is done, see García 1993; for a thorough criticism of the model and the ideologies behind it, see Mohanty, forthcoming. This model fits the United Nation's old definition of linguistic genocide – see Skutnabb-Kangas 1993, in press a, b).

22 An exception could be native speakers of the majority language of the host country, where this is different from the language of instruction, e.g. native (Austrian) German speakers in the Vienna International School might, as a rule, become high level bilingual and biliterate in German and English.

23 This stage roughly corresponds to the emergence of what Jim Cummins (1980a, 1981b) calls BICS (Basic Interpersonal Communicative Skills) or context-embedded language.

24 Ajit K. Mohanty summarizes his extensive empirical studies in India, studies where many of the methodological shortcomings of much of Western research into the relationship between bilingualism and cognition have been corrected for, as follows: "... bilingualism or the ability to communicate in two linguistic codes fosters metalinguistic and metacognitive development which makes them [the Kond children studied] cognitively more flexible, endows them with a capacity to control their own cognitive processes more effectively, gives them a better analytic and objective orientation and enhances their sensitivity to communicative input." (Mohanty, forthcoming, 81).

25 For some of the relevant applications of theories on macro-societal aspects of

education to minority education, see references to Cummins, Cameron et al., Heller, in the bibliography.

26 See e.g. the evaluation by Ramirez et al. 1991, where none of the groups evaluated had developed anything approaching full bilingualism by the end of grade 6; see also Dolson & Lindholm, this volume. In the Finnish study of working class immigrant minority children in mother tongue maintenance classes in two municipalities in Sweden, children who had most of their education through the medium of Finnish in grades 1-6 and a fair amount still in grades 7-9, did almost as well as Finnish children in Finland on a Finnish language test and somewhat but not significantly better than Swedish *middle class* children in parallel classes in the same schools on a Swedish language test, in grade 9 (see e.g. Skutnabb-Kangas 1987, 1991a, 1993a, 1994a; see also Eriksson 1994 for long-term results).

27 On mother tongue definitions, see Skutnabb-Kangas, 1984, chapter 2; 1988; 1990, chapter 2, "Concept definitions". We use here the following definition: "the mother tongue is the language (or the languages) one has learned first and identifies with". This definition (which takes into consideration the varying degrees of linguistic human rights, enjoyed by diffrent language groups) thus disregards both the person's *competence* in the mother tongue and whether the person *uses* the mother tongue, for instance, for official purposes/functions. Both a competence definition ("the language best known") and a functional definition ("the language used most") ignore the fact that the possibility of developing a mother tongue and using it outside the home crucially depends on power relations between speakers of different languages which an individual with a specific mother tongue cannot influence much as an individual.

28 An example could be that Spanish MT children in New York should be exposed to Puerto Rican, Dominican, Cuban, Castillian, Mexican, Guatemalan, New York and Californian Spanishes, spoken/written both by monolinguals and by bilinguals, as a first, a second and maybe even a third language.

29 See Beutel 1990a,b and Ada & Beutel, forthcoming, for powerful, empirically based reflections on how this can be done.

30 For more on whole language curricula and its implementation, see especially, Goodman, Kenneth, E. Brooks Smith, Robert Meredith and Yetta Goodman, 1987. *Language and Thinking in School. A Whole Language Curriculum*. New York: Richard C. Owen. For a look at whole language practices in bilingualism classrooms, see especially, Ada, Alma Flor. 1987. *A children's literature-based whole language approach to creative reading and writing*. Northvale, New Jersey: Santillana; Edelsky, Carole, 1986. *Writing in a Bilingual Program: Había una vez*. Norwood, NJ: Ablex. For a recent questioning of whole language practices with language minority students, see, Reyes, María de la Luz. 1992. Challenging Venerable Assumptions: Literacy instruction for

linguistically different students. *Harvard Educational Review* 62: 427-446.

31 See Ada et al., 1993, for an excellent example of this type of materials.

32 For more on portfolios and alternative assessment, see Mindy Kornhaber and Howard Gardner. 1993. *Varieties of Excellence.* New York: National Center for Restructuring Education, Schools, and Teaching, Teachers College, Columbia University. Also see Linda Darling-Hammond, Jacqueline Ancess & Beverly Falk (1994). *Alternative Assessment in Action. Case Studies of Schools and Students.* New York: Teachers College Press.

33 In fact our own ratings were not always in agreement for every detail either, except for the European School where we based it mainly on Hugo Baetens Beardsmore's description rather than thinking of the variation. In all the other models, the factual variation is enormous, and both of us are obviously familiar with different schools, in addition to the shared principles and experiences.

34 According to statistics from the different European Schools, many of them in fact do have a much more socially varied student body than the Brussels school which has been studied most. One of us had a long discussion about this recently with several of the teachers in the Brussels school – thanks again!

35 We know that many two-way teachers and administrators would agree with several of our points here. Our criticism should not be seen as criticism of those who have conceived the model or those who teach in it. Both of us are impressed and moved by the unselfish enthuasiasm and high-level professionalism and commitment we have experienced in the two-way programmes we have visited. The changes we propose can only come about in a different political climate which may not exist – yet.

CONSOLIDATED BIBLIOGRAPHY

Abbi, Anvita (Ed.) (1986). *Studies in bilingualism*. Delhi: Bahri Publications.

Abdoolcader, Levane (1989). *Sydney Voices: a Survey of Languages Other Than English in Catholic Schools*. Sydney: Catholic Education Office.

Ada, Alma Flor (1987). *A children's literature-based whole language approach to creative reading and writing*. Northvale, New Jersey: Santillana.

Ada, Alma Flor (1988). The Pajaro Valley Experience: Working with Spanish-Speaking Parents to Develop Children's Reading and Writing Skills Through the Use of Children's Literature. In Skutnabb-Kangas & Cummins (Eds.), 223-238.

Ada, Alma Flor, Harris, Violet J. & Hopkins, Lee Bennett (1993). *A chorus of cultures. Developing literacy through multicultural poetry. Poetry Anthology*. Carmel, CA: Hampton-Brown Books.

Ada, Alma Flor & Beutel, Constance, forthcoming, *Participatory Research as a Dialogue for Social Action*, San Francisco.

Alatis, James A. (Ed.) (1970). *Bilingualism and Language Contact: Anthropological, Linguistic, Psychological, and Sociological Aspects*. Report of the Twenty-first Annual Round Table Meeting on Linguistics and Language Studies. Washington, D.C.: Georgetown University Press.

Alatis, James A. (Ed.) (1978). *International Dimensions of Bilingual Education*. Georgetown University Round Table on Languages and Linguistics 1978. Washington, D.C.: Georgetown University Press.

Alatis, James A. (Ed.) (1980). *Current Issues in Bilingual Education*. Georgetown University Round Table on Languages and Linguistics 1980. Washington, D.C.: Georgetown University Press.

Alatis, James A. (Ed.) (1994). Georgetown University Round Table on Languages and Linguistics 1993. Washington, D.C.: Georgetown University Press.

Alfredsson, Gudmundur (1991). Minority Rights: Equality and Non-Discrimination. In Krag & Yukhneva (Eds.) 19-41.

Ammon, Ulrich 1991 *Die internationale Stellung der deutschen Sprache*, Berlin: De Gruyter.

Ammon, Ulrich 1994 The Present Dominance of English in Europe. With an Outlook on Possible Solutions to the European Language Problem, *Sociolinguistica* 8, 1994, 1-14.

Andersson, Theodore & Boyer, Mildred (1978). *Bilingual Schooling in the United States.* Austin, Texas: National Educational Laboratory Publishers, 2nd edition.

Andrýsek, Oldrich (1989). *Report on the definition of minorities.* Netherlands Institute of Human Rights, Studie- en Informatiecentrum Mensenrechten (SIM), SIM Special No 8.

Annamalai, E. (1986). Bilingualism through schooling in India. In Abbi (Ed.).

Arnau, Joaquim, Boada, Humbert & Forns, Maria (1990). *Els programes d'immersió al Català: una avaluació inicial.* Barcelona: Serveid'Ensenyament del Català del Departament d'Ensenyament de la Generalitat de Catalunya. (unpublished report).

Arnau, Joaquim, Comet, Cinta, Serra, Josep Maria & Vila, Ignasi (1992). *La educación bilingüe.* Barcelona: ICE.UB/Horsosri.

Arnau, Joaquim & Serra, Josep Maria (1992). Un model d'anàlisi per a l'avaluació de la competència oral dels alumnes castellanoparlants que assisteixen a un programa d'immersió. In *Ponencies, comunicacions i conclusions del Segons simposi sobre l'ensenyament del català a no-catalanoparlants.* Vic: EUMO, 145-156.

Artigal, Josep Maria (1987). Le programme de "bain de langue" pour l'enseignement de la langue à des enfants d'immigrés dans les écoles maternelles de Catalogne. *Revue de Phonetique Appliquée,* 82-83-84 (1987), 134-142.

Artigal, Josep Maria (1991a). *The Catalan Immersion Program: an European point of view.* Norwood, N.J.: Ablex.

Artigal, Josep Maria (1991b). The Catalan immersion program: the joint creation of shared indexical territory. *Journal of Multilingual and Multicultural Development,* 12(1&2), 21-33.

Artigal, Josep Maria (1992). Some considerations about why a new language is acquired by being used. *International Journal for Applied Linguistics,* 2(2), 221-240.

Artigal, Josep Maria (1993). Catalan and Basque Immersion programmes. In Baetens Beardsmore (Ed.), 30-53.

Artigal, Josep Maria (1994). The L2 kindergarten teacher as a territory maker. In Alatis (Ed.), 452-468.

Baetens Beardsmore, Hugo (1988). Who's Afraid of Bilingualism?. In *Euskara Biltzarra/Congreso de la Lengua Vasca,* vol. II, Vitoria-Gasteiz, 75-90.

Baetens Beardsmore, Hugo (1993). *The European School Experience in Multilingual Education.* Brussels: Vrije Universiteit Brussel and Université Libre de Bruxelles.

Baetens Beardsmore, Hugo & Anselmi, Gulia (1991). Code-Switching in a

Heterogeneous, Unstable, Multilingual Speech Community. In *Papers for the Symposium on Code-Switching in Bilingual Studies; Theory, Significance and Perspectives*, Strasbourg, European Science Foundation, vol. II, 405-436.

Baetens Beardsmore, Hugo & Kohls, Jürgen (1988). Immediate Pertinence in the Acquisition of Multilingual Proficiency: the European Schools. *The Canadian Modern Language Review*, 44(2), 240-260.

Baetens Beardsmore, Hugo & Lebrun, Nathalie (1991). Trilingual Education in the Grand Duchy of Luxembourg. In García (Ed.), 107-122.

Baetens Beardsmore, Hugo & Swain, Merrill (1985). Designing Bilingual Education: aspects of Immersion and 'European School Models'. *Journal of Multilingual and Multicultural Development*, 6(1), 1-15.

Baetens Beardsmore, Hugo (Ed.) (1993). *European Models of Bilingual Education*, Clevedon & Philadelphia: Multilingual Matters.

Baker, Colin (1993). *Foundations of Bilingual Education and Bilingualism*. Clevedon & Philadelphia: Multilingual Matters.

Baker, Keith & de Kanter, Adriane (1981). *Effectiveness of Bilingual Education: A Review of the Literature*, Final Draft. Washington, D.C.: U.S.Department of Education.

Baldauf, Jr., Richard & Luke, Allan (Eds.) (1990). *Language Planning and Education in Australasia and the South Pacific*. Clevedon & Philadelphia: Multilingual Matters.

Balkan, L. (1970). *Les effets de bilinguisme français-anglais sur les aptitudes intellectuelles*. Bruxelles: AIMAV.

Barona, Andres & Garcia, Eugene (Eds.) (1990). *Children at Risk: Poverty, Minority Status and Other Issues in Educational Equity*. Washington, D.C.: National Association of School Psychologists.

Bel, Aurora (1989). La competencia linguistica de los alumnos de immersion. In *Actas do I Simpósio Internacional de Didáctica da Lingua e a Literatura*. Santiago: Universidade de Santiago de Compostela, 209-219.

Bel, Aurora (1990). El programa d'immersió: alguns resultats. *Escola Catalana*, 274, 26-27.

Bel, Aurora (1991). *Deu anys de normalització lingüística a l'ensenyament, 1978-1988*. Barcelona: SEDEC, Departament d'Ensenyament, Generalitat de Catalunya.

Ben-Zeev, Sandra (1977a). Mechanisms by which chilhood bilingualism affects understanding of language and cognitive structures. In Hornby (Ed.), 29-55.

Ben-Zeev, Sandra (1977b). The influence of bilingualism on cognitive development and cognitive strategy. *Child Development*, 48(4), 1009-1018.

Bentahila, Abdelali (1983). *Language Attitudes Among Arabic-French Bilinguals in Morocco*. Clevedon: Multilingual Matters.

Berman, Paul et al. (1992). *Meeting The Challenge of Language Diversity (Volume II, Findings and Conclusions)*. Berkeley: BW Associates, 1-223.

Bernaus, Mercé (1993). *Introducció d'una tercera llengua des de l'educació infantil. Avaluació curs 1992-93.* Barcelona: Centre de Recursos de Llengües Estrangeres, Departament d'Ensenyament, Generalitat de Catalunya. (unpublished report).

Bernaus, Mercé (1994). *The role of motivation in the learning of a third language at the age of four.* Barcelona: Centre de Recursos de Llengües Estrangeres, Departament d'Ensenyament, Generalitat de Catalunya. (unpublished report).

Besikci, Ismail (1990). A Nation Deprived of Identity: The Kurds, Report to Minority Rights Conference. In *Minority Rights, Policies and Practice in South-East Europe.*

Beutel, Constance (1990a). To transform the world: all the rest is commentary. *CABE Newsletter,* 12(6), 3-13.

Beutel, Constance (1990b). Education for whom and for what? *The Newsletter for the North American Center for Active Learning through Drama,* 1(4), 1-3.

Bialystok, Ellen (1991). Metalinguistic dimensions of bilingual language proficiency. In Bialystok (Ed.), 113-140.

Bialystok, Ellen (Ed.) (1991) *Language processing in bilingual children.* Cambridge: Cambridge University Press.

Black, Paul (1990) Some Competing Goals in Aboriginal Language Planning. In Baldauf & Luke (Eds.), 80-88.

Boada, Humbert & Forns, Maria (in press). The speaker and listener referential communication skills on Catalan Immersion programmes. In *First European Conference on the Evaluation of Immersion Programmes.* Vaasa/Vasa: Continuing Education Center, University of Vaasa/Vasa, Finland.

Boixaderas, Rosa, Canal, Imma & Fernandez, Estela (1992). Avaluació dels nivells de llengua Catalana, Castellana i Matemàtiques en alumnes que han seguit el programa d'immersió lingüística i en alumnes que no l'han seguit. In *Ponencies, comunicacions i conclusions del Segons simposi sobre l'ensenyament del català a no-catalanoparlants.* Vic: EUMO, 165-182.

Brock-Utne, Birgit (1993). *Education in Africa,* Rapport Nr. 3, Oslo: University of Oslo, Institute for Educational Research.

Burke, Mary Ann (1992). Canada's immigrant children. *Canadian Social Trends,* Spring 1992, 15-20.

Byram, Michael & Leman, Johan (Eds.) (1990). *Bicultural and Trilingual Education. The Foyer Model in Brussels.* Clevedon & Philadelphia: Multilingual Matters.

Byrne, Heidi (Ed.) (1992). *Languages for a Multicultural World in Transition.* Illinois: National Textbook Company.

Cameron, Deborah, Frazer, Elizabeth, Harvey, Penelope, Rampton, M.B.H., and Richardson, Kay (1992). *Researching language. Issues of power and method.* London & New York: Routledge.

Carder, Maurice W. (1991). The role and development of ESL programmes in international schools. In Joniez & Harris (Eds.).

Capotorti, Francesco (1979). *Study of the Rights of Persons Belonging to Ethnic, Religious and Linguistic Minorities*. New York: United Nations.

CDE 1981 = California State Department of Education (1981). *Schooling and Language Minority Students: A Theoretical Framework*. Los Angeles: Evaluation, Dissemination and Assessment Center, California State University.

CDE 1982 = California State Department of Education (1982). *Basic principles for the education of language minority students, an overview*. Sacramento: Office of Bilingual Bicultural Education.

CDE 1984 = California Department of Education (1984). *Studies on Immersion Education: A Collection for U.S. Educators*. Sacramento: Bilingual Education Office.

CDE 1986 = California Department of Education (1986). *Beyond Language: Social & Cultural Factors in Schooling Language Minority Students*. Los Angeles: Evaluation, Dissemination and Assessment Center, California State University.

CDE 1990 = California Department of Education (1990). *California Basic Educational Data System Report: Foreign Language Classes*. Sacramento: California Department of Education.

CDE 1991 = California Department of Education (1991). *Remedying the Shortage of Teachers for Limited-English-Proficient Students*. Sacramento: Bilingual Education Office.

CDE 1992 = California Department of Education (1992). *Databical Language Census Reports*. 92-8B, Sacramento: Bilingual Education Office.

California Tomorrow (1992). *California Perspectives*. San Francisco: An Anthology from The California Tomorrow Organization.

Campbell, Russell (1984). The Immersion Education Approach to Foreign Language Teaching. In CDE 1984, 114-143.

Canale, Michael & Swain, Merrill (1980). Theoretical bases of communicative approaches to second language teaching and testing. *Applied Linguistics*, 1, 1-47.

Cenoz, Jasone, Lindsay, Diana & Espi, María Jesús (1992). *Introducción de una tercera langua desde la educación infantil. Evaluación curso 1991-92*. Donostia/San Sebastian: Guipuzkoa Ikastolen Elkartea. (unpublished report).

Cenoz, Jasone, Lindsay, Diana & Espi, María Jesús (1993). *Introducción de una tercera langua desde la educación infantil. Evaluación curso 1992-93*. Donostia/San Sebastian: Guipuzkoa Ikastolen Elkartea. (unpublished report).

Centre of African Studies (1986). *Language in education in Africa*, Seminar proceedings 26, Proceedings of a seminar at the Centre of African Studies, University of Edinburgh, 29-30 November, 1985. Edinburgh: Centre of African Studies.

Chilton, Pearce, J. (1992). *Evolution's End: Claiming the Potential of Our Intelligence*. San Francisco: Harper Collins Publishers.

Christian, Donna 1994 Students learning through two languages, Paper presented at 28th Annual TESOL Convention, Baltimore, Maryland, March 12 1994.

Christian, Donna & Mahrer, Cindy (1992). *Two-Way Bilingual Programs in the United States, 1991-1992*. Washington, D.C.: National Center for Research on Cultural Diversity and Second Language Learning.

Christian, Donna & Mahrer, Cindy (1993). *Two-Way Bilingual Programs in the United States, 1992-1993 Supplement*. Washington, D.C.: National Center for Research on Cultural Diversity and Second Language Learning.

Christian, Donna & Montone, Chris (1994). *Two-Way Bilingual Programs in the United States, 1993-1994 Supplement*. Washington, D.C.: National Center for Research on Cultural Diversity and Second Language Learning.

Clark, M. & Handscombe, Jean (Eds.) (1983). *On TESOL '82. Pacific Perspectives on Language Learning and Teaching*. Washington, D.C.: Teachers of English to Speakers of Other Languages.

Clyne, Michael (Ed.) (1986). *An Early Start: Second Language at Primary School*. Melbourne: River Seine.

Collier, Virginia P. (1987). Age and rate of acquisition of second language for academic purposes. *TESOL Quarterly*, 21, 617-641.

Corson, David (1993). *Language, Minority Education and Gender. Linking Social Justice and Power*. Clevedon/Philadelphia/Adelaide: Multilingual Matters.

Crawford, James (1989). *Bilingual Education: History, Politics, Theory and Practice*. Trenton, New Jersey: Crane Publishing Company.

Cummins, Jim (1978). Immersion programs: The Irish experience. *International Review of Education*, 24, 273-282.

Cummins, Jim (1979). Linguistic interdependence and the educational development of children. *Review of Educational Research*, 49, 222-251.

Cummins, Jim (1980a). The construct of language proficiency in bilingual education. In Alatis (Ed.), 81-103.

Cummins, Jim (1980b). The Cross Lingual Dimensions of Language Proficiency: Implications for Bilingual Education and the Optimal Age Issue. *Tesol Quarterly*, 14(2), 175-187.

Cummins, Jim (1981). The Role of Primary Language Development in Promoting Educational Success for Language Minority Students. In CDE 1981, 3-49.

Cummins, Jim (1984a). *Bilingualism and Special Education Issues in Assessment and Pedagogy*. Clevedon: Multilingual Matters.

Cummins, Jim (1984b). Bilingualism and cognitive functioning. In Shapson & D'Oyley (Eds.), 55-67.

Cummins, Jim (1984c). The Minority Language Child. In Shapson & D'Oyley (Eds.), 71-92.

Cummins, Jim (1987). Bilingualism, language proficiency, and metalinguistic development. In Homel, Palij & Aaronson (Eds.), 57-73.

Cummins, Jim (1989). *Empowering Minority Students*, Sacramento: California Association for Bilingual Education.

Cummins, Jim (1991). The development of bilingual proficiency from home to school: A longitudinal study of Portuguese-speaking children. *Journal of Education*, 173(2), 85-98.

Cummins, Jim (1992). Interpretations of the Calgary RCSSD #1 Literacy Immersion Project Year 3 data. Report submitted to the Calgary Roman Catholic Separate School Division, September.

Cummins, Jim (1994a). From Coercive to Collaborative Relations of Power in the Teaching of Literacy. In Ferdman, Weber & Ramirez (Eds.), 295-331.

Cummins, Jim (1994b). The socioacademic achievement model in the context of coercive and collaborative relations of power. In De Villar, Faltis & Cummins (Eds.), 363-390.

Cummins, Jim (1994c). The discourse of disinformation: the debate on bilingual education and language rights in the United States. In Skutnabb-Kangas & Phillipson (Eds.), 159-177.

Cummins, Jim & Danesi, Marcel (1991). *Heritage languages: The development and denial of Canada's linguistic resources*. Toronto: Garamond/Our Schools, Our Selves.

Curtis, Jan (1988). Parents, schools and racism: Bilingual education in a Northern California town. In Skutnabb-Kangas & Cummins (Eds.), 278-298.

Cziko, Gary A. (1992). The evaluation of bilingual education: from necessity to probability to possibility. *Educational Researcher*, 21(2), 10-15.

Dakin, J., Tiffen, B. & Widdowson, Henry G. (Eds.) (1968). *Language and Education*. Oxford: Oxford University Press.

Darling-Hammond, Linda, Ancess, Jacqueline & Falk, Beverly (1994). *Alternative Assessment in Action. Case Studies of Schools and Students*. New York: Teachers College Press.

de Varennes, Fernand (in press). *Language minorities and human rights*. Dortrecht: Martinus Nijhoff.

De Villar, Robert A., Faltis, Christian, J. & Cummins, James P. (Eds.) (1994). *Cultural diversity in schools: From rhetoric to practice*. Albany, NY: State University of New York Press.

DeAvila, Edward, Cohen, Elisabeth G. and Intili, J.A. (1981). *Multicultural improvement in cognitive abilities*. Sacramento: Final report to California State Department of Education.

Declaration on Languages of the Peoples of Russia (1991). On Languages of the Peoples of the Russian Federation. In *Collected Legislative Acts of the Russian Federation*, 4th issue, Edited by the Supreme Soviet of the Russian Federation. Moscow. (in Russian).

Derman-Sparks, Louise (1989). *Antibias Curriculum: Tools for Empowering Young Children*. Washington, D.C.: National Association for the Education of Young Children.

Diaz, Rafael (1986). Bilingüísmo y inteligencia: una revisión. In Siguan (Ed.), 41-51.

Diaz, Rafael & Klinger, C. (1991). Towards an explanatory model of the interaction between bilingualism and cognitive development. In Bialystok (Ed.), 167-192.

Diaz, Stephen, Moll, Luis & Mehan, Hugh (1986). Sociocultural Resources in Instruction: A Context-Specific Approach. In CDE 1986, 187-230.

Dodson, Carl (1985). *Bilingual Education: Evaluation, Assessment and Methodology*, Cardiff: University of Wales Press.

Dolson, David P. (1985a). *The Application of Immersion Education in the United States*. Rosslyn, VA: National Clearinghouse for Bilingual Education.

Dolson, David P. (1985b). The effects of Spanish home language use on the scholastic performance of Hispanic pupils. *Journal of Multilingual and Multicultural Development* 6(2), 135-155.

Dolson, David P. (1993). Multicultural Education for Superior Scholastic Performance: The Struggle for Social Justice. Paper presented at Institute for Two-Way Bilingual Programs, Manhattan Beach, California, July.

Dolson, David P. and Mayer Jan (1992). Longitudinal Study of Three Program Models for Language Minority Students: A Critical Examination of Reported Findings. *Bilingual Research Journal* 16(1&2), 105-158.

Drexel-Andrieu, Irène (1993). Bilingual geography: a Teacher's Perspective. In Baetens Beardsmore (Ed.), 174-183.

Duff, Patricia A. (1991). Innovations in Foreign Language Education: an Evaluation of Three Hungarian-English Dual-Language Schools. *Journal of Multilingual and Multicultural Development* 12(6), 459-476.

ECIS 1992 = European Council of International Schools (1992). *The International Schools Directory 1992*. European Council of International Schools, Inc.: Petersfield, Hampshire.

Edelsky, Carole (1986). *Writing in a Bilingual Program: Había una vez*. Norwood, NJ: Ablex.

Eide, Asbjørn (1994) *New approaches to minority protection*, London: Minority Rights Group International.

Eriksson, Riitta 1994 *Biculturalism in Upper Secondary Education. The Long Term Effects of Finnish Language Programs on Students' Educational and Occupational Careers - A Swedish Case Study*, Stockholm: Stockholm University, Institute of International Education.

Fazio, Lucy L. (1993). Influence of supplementary mother tongue instruction on minority children's second language performance. Paper presented at the 24th annual conference of the Canadian Association of Applied Linguistics, Ottawa, June.

Ferdman Bernardo, Weber, Rose-Marie & Ramirez, Arnulfo G. (Eds.) (1994). *Literacy Across Languages and Cultures*. Albany: State University of New York Press.

Ferguson, Charles A. (1959). Diglossia. *Word*, 15, 325-340.

Ferguson, Charles A., Houghton, Catherine & Wells, Marie H. (1977). Bilingual Education: An International Perspective. In Spolsky & Cooper (Eds.), 159-174.

FIPLV (1993). *Language policies for the world of the twenty-first century: Report for UNESCO.* no place: World Federation of Modern Language Associations.

Fishman, Joshua A. (1971). The Sociology of Language: An Interdisciplinary Social Science Approach to Language in Society. In Fishman (Ed.), 217-404.

Fishman, Joshua A. (1976). *Bilingual Education: An International Sociological Perspective,* Rowley, Mass.: Newbury House.

Fishman, Joshua A. (1980). Minority language maintenance and the ethnic mother-tongue school. *Modern Language Journal*, 64, 167-172.

Fishman, Joshua A. (1989). *Language & Ethnicity In Minority Sociolinguistic Perspective,* Clevedon & Philadelphia: Multilingual Matters.

Fishman, Joshua A., Cooper, Robert L. & Ma, Roxana (1971). *Bilingualism in the Barrio,* Language Science Monographs. Bloomington, Ind.: Indiana University.

Fishman, Joshua A. (Ed.) (1971). *Advances in the Sociology of Language, Volume 1.* The Hague: Mouton.

Forns Maria & Gómez-Benito, Juana (in press). The cognitive, linguistic and adaptative development, and academic achievement of Pre-school children within the Catalan Immersion Programme. In *First European Conference on the Evaluation of Immersion Programmes.* Vaasa/Vasa: Continuing Education Center. University of Vaasa/Vasa, Finland.

García, Ofelia (1988). The education of biliterate and bicultural children in ethnic schools in the United States. In *Essays by the Spencer Fellows of the National Academy of Education*, Vol. IV, 19-78.

García, Ofelia (1992). Societal multilingualism in a multicultural world in transition. In Byrne (Ed.), 1-27.

García, Ofelia (1993). Understanding the societal role of the teacher in transitional bilingual education classrooms: Lessons from Sociology of Language. In Zondag (Ed.), 25-37.

García, Ofelia (Ed.) (1991). *Bilingual Education: Focusschrift in Honor of Joshua A. Fishman.* Volume I. Amsterdam & Philadelphia: John Benjamins.

García, Ofelia & Otheguy, Ricardo (1985). The Masters of Survival Send Their Children to School: Bilingual Education in the Ethnic Schools of Miami. *The Bilingual Review,* 12, 3-20.

García, Ofelia & Otheguy, Ricardo (1988). The bilingual education of Cuban American children in Dade County's ethnic schools. *Language and Education* 1, 83-95.

Gardner, Robert C. (1979). Social Psychological Aspects of Second Language Acquisition. In Giles & StClair (Eds.), 193-220.

Gass, Susan & Madden, Carolyn (Eds.) (1985). *Input in Second Language Acquisition.* Rowley, Mass.: Newbury House.

Genesee, Fred (1976). The Suitability of Immersion Programs for All Children. *Canadian Modern Language Review,* 32(5), 494-515.

Genesee, Fred (1985). Second language learning through immersion: A review of U.S. programs. *Review of Educational Research* 55(4), 541-561.

Genesee, Fred (1987). *Learning Through Two Languages: Studies of Immersion and Bilingual Education.* Cambridge, MA: Newbury House.

Genesee, Fred, Tucker, G. Richard & Lambert, Wallace E. (1976). An Experiment in Trilingual Education: report 3. *The Canadian Modern Language Review,* 34, 621-643.

Gerard, W. (1993). Broken English. *Toronto Star,* June 20, B1, B7.

Gersten, Russell, Woodward, Joan & Schneider, Susan (1992). *Bilingual Immersion: A Longintudinal Evaluation of the El Paso Program.* Washington, D.C.: READ Institute.

Gibbons, John (1994). Depth or breadth: some issues in LOTE teaching. *Australian Review of Applied Linguistics* 17(1), 1-22.

Gibbons, John, White, William & Gibbons, Pauline (1994). Combating educational disadvantage among Lebanese Australian children. In Skutnabb-Kangas & Phillipson (Eds.), 253-262.

Giles, Howard & StClair, Robert (Eds.) (1979). *Language and Social Psychology.* Oxford: Basil Blackwell.

Goodman, Kenneth, E., Smith, Brooks, Meredith, Robert & Goodman, Yetta (1987). *Language and Thinking in School. A Whole Language Curriculum.* New York: Richard C. Owen.

Gronemeyer, Marianne (1992). Helping. In Sachs (Ed.), 53-69.

Guasch, Oriol et al. (1990). L'aprenentatge de l'escriptura i els programes d'immersió: anàlisi de textos de nens de 4t d'EGB. In *Ponencies, comunicacions i conclusions del Segons simposi sobre l'ensenyament del català a no-catalanoparlants.* Vic: EUMO, 183-192.

Guthrie, Grace (1985). *A School Divided: An Ethnography of Bilingual Education in a Chinese Community.* Hillsdale: Lawrence Erlbaum.

Göncz, Lajos & Kodžopeljić, Jasmina (1991). Exposure to two languages in the preschool period: metalinguistic development and the acquisition of reading. *Journal of Multilingual and Multicultural Development,* 12(3), 137-163.

Haarman, Harald (1979-1984). *Elemente einer Soziologie der kleinen Sprachen Europas.* Bd.1, 1983; Bd. 2, 1979; Bd. 3, 1984. Hamburg: H.Buske.

Hakuta, Kenji (1986). *Mirror of language: The debate on bilingualism.* New York: Basic Books.

Hamel, Rainer Enrique (1994a). Indigenous education in Latin America: policies and legal frameworks. In Skutnabb-Kangas & Phillipson (Eds.), 271-287.

Hamel, Rainer Enrique (1994b). Linguistic rights for Amerindian people in Latin

America. In Skutnabb-Kangas & Phillipson (Eds.), 289-303.

Harley, Birgit, Allen, Patrick, Cummins, Jim & Swain, Merrill (1991). *The development of second language proficiency*. Cambridge: Cambridge University Press.

Harris, Stephen 1990 *Two-way Aboriginal Schooling. Education and Cultural Survival.* Canberra: Aboriginal Studies Press.

Hawkesworth, Dorrit (1988). Incongruity of Sexual Norms and Behaviour in the Danish State Schools: Notes for Discussion. In Jørgensen, Hansen, Holmen & Gimbel (Eds.), 221-226.

Heath, Shirley Brice (1986). Sociocultural Contexts of Language Development. In CDE 1986, 143-186.

Helle, Tuija (in press). Directions in bilingual education: Finnish comprehensive schools in perspective. *International Journal of Applied Linguistics*.

Heller, Monica (1994). *Crosswords. Language Education and Ethnicity in French Ontario.* Contributions to the Sociology of Language, 66. Berlin & New York: Mouton de Gruyter.

Helsinki Watch (1990). *Destroying ethnic identity. The Kurds of Turkey. An update,* September 1990. New York & Washington, D.C..

Hernández-Cháves, Eduardo (1984). The Inadequacy of English Immersion Education as an Educational Approach for Language Minority Students in the United States. In CDE 1984, 144-183.

Hettne, Björn (1987). *Etniska konflikter och internationella relationer*, Rapport 6 från DEIFO. Stockholm: DEIFO (Delegationen för invandrarforskning).

Hettne, Björn (1990). *Development Theory and the Three Worlds*. Harlow: Longman.

Holt, Daniel (1993). *Cooperative Learning: A Response to Linguistic and Cultural Diversity*. Language in Education Series: ERIC Clearinghouse on Languages and Linguistics. McHenry, Illinois: Delta Systems Company.

Homel, Peter, Palij, Michael & Aaronson, Doris (Eds.) (1987). *Childhood bilingualism: Aspects of linguistic, cognitive and social development*. Hillsdale, NJ: Lawrence Erlbaum Associates Publishers.

Hornberger, Nancy H. (1991). Extending enrichment bilingual education: Revisiting typologies and redirecting policy. In García (Ed.) 1991, 215-234.

Hornby, Peter A. (Ed.) 1977. *Bilingualism. Psychological, social and educational implications*. New York: Academic Press.

Housen, Alex (1993). The Expression of Temporality in the English Interlanguage of French, Dutch and German Child Learners of English, Paper presented at AILA '93, Amsterdam.

Housen, Alex & Baetens Beardsmore, Hugo (1987). Curricular and Extra-Curricular Factors in Multilingual Education. *Studies in Second Language Acquisition*, 9, 83-102.

Human Rights in Kurdistan (1989). *Documentation of the international conference on human rights in Kurdistan*, 14-16 April 1989, Hochschule Bremen. Bremen: The Initiative for Human Rights in Kurdistan.

Ianco-Worral, Anita D. (1972). Bilingualism and cognitive development. *Child Development*, 43, 1390-1400.

Illich, Ivan (1992). Needs. In Sachs (Ed.), 88-101.

International Baccalaureate Examinations Office (IBEX) (1992). *Language A2, Development Working Party; Report of Meeting 20-22 November 1992*. Cardiff: IBEX.

Jonietz, Patricia L. and Harris, D. (Eds.) (1991). *World Yearbook of Education 1991: International Schools and International Education*. London: Kogan Page.

Jordan, Deirdre (1988). Rights and claims of indigenous people: Education and the reclaiming of identity. In Skutnabb-Kangas & Cummins (Eds.), 189-222.

Jørgensen, Jens N., Hansen, Elisabeth, Holmen, Anne & Gimbel, Jørgen (Eds.) (1988). *Bilingualism in Society and School*, Clevedon & Philadelphia: Multilingual Matters,

Kagan, Spencer (1986). Cooperative learning and sociocultural factors in schooling. In CDE 1986, 231-298.

Kāretu, Timoti (1994). Māori language rights in New Zealand. In Skutnabb-Kangas & Phillipson (Eds.), 209-218.

Keep, Linda (1993). *French immersion attrition: Implications for model building*. Doctoral dissertation, The University of Alberta.

Khubchandani, Lachman M. (1983). *Plural Languages, Plural Cultures: Communication, Identity and Sociopolitical Change in Contemporary India*. An East-West Center Book. Honolulu: The University of Hawaii Press.

Kornhaber, Mindy & Gardner, Howard (1993). *Varieties of Excellence*. New York: National Center for Restructuring Education, Schools, and Teaching, Teachers College, Columbia University.

Krag, Helen & Yukhneva, Natalia (Eds.) (1991). *The Leningrad Minority Rights Conference. Papers*. Copenhagen: The Minority Rights Group in Denmark.

Krashen, Stephen (1981a). *Second Language Acquisition and Second Language Learning*, Oxford, Pergamon.

Krashen, Stephen (1981b). Bilingual education and second language acquisition. In CDE 1981, 51-70.

Krashen, Stephen & Biber, Douglas (1988). *On Course: Bilingual Education's Successes in California*, Sacramento, CA: California Association for Bilingual Education.

Lambert, Wallace E. (1978). Some cognitive and sociocultural consequences of being bilingual. In Alatis (Ed.), 214-229.

Lambert, Wallace E. (1987). The effects of bilingual and bicultural experiences on children's attitudes and social perspectives. In Homel, Palij & Aaronson (Eds.), 197-221.

Lambert, Wallace E. & Tucker, G.Richard (1972). *Bilingual education of children. The*

St.Lambert experiment. Rowley, M.A.: Newbury House.

Lapkin, Sharon, Swain, Merrill, & Shapson, Stan (1990). French immersion research agenda for the 90s. *Canadian Modern Language Revue/ La Revue canadienne des language vivantes*, 46(4), 638-674.

Laundry, R. & Allard, R. (1991). Can schools promote additive bilingualism in minority group children? In Malave & Duquette (Eds.), 198-231.

Leman, Johan (1993). The Bicultural Programmes in the Dutch-Language School System in Brussels. In Baetens Beardsmore (Ed.), 86-99.

Leontiev, Alexei A. (1991). Bilingualism and Bilingual Education in the USSR. *Korean Linguistics and Korean Language Education in the USSR*. Seoul: The Korean Society of Bilingualism, 195-205.

Leontiev, Alexei A. (1994). Linguistic Human Rights and Educational Policy in Russia. In Skutnabb-Kangas & Phillipson (Eds.), 63-70.

Leontiev, Alexei A., in press *Cultures and Languages of Our Peoples*. Moscow: MIDES Publishing House. (in Russian).

Leopold, Werner (1970). *Speech Development of a Bilingual Child*, Vols I-IV. New York: AMS Press.

Lewis, Glyn E. (1972). *Multilingualism in the Soviet Union*. The Hague: Mouton.

Liljeström, Rita, Noren-Björn, Eva, Schyl-Bjurman, Gertrud, Örn, Birgit, Gustafsson, Lars H. & Löfgren, Orvar (1982). *Kinas barn och våra*. Lund: Liber.

Liljeström, Rita, Noren-Björn, Eva, Schyl-Bjurman, Gertrud, Örn, Birgit, Gustafsson, Lars H. & Löfgren, Orvar (1985). *Young Children in China*. Clevedon, Avon: Multilingual Matters.

Lindholm, Kathryn J. (1990). Bilingual immersion education: Educational equity for language-minority students. In Barona & Garcia (Eds.), 77-89.

Lindholm, Kathryn J. (1991). Theoretical assumptions and empirical evidence for academic achievement in two languages. *Hispanic Journal of Behavioral Sciences*, 13, 3-17.

Lindholm, Kathryn J. (1992). Two-way bilingual/immersion education: Theory, conceptual issues, and pedagogical implications. In Padilla & Benavides (Eds.), 195-220.

Lindholm, Kathryn J. (1994). Promoting positive cross-cultural attitudes and perceived competence in culturally and linguistically diverse classrooms. In De Villar, Faltis & Cummins (Eds.), 189-206.

Lindholm, Kathryn J. & Aclan, Zierlein (1991). Bilingual proficiency as a bridge to academic achievement: Results from bilingual immersion programs. *Journal of Education*, 173, 99-113.

Little Hoover Commission (1993). *A Chance To Succeed: Providing English Learners with Supportive Education*. Sacramento: Little Hoover Commission.

Lo Bianco, Joseph (1987). *National Policy on Languages*. Canberra: Australian Government Publishing Service.

Lo Bianco, Joseph (1990). Making Language Policy: Australia's Experience. In Baldauf & Luke (Eds.), 47-79.

Long, Michael H. (1981). Input, interaction and second language acquisition. In Winitz (Ed.), 379.

Lorch, S. C., McNamara, Timothy F. & Eisokovits, Edina (1992). Late Hebrew Immersion at Mount Scopus College, Melbourne: Towards complete Hebrew fluency for Jewish day school students. *Working Papers in Language and Language Education*, 2(1), 1-29.

Lummis, Douglas C. (1992). Equality. In Sachs (Ed.), 38-52.

Magga, Ole Henrik (1994). The Sámi Language Act. In Skutnabb-Kangas & Phillipson (Eds.), 219-233.

Malakoff, M. & Hakuta, Kenji (1991). Translation skill and metalinguistic awareness in bilinguals. In Bialystok (Ed.), 141-166.

Malave, L. M. & Duquette, G. (Eds.) (1991). *Language, culture & cognition*. Clevedon, England: Multilingual Matters.

Maurais, Jacques (1992). "Redéfinition du statut des langues en Union Soviétique." *Language Problems and Language Planning*, 16(1), 1-20.

McLaughlin, Daniel (1992). *When literacy empowers. Navajo language in print*. Albuquerque: University of New Mexico Press.

McLaughlin, Daniel & Tierney, William G. (Eds.) (1993). *Naming silenced lives: personal narratives and the process of educational change*. New York: Routledge.

Milk, Robert D. (1993). Bilingual Education and English As A Second Language: The Elementary School. In *Bilingual Education: Politics, Practice, Research*. Chicago: The National Society for the Study of Education, 88-112.

Milroy, Lesley (1980). *Language and Social Networks*. Oxford: Blackwell.

Minority Rights Group (Ed.) (1994). *Education Rights and Minorities*. London: Minority Rights Group.

Minority Rights, Policies and Practice in South-East Europe, Reports for the Conference at Christiansborg, Copenhagen, March 30th - April 1st 1990 (1990). Copenhagen: The Danish Helsinki Committee & The Minority Rights Group.

Mohanty, Ajit K. (forthcoming). *Bilingualism in a Multilingual Society. Psychosocial and Pedagogical Implications*.

Moore, Helen (1991). Teaching English to speakers of other languages: an Australian perspective. Paper at ACTA/ATESOL 7th Annual Summer School "TESOL in Context". Sydney.

Murphy, Edna (Ed.) (1990). *ESL: A Handbook for Teachers and Administrators in International Schools*. Clevedon, Avon: Multilingual Matters.

National Commission on Excellence in Education (1983). *A nation at risk: The imperative for educational reform*. Washington, D.C.: U.S. Department of Education.

Nieto, Sonia (1992) *Affirming diversity. The sociopolitical context of multicultural education*. New York & London: Longman.

Ngũgĩ, wa Thiong'o (1987). *Decolonising the mind. The politics of language in African literature*. London: James Currey.

Obura, Anna (1986). Research issues and perspectives in language in education in Africa: an agenda for the next decade. In *Centre of African Studies*, 413-444.

Ogbu, John & Matute-Bianchi, María Eugenia (1986). Understanding Sociocultural Factors: Knowledge, Identity, and School Adjustment. In CDE 1986, 73-142.

Otero-Lamas, Antonio (1994). L'Ecole Européenne et la formation de la jeunesse, *Schola Europaea* VI, No 120, 22-31.

Padilla, Raymond V. & Benavides, Alfredo H. (Eds.) (1992). *Critical Perspectives on Bilingual Education Research*. Tempe, Arizona: Bilingual Review Press/Editorial Bilingüe.

Pattanayak, Debi Prasanna (1981). *Multilingualism and Mother-Tongue Education*. Delhi: Oxford University Press.

Pattanayak, Debi Prasanna (1984). Language policies in multilingual states. In Gonzales, A. (Ed.) *Panagani. Language planning, implementation and evaluation*. Manila: Linguistic Society of the Philippines. (quoted in Mohanty, forthcoming, 166).

Pattanayak, Debi Prasanna (1986). Educational use of the mother tongue. In Spolsky (Ed.), 5-15.

Pattanayak, Debi Prasanna (1988). Monolingual myopia and the petals of the Indian lotus: do many languages divide or unite a nation? In Skutnabb-Kangas & Cummins (Eds), 379-389.

Pattanayak, Debi Prasanna (Ed.) 1991. *Multilingualism in India*, Clevedon: Multilingual Matters.

Pattanayak, Debi Prasanna (1992). Mothertongue awareness. Lecture given at Cambridge University, U.K., September 1992, manuscript.

Paulston, Cristina Bratt (1982). *Swedish Research and Debate About Bilingualism*. Stockholm: Skolöverstyrelsen (National Swedish Board of Education).

Peal, Elisabeth & Lambert, Wallace E. (1962). The relation of bilingualism to intelligence. *Psychological Monographs*, 1962, 76(27), 1-23.

Peura, Markku & Skutnabb-Kangas, Tove (Eds.) 1994. *"Man kan vara tvåländare också." Om sverigefinnarnas väg från tystnad till kamp*, ("You can be bicountrial too". The road of the Sweden Finnish minority from silence to struggle), Stockholm: Sverigefinländarnas arkiv.

Phillips, Alan (1994). Introduction. In Eide (1994), 5-8.

Phillipson, Robert (1992). *Linguistic imperialism*. Oxford: Oxford University Press.

Phillipson, Robert (1994). English language spread policy. *International Journal of the*

Sociology of Language, 107, 7-24.

Phillipson, Robert, Rannut, Mart & Skutnabb-Kangas, Tove (1994). Introduction. In Skutnabb-Kangas & Phillipson (Eds.), 1-22.

Phillipson, Robert & Skutnabb-Kangas, Tove (1994). English, panacea or pandemic. *English only? in Europe/in Europa/en Europe, Sociolinguistica* 9, International Yearbook of European Sociolinguistics, 73-87.

Phillipson, Robert, Kellerman, Eric, Selinker, Larry, Sharwood Smith, Mike & Swain, Merrill (Eds.) (1991). *Foreign/Second Language Pedagogy Research: a commemorative volume for Claus Faerch*. Clevedon: Multilingual Matters.

Ramirez, J. David (1992). Executive Summary. *Bilingual Research Journal*, 16(1&2), 1-62.

Ramirez, J. David, Pasta, David J., Yuen, Sandra D., Billings, David K. & Ramey, Dena R. (1991). *Longitudinal study of structured immersion strategy, early-exit, and late-exit bilingual education programs for language minority children (Vols. 1-2)*. San Mateo, CA: Aguirre International.

Ramirez, J. David., Yuen, Sandra D. & Ramey, Dena R. (1991). *Executive Summary: Final report: Longitudinal study of structured English immersion strategy, early-exit and late-exit transitional bilingual education programs for language-minority children, Submitted to the U.S.Department of Education*. San Mateo, CA: Aguirre International.

Rannut, Ülle 1992 *Keelekümblus*, Tallinn: Keeleameti toimetised nr 3.

Reyes, María de la Luz (1992). Challenging Venerable Assumptions: Literacy instruction for linguistically different students. *Harvard Educational Review* 62, 427-446.

Rhodes, Nancy & Schreibstein, Alice (1983). *Foreign Language in the Elementary School: A Practical Guide*. Washington, D.C.: Center for Applied Linguistics.

Ribes, David (1993). *Els programes d'immersió al català: avaluació d'alguns aspectes del rendiment escolar*. Unpublished Ph. D. dissertation. Universitat de Barcelona.

Rosenberg, Thomas (1994). *Svenskfinlands sönderfall. Texter till minnet av ett folk*. (The disintegration of Swedish Finland. Texts in rememberance of a people). Vasa: Institutet för finlandssvensk samhällsforskning.

Rubagumya, Casmir M. 1991 *Language, social values and inequality in Tanzania: reinterpreting triglossia*, Lancaster University, Department of Linguistics and Modern English Language, Centre for Language in Social Life, Working Papers 26.

Rubagumya, Casmir M. (Ed) 1990 *Language in education in Africa: A Tanzanian perspective*, Clevedon: Multilingual Matters.

Sachs, Wolfgang (1992). One World. In Sachs (Ed.), 102-115.

Sachs, Wolfgang (Ed.) (1992). *Development Dictionary. A Guide to Knowledge as Power*. London & New Jersey: Zed Books.

Sahgal, Anju (1992). *Bilingualism and scholastic achievement*. Unpublished PhD Thesis. Delhi: University of Delhi.

Schola Europaea.

SEDEC (1983). *Quatre anys de català a l'escola*. Barcelona: Departament d'Ensenyament, Generalitat de Catalunya.

Serra, Josep Maria (1990). Resultados académicos y desarrollo cognitivo en un programa de inmersión dirigido a escolares de nivel sociocultural bajo. *Infancia y Aprendizaje*, 47, 55-65.

Shapson, Stan & D'Oyley, Vincent (Eds.) (1984). *Bilingual and Multicultural Education: Canadian Perspectives*. Clevedon: Multilingual Matters.

Sharp, Derrick (1973). *Language in Bilingual Communities*. London: Arnold.

Sierra, Josy (1991). La inmersión y la enseñanza bilingüe en el País Vasco. *Comunicación, Lenguaje y Educación*, 10, 41-55.

Sierra, Josy & Olaziregi, Ibon (1987). *PIR-5 Hizkuntz testa. B eta D ereduetako 5-6 uteko haurrentzat*. Vitoria-Gasteiz: Servicio Central de Publicaciones del Gobierno Vasco.

Sierra, Josy & Olaziregi, Ibon (1989). *EIFE 2. La enseñanza del euskera: influencia de los factores. Estudio de 5º de EGB en los modelos A, B y D*. Vitoria-Gasteiz: Servicio Central de Publicaciones del Gobierno Vasco.

Sierra, Josy & Olaziregi, Ibon (1990). *EIFE 3. La enseñanza del euskera: influencia de los factores. Estudio de 2º de EGB en los modelos A, B y D*. Vitoria-Gasteiz: Servicio Central de Publicaciones del Gobierno Vasco.

Sierra, Josy & Olaziregi, Ibon (1991). *EIFE 3. Influence of factors on the learning of Basque: Study of the models A, B, and D in second year Basic General Education*. Vitoria-Gasteiz: Department of Education, Universities and Research, Government of the Basque Country.

Siguan, Miquel (1992). *España plurilingüe*. Madrid: Alianza Editorial.

Siguan, Miquel (Ed.) (1986). *Las lenguas minoritarias i la educación*. Barcelona: ICE-Universitat de Barcelona.

Silence is killing them. Annual report 1993, "On the Situation of Human Rights in Northern Kurdistan and the Kurds in Turkey" (1994). Bremen: International Association for Human Rights in Kurdistan.

Siren, Ulla (1991). *Minority language transmission in early childhood: Paternal intention and language use*. Stockholm: Institute of International Education, Stockholm University.

Skutnabb-Kangas, Tove (1984). *Bilingualism or Not: the Education of Minorities*, Clevedon, Multilingual Matters.

Skutnabb-Kangas, Tove (1987). *Are the Finns in Sweden an Ethnic Minority? Finnish Parents Talk about Finland and Sweden*. Working Paper 1, Research Project The Education of The Finnish Minority in Sweden, Roskilde: Roskilde Universitetscenter.

Skutnabb-Kangas, Tove (1988). Multilingualism and the education of minority children. In Skutnabb-Kangas & Cummins (Eds.), 9-44.

Skutnabb-Kangas, Tove (1990a). Legitimating or delegitimating new forms of racism - the role of researchers. In Gorter et al. (Eds.), 77-100.

Skutnabb-Kangas, Tove (1990b). *Language, Literacy and Minorities*. London: The Minority Rights Group.

Skutnabb-Kangas, Tove (1991a). Bicultural Competence and Strategies for Negotiating Ethnic Identity. In Phillipson et al. (Eds.), 307-332.

Skutnabb-Kangas, Tove (1991b). Swedish strategies to prevent integration and national ethnic minorities. In García (Ed.), 25-42.

Skutnabb-Kangas, Tove (1993a). Linguistic human rights in the education of minorities. Paper presented at Conference on Multilingualism and Ethnicity in Europe, Bratislava, 21-25 August 1993.

Skutnabb-Kangas, Tove (1993b). Identitet og strategier i flersprogede familier: interview med Tiina Rinne Toh & Eric Toh, Mustafa Hussain & Ida Høgsbro, Gulda Bozarslan & Mehmet Bozhan (Identity and strategies in multilingual families: interview with TRT & ET, MH & IH, GB & MB). In Skutnabb-Kangas, Holmen & Phillipson (Eds.), 190-199.

Skutnabb-Kangas, Tove (1994a). Sverigefinnar förhandlar om etnisk identitet (The Sweden Finns negotiate about ethnic identity). In Peura & Skutnabb-Kangas (Eds.), 98-128.

Skutnabb-Kangas, Tove (1994b). Språkliga mänskliga rättigheter, invandrade minoriteter och makt (Linguistic human rights, immigrant minorities and power). In Peura & Skutnabb-Kangas (Eds.), 73-83.

Skutnabb-Kangas, Tove (in press, a). Language and demands for self-determination. In Clark, Don et al (Eds.) *Self-Determination: International Perspectives*. London: The Macmillan Press.

Skutnabb-Kangas, Tove (in press, b). Educational language choice - multilingual diversity or monolingual reductionism? In Hellinger, Marlis & Ammon, Ulrich (Eds.) *Contrastive Sociolinguistics*, Part III, Language planning and language politics. Berlin & New York: Mouton de Gruyter.

Skutnabb-Kangas, Tove & Bucak, Sertaç (1994). Killing a mother tongue - how the Kurds are deprived of linguistic human rights. In Skutnabb-Kangas & Phillipson (Eds.), 347-370.

Skutnabb-Kangas, Tove & Peura, Markku (1994) Den sverigefinska minoriteten i världen (The Sweden Finnish minority from a global point of view). In Peura & Skutnabb-Kangas (Eds.), 154-170.

Skutnabb-Kangas, Tove & Phillipson, Robert (1989). *Wanted! Linguistic Human Rights*, Roskilde: Roskilde University, ROLIG-papir 44.

Skutnabb-Kangas, Tove & Phillipson, Robert (1994). Linguistic human rights, past and present. In Skutnabb-Kangas & Phillipson (Eds.), 71-110.

Skutnabb-Kangas, Tove & Cummins Jim (Eds.) (1988). *Minority Education: From Shame to Struggle*. Clevedon/Philadelphia: Multilingual Matters.

Skutnabb-Kangas, Tove, Holmen, Anne & Phillipson, Robert (Eds.) 1993. *Uddannelse af minoriteter* (The Education of minorities), Københavnerstudier i tosprogethed 18, Copenhagen: Danmarks Lærerhøjskole, Center for multikulturelle studier.

Skutnabb-Kangas, Tove & Phillipson, Robert (Eds., in collaboration with Mart Rannut) (1994) *Linguistic Human Rights. Overcoming Linguistic Discrimination*. Contributions to the Sociology of language, 67. Berlin & New York: Mouton de Gruyter.

Smolicz, J.J. (1986). National Language Policy in the Philippines. In Spolsky (Ed.), 96-116.

Spener, David (1988). Transitional Bilingual Education and The Socialization of Immigrants. *Harvard Educational Review* 58: 2 (May).

Spolsky, Bernard (Ed.) (1986). *Language and education in multilingual settings*, Clevedon & Philadelphia: Multilingual Matters.

Spolsky, Bernard & Cooper, Robert (Eds.). *Frontiers of Bilingual Education*. Rowley, Mass.: Newbury House.

Stairs, Arlene 1988 Beyond cultural inclusion. An Inuit example of indigenous education development. In Skutnabb-Kangas & Cummins (Eds.), 308-327.

Stanford Working Group (1993). *Federal Education Programs for Limited-English-Proficient Students: A Blueprint for the Second Generation*. Stanford, CA: Stanford University.

Stavenhagen, Rodolfo (1988). Old and New Racism in Europe. In *New Expressions of Racism. Growing Areas of Conflict in Europe*, SIM Special No. 7, 1988, Utrecht: Netherlands Institute of Human Rights, 23-30.

Stavenhagen, Rodolfo (1990). *The Ethnic Question. Conflicts, Development, and Human Rights*, Tokyo: United Nations University Press.

Swain, Merrill (1981). Bilingual education for majority and minority language children. *Studia Linguistica*, 35(1-2), 15-32.

Swain, Merrill (1981). Time and Timing in Bilingual Education. *Language Learning*, 31.

Swain, Merrill (1984). A review of immersion education in Canada: Research and evaluation studies. In CDE 1984, 87-112.

Swain, Merrill (1985). Communicative Competence: Some Roles of Comprehensible Input and Comprehensible Output in its Development. In Gass & Madden (Eds.), 235-253.

Swain, Merrill (1987). *The case for focussed input: Contrived but authentic - Or, how content teaching needs to be manipulated and complemented to maximize second language learning*. Plenary paper presented at TESOL '87 conference, Vancouver, B.C.

Swain, Merrill (1991). Manipulating and complementing content teaching to maximize second language learning. In Phillipson et al. (Eds.), 234-250.

Swain, Merrill & Lapkin, Sharon (1982). *Evaluating Bilingual Education: a Canadian case study*. Clevedon: Multilingual Matters.

Swain, Merrill & Lapkin, Sharon (1986). Immersion French in secondary schools: "The goods" and "the bads". *Contact*, 5(3), 2-9.

Swain, Merrill, Lapkin, Sharon, Rowen, Norman, Hart, Doug (1990). The Role of Mother Tongue Literacy in Third Language Learning. *VOX, The Journal of the Australian Advisory Council on Languages and Multicultural Education*, 4, 111-121.

Taylor, Shelley K. (in press). Trilingualism by design?: Contextual factors in the educational experience of Mi'kmaq pupils in French Immersion. *Proceedings of the Lancaster University Conference on Bilingual Classroom Discourse, July 1993*. Lancaster: Lancaster University, Centre for Language in Social Life.

Thornberry, Patrick (1991). *International Law and the Rights of Minorities*. Oxford: Clarendon Press.

Thornberry, P. (1993). UN support for linguistic minorities. *Contact Bulletin*, 10(1), 1-2.

Tosi, Arturo (1984). *Immigration and Bilingual Education*, Oxford: Pergamon Press.

Tosi, Arturo (1989). *Feasibility Study No. 1: Bilingualism in the IB*. London: International Baccalaureate and Institute of Education, University of London. Unpublished report.

Toukomaa, Pertti & Skutnabb-Kangas, Tove (1977). *The intensive teaching of the mother tongue to migrant children of pre-school age and children in the lower level of comprehensive school*. Helsinki: The Finnish National Commission for UNESCO.

Troike, Rudolph C. (1986). *Improving conditions for success in bilingual education programs*. Prepared for Committee on Education and Labor, U.S. House of Representatives.

Truchot, Claude 1990 *L'anglais dans le monde contemporain*, Paris: Le Robert.

Truchot, Claude 1994 La France, l'anglais, le français et l'Europe, *Sociolinguistica* 8, 1994, 15-25.

Tsuda, Yukio (1986). *Language, inequality and distortion in intercultural communication. A critical theory approach*. Amsterdam & Philadelphia: John Benjamins.

Tsuda, Yukio (1988). *Language, education and intercultural communication*. Policy Research Project on Internationalization of Japanese Economy, Faculty of Economics, Nagasaki University.

Tsuda, Yukio (1992). The dominance of English and linguistic discrimination. *Media Development* 1, 32-34.

Tsuda, Yukio (1994). The Diffusion of English: Its Impact on Culture and Communication. *Keio Communication Review* 16, 49-61.

Tucker, Richard G., Otanes, Fe T. & Sibanes, B.P. (1970). An Alternate Days Approach to Bilingual Education. In Alatis (Ed.), 281-300.

UNESCO (1953). *The use of vernacular languages in education*. Paris: Monographs on Fundamental Education.

van Ek, Jan A. and Trim, John L. M. (1991). *Threshold Level*. Strasbourg: Council of Europe.

Veltman, Calvin J. (1988). *The future of the Spanish language in the United States*. Washington, D.C.: Hispanic Development Project.

Verhoeven, Ludo (1991). Predicting minority children's bilingual proficiency: Child, family, and institutional factors. *Language Learning*, 41(2), 205-233.

Vial, Santi (1994). *Distribució d'unitats i d'alumnes que tenen el percentatge adient d'alumnes castellanoparlants per a poder aplicar el programa d'immersió.* Barcelona: SEDEC, Departament d'Ensenyament, Generalitat de Catalunya. (unpublished report).

Vial, Santi (1994). *Distribució d'unitats i d'alumnes que tenen el percentatge adient d'alumnes castellanoparlants per a poder aplicar el programa d'immersió.* Barcelona: SEDEC, Departament d'Ensenyament, Generalitat de Catalunya. (unpublished report).

Vigil, James D. (1980). *From Indians to Chicanos: A Sociocultural History.* St. Louis, Missouri: C. V. Mosby Company.

Vila, Ignasi (1985). *Reflexions sobre l'educació bilingue: llengua de la llar i llengua d'instrucció.* Barcelona: Direcció General d'Ensenyament Primari, Generalitat de Catalunya.

Vila, Ignasi (1993). *La normalització linguistica a l'ensenyament no universitari de Catalunya.* Barcelona: Servei d'Ensenyament del Català del Departament d'Ensenyament de la Generalitat de Catalunya.

Wagner Gough, J. & Hatch, Evelyn (1975). The Importance of Input Data in Second Language Acquisition. *Language Learning*, 25, 297-307.

Widdowson, Henry G. (1968). The Teaching of English through Science. In Dakin et al. (Eds.), 115-175.

Winitz, H. (Ed.) (1981). *Native Language and Foreign Language Acquisition.* New York: Annals of the New York Academy of Sciences.

Wink, Joan (1994). I am not a LAP. *TESOL Matters*, February/March.

Wittrock, M. (Ed.) (1986). *Handbook of Research on Teaching*, Third Edition, New York: Macmillan.

Wong Fillmore, Lily (1983). The Language Learner as an Individual. In Clark & Handscombe (Eds.).

Wong Fillmore, Lily (1985). When Does Teacher Talk Work as Input? in Gass & Madden (Eds.), 17-50.

Wong Fillmore, Lily (1991). Second language learning in children: A model of language learning in social context. In Bialystok (Ed.), 49-69.

Wong Fillmore, Lily & Valadez, Concepcion (1986). Teaching Bilingual Learners. In Wittrock (Ed.), 648-685.

Zondag, Koen (Ed.) (1993). *Bilingual Education in Friesland: Facts and Prospects.* Leeuwarden, The Netherlands: Gemeenschappelijk Centrum voor Onderwijsbegeleiding in Friesland.

SUBJECT INDEX

NAME INDEX

NOTES ON CONTRIBUTORS

Prof. E. **Annamalai**
  Director, Central Institute of Indian
  Languages
  Mysore, INDIA

Dr. Josep Maria **Artigal**
  Second Language Acquisition for
  Children under Seven
  Barcelona, Catalonia, SPAIN

Prof. Hugo **Baetens Beardsmore**
  Vrije Universiteit Brussel
  Brussel, BELGIUM

Maurice **Carder**
  Head, ESL and Mother-Tongue
  Department, Vienna International
  School
  Vienna, AUSTRIA

Prof. Jim **Cummins**
  Modern Language Center, Ontario
  Institute for Studies in Education
  Toronto, Ontario, CANADA

Dr. David **Dolson**
  Bilingual Education Office, State
  Department of Education
  Sacramento, California, U.S.A.

Prof. Ofelia **García**
  School of Education, The City College

of New York
New York, U.S.A.

Prof. John **Gibbons**
  Department of Linguistics, University
  of Sydney
  New South Wales, AUSTRALIA

Prof. Alexei A. **Leontiev**
  Russian Academy of Science
  Moscow, RUSSIA

Prof. Kathryn **Lindholm**
  School of Education - Division of
  Teacher Education, San Jose State
  University
  San Jose, California, U.S.A.

Mart **Rannut**
  Director General
  (Estonian Language Board); Eesti
  Vabariigi Riiklik Keeleamet
  Tallinn, ESTONIA

Ülle **Rannut**
  Acting Director, Lexicon
  Tallinn, ESTONIA

Dr. Tove **Skutnabb-Kangas**
  Department of Languages and
  Culture, Roskilde University
  Roskilde, DENMARK